Authority, Community and Conflict

edited by

Madonna Kolbenschlag

Sheed & Ward

Sheed & Ward™ is a service of National Catholic Reporter Publishing,
Inc.

Library of Congress Catalog Card Number: 85-73300

ISBN: 0-934134-49-9

Published by: Sheed & Ward
            115 E. Armour Blvd. P.O. Box 281
            Kansas City, MO 64141-0281

To order, call: (800) 821-7926

Contents

Introduction

Madonna Kolbenschlag

On May 9, 1983, Agnes Mary Mansour of Michigan, a Sister of Mercy, was faced with two undesirable choices by church authorities: either resign from her post as director of the Michigan Department of Social Services or be subject to a canonical process of imposed dismissal from her religious vows and community.

Mansour's dilemma, fueled for weeks by the media, by raucous pressure groups and by threatened hierarchs, sketched an unfortunate scenario that presaged several subsequent interactions between Vatican officials and U.S. women religious. The Mansour case had implications that went far beyond the immediate participants, touching the very meaning of church, the role of the laity, and — in particular — exposing the vulnerability of Catholic lay women who would be candidates for political office.

Most of all, it provided evidence of the diverse, even disparate understandings of authority, power and fidelity that prevail in the church today. It revealed the stark impasses and incompatibilities that can arise when sincere people try to balance the virtues of citizenship and a sense of Gospel "mission" with church discipline.

To some observers, the agon that ensued between the Sisters of Mercy of the Union and the Vatican officials was a classic incidence of patriarchal abuse of power, even an act of retribution against Sr. Theresa Kane for her public intervention before John Paul II on behalf of women in 1979.

To others it was a necessary and unequivocal reassertion of ecclesial authority, long overdue in the wake of the "experimentation" and secularization that followed Vatican II.

To many it seemed at the very least to be a failure of prudence on the part of some, and a failure to observe the counsel of "charity in all things" on the part of others.

The decision of Agnes Mary Mansour and of her sister peers — Elizabeth Morancy in the Rhode Island legislature and Arlene Violet, now attorney general of Rhode Island — was in many ways inevitable, given the social, spiritual, psychological and professional development of U.S. religious women since Vatican II.[1] The choice of the American women, electing to serve their people in government as an expression of their religious commitment, as well as the choice of their superiors not to contravene consciences and their concern to maintain fidelity to the communal process and charism — a disposition seemingly contrary to Roman discipline and the traditional obedience to fiat expected of religious — is in fact a consciousness nurtured on papal and pastoral teachings since Vatican II, especially those related to social justice and the concept of church. These events also reveal a clear and unequivocal expression of enculturation: the translation of a Gospel commitment and charism into the "scandal of the particular," namely the cultural context of a post-1960's United States.

In the past the clash between hierarchs and dissidents has been enacted behind closed doors and via sealed missives. Silence and secrecy have been obstacles to the discernment of truth and authentic moral judgment. Our purpose in this volume is to provide access to key documents which have not been made public up to now, and to assessments of the events and issues surrounding the conflict between the Vatican and the Sisters of Mercy over the three sisters who have pursued political offices. We do this in order to encourage reflection by the people of God on the moral pedagogy involved in these ecclesial/political events and the pastoral consequences for all of us.

Leonardo Boff has expressed these concerns eloquently in his book, *Church, Charism and Power:* "The fundamental charismatic structure of the Church means that each individual has his or her place in the community, a place that is determined by the individual's charism; it also means that each one co-constitutes the Church. If the individual loses his or her place, or if that place is taken away, then the community is affected not only on a moral level but is also attacked at its core and even demoralized."[2]

It is our hope that the encounters recorded in this volume will shed light on our mutual struggle toward truth, authenticity and unity.

ACKNOWLEDGEMENTS

I wish to offer a special word of thanks to Sister Helen Marie Burns, RSM, for her contribution to this volume as both witness and historian, to her staff, and to other members of the Mercy Administrative Team — both past and present — for the access and assistance they provided throughout the course of this project. I am particularly indebted to those women who gave permission for their personal documents to be used in the research, and to Mr. Robert Heyer for his editorial assistance.

1. My recent publication, *Between God and Caesar* (Paulist Press, 1985) provides a thorough documentation of these developments among American women religious.

2. Leonardo Boff, *Church, Charism and Power* (Crossroad Press, 1985), p. 160

I. Case Study:

The Experience of Sisters of Mercy of the Union in Public Office

Helen Marie Burns, RSM

All our past and future rest in our present. We know this to be true and understand it most dramatically in certain moments of life. The Sisters of Mercy of the Union experienced such a moment in recent years when the selection of political office as a mode of service for their members — a natural evolution of the congregation's struggle to do the work of justice — brought individual members, leadership, and the membership-at-large into conflict with the Congregation for Religious and Secular Institutes and, so it would seem, with Pope John Paul II. The story bears recording and reflection for it has found resonance in many hearts and many spirits, and issues imbedded in the story continue to disturb the community of believers.

In April 1977 the Tenth General Chapter of the Sisters of Mercy of the Union pledged the congregation to "a deeper degree of inter-province solidarity in order . . . to direct our human and material resources to the promotion of justice within the world community, the Church community, and our own community." The same chap-

1

ter approved a statement concerning our relationship within the
church which called for efforts to bring about the full potential of
the church by taking responsibility as Sisters of Mercy for leadership for change. This approval paved the way for the establishment
at the generalate level of a Mercy Church-Institute Committee to
be advisory to the Mercy administrative team relative to stances
and possible strategies or actions and, pro-actively, relative to
recommendations of steps to be taken or positions to be articulated
on issues determined by the committee to be significant. As early
as October 1979, the minutes of the Church-Institute Committee
recorded: "future agenda items were also surfaced. They were
. . . church-state relationship, e.g., church's role in public policy
and legislation; political ministry; taxation of churches and religious congregations. . ."

In March 1980, the eleventh general chapter identified among
priorities for the '80's "a ministerial direction which focuses on
the need for a more just world: analysis of issues and social
realities, service to materially poor, international consciousness,
coalition building, and service to women." This chapter also recognized the '77 statement on relationship within the church as a
"substantive beginning of an articulation of our relationship" and
called for a task force to further that articulation.

Sister Agnes Mary Mansour and Sister Arlene Violet participated in both Chapters as delegates from their respective
provinces. They and other delegates committed themselves and
the Sisters of Mercy of the Union to serious consideration of efforts
toward systemic change and to active participation in development
of the church's understanding of critical issues. These chapter
statements both revealed and awakened a growing concern for
the work of justice within the congregation. Expressions of this
concern were myriad, but became most problematic in the circumstances which converged on the choice to seek political office
as a means to address systemic change.

Oddly enough, early experiences of political office — prior to
the 1978 papacy of John Paul II, prior to the 1980 release of the
document entitled *Religious Life and Human Promotion,* prior to
the 1983 revision of canon law — happened with relative ease.
The first instance of the Sisters of Mercy of the Union in elected

was defeated in August in her bid for the congressional seat in District #17. The question of Sister Arlene Violet's candidacy also became somewhat moot since she was narrowly defeated in her bid for attorney general in the November elections. Again, quietly and somewhat unobtrusively, Sister Elizabeth Morancy won her *third* term in the state House of Representatives in Rhode Island in the same November elections.

While the Mercy Church-Institute Committee moved toward finalization of a position paper relative to elective office for religious, circumstances were converging which would soon bring the issue again into the media. Early in December 1982, Sister Agnes Mary informed Sister Helen Marie Burns that Governor-elect James Blanchard was considering her for a state-level cabinet appointment. Sister Helen Marie again consulted with her administrative team. They reviewed the nearly two-year on-going discussion with Sister Agnes Mary relative to their mutual agreement that it was timely to offer her resignation as President of Mercy College of Detroit. They also discussed her interest in political office and the current ecclesial climate for such a choice. The administrative team determined to support the prospective appointment if Archbishop Szoka was supportive or, at least, not opposed. Sister Helen Marie telephoned Archbishop Szoka who expressed his approval for the appointment and reflected his concern — should it be the Department of Social Services — for a clear stand relative to the abortion issue. Both agreed that Sister Agnes Mary should discuss this matter personally with Archbishop Szoka and that Sister Helen Marie would communicate this to Sister Agnes Mary.

On December 20, 1982, Sister Agnes Mary called Sister Helen Marie to say that the appointment to the Department of Social Services was confirmed and that, in spite of several attempts, she had not yet been able to set up an appointment with the archbishop. On December 27 and 28, Sister Agnes Mary left messages at Archbishop Szoka's office stating that she was trying to set up an appointment with him. By now she and the provincial administrative team were aware that a public announcement of her appointment would be made on December 29, 1982.

On the morning of the 29th, while Sister Agnes Mary traveled to Lansing for a press conference, Sister Helen Marie reached the archbishop by telephone to inform him of the appointment to be announced later that day. By late afternoon of the same day, Sister Agnes Mary also reached the archbishop by telephone to discuss with him at length the appointment and his concerns relative to the abortion issue. Sister Agnes Mary recalls that Archbishop Szoka told her to make clear her stand on abortion; to say, relative to the Medicaid payments for abortion, that she was upholding the law and not to comment further in the matter of Medicaid. She was uncertain when she concluded the conversation whether the archbishop continued his support or not. She felt she had been unambiguous in her stand and was not certain the archbishop could support her approach.

Archbishop Szoka recalls that their conversation lasted at least one and one-half hours and that he explained to Sister Agnes Mary the absolute necessity for her to take a clear stand against Medicaid payments for abortion and that if she did not take such a position, she would not have his support. The Archbishop's support appeared clear and firm, however, in a *Detroit Free Press* article on December 31, 1982, which quotes his response to her appointment: "A lot is being made about the fact that the D.S.S. (uses Medicaid funds) to pay for abortions," he said. "It's creating a problem where there is none. . . . As a sister, Sister Mansour must be in accord with the church. But in her job she has to follow the laws of the state, even if she doesn't agree with them. . . . The fact that her appointment encompasses so many of the areas women religious have traditionally worked in — the poor, foster children, welfare — could give a powerful witness to the Christian dimension of the D.S.S."

Throughout January and February, media coverage in Michigan and elsewhere raised controversy relative both to Sister Agnes Mary's appointment and Medicaid funding for abortion. The provincial administrator (Detroit) and the president received a steady, though not overwhelming, stream of letters regarding the announcement of Sister Agnes Mary's appointment. Most of these letters opposed the appointment as detrimental to right-to-life efforts in the State of Michigan and an affront to the church's teaching on abortion. In mid-February an ad appeared in the *Wall*

Street Journal and in other major newspapers depicting Sister Agnes Mary and Archbishop Szoka as "baby killers." Postcards similar in tone to the ad, began to deluge the archbishop's office.

Around this time the Mercy Church-Institute Committee completed its position paper on elective office for religious and submitted it to the Mercy administrative team. The team released the position paper to several consultants for their critique. Among the consultants were Sisters Agnes Mary Mansour, Elizabeth Morancy, and Arlene Violet.

In early February, Sister Helen Marie, aware that Sister Agnes Mary's confirmation hearing (scheduled for March 8, 1983) could generate additional media coverage and aware that she would be out of the state on provincial business from February 8 to February 19, called Archbishop Szoka's office to inform him of the circumstances surrounding the hearing and to offer times she could be available to meet with him before the hearing if he desired. Both concerns were given to Father Kevin Britt, the archbishop's secretary, to be forwarded to the archbishop. There was no response from the archbishop.

On February 14, the archbishop, at his own request, met with Sister Agnes Mary at his residence. This session lasted about one hour. Archbishop Szoka reported that he said he intended to publicly state his opposition to Sister Agnes Mary's continuing as Director of the Department of Social Services and would call for her resignation unless she clearly stated her opposition to Medicaid funding. Sister Agnes Mary, however, understood him to say that he would have to go to her religious superiors so that they could ask her to change her position. On February 21, Sister Agnes Mary shared information with Sister Helen Marie regarding the meeting with Archbishop Szoka and her concern that he intended to withdraw his support for her appointment.

On February 23, 1983, at 8:45 a.m., Sister Helen Marie received a letter from Archbishop Szoka informing her that he had withdrawn his support for Sister Agnes Mary's appointment and that he would ask for her resignation at a news conference at 10:15 a.m. that same morning. Attempts to reach Archbishop Szoka prior to the news conference failed, so Sister Helen Marie and her provincial administrative team issued a press release basically stating they needed time "to consider all the elements implied, including: a) the religious community's traditional involvement in social services; b) their support for Sister Agnes Mary Mansour in accepting the appointment as Director of Social Services; and c) their respect for the Archbishop's authority."

Immediately the provincial administrative team began a series of consultations with Sister Agnes Mary, the sisters of the province, Sister M. Theresa Kane and the Mercy administrative team, with moral theologians, canon lawyers, other major superiors, and other Michigan Bishops. These consultations were varied and extensive and coterminous with the Mercy administrative team's activities relative to the Mercy Church-Institute Committee's position paper on elective office for religious and to related inquiries concerning the new code of canon law. On February 28, two members of the provincial administrative team met privately with Archbishop Szoka. On March 4, the entire provincial administrative team met with Archbishop Szoka, Father Kevin Britt, and Bishop Dale Malezak. The meetings yielded no openings for compromise or further discussion.

On March 5, 1983, the provincial administrative team issued a press release that indicated there was not sufficient clarity at this time for them to judge that Sister Agnes Mary's resignation would be for the greater good. Conversation continued with other Michigan bishops in an attempt to gather Church leaders in Michigan for a re-examination of the situation in order to resolve the obvious differences of opinion regarding the serious pastoral concerns involved.

These conversations were interrupted by Sister Helen Marie's yearly visit (March 7-20) with the province's Sisters in Argentina. Media coverage heightened, however, with the March 8 confirmation hearing. On that date, Sister Agnes Mary testified before the Michigan State Senate Committee and was overwhelmingly confirmed as Director of the Department of Social Services. In a prepared statement she testified that while she was opposed to abortion, she could tolerate Medicaid funding. She did not see the elimination of such funding as the way to change the circumstances surrounding the choice of abortion.

On March 10, 1983, Archbishop Szoka presented a report of the

situation to the Holy See through the office of the apostolic delegate, Archbishop Pio Laghi. On March 23, Archbishop Laghi held
a meeting with Mercy President, Sister M. Theresa Kane, and
Sister Emily George, a member of the Mercy administrative team.
He presented to Sr. M. Theresa a letter informing her that CRIS
wished her to tell Sister Agnes Mary to resign as Director of the
Department of Social Services. Verbally, Archbishop Laghi
suggested that refusal to resign by Sister Agnes Mary could lead
to her dismissal and that refusal to transmit this order by Sister
M. Theresa could subject her to serious canonical consequences.
Sister M. Theresa stated that she had planned to leave for retreat
on March 27 and wondered if she should cancel it. Archbishop
Laghi saw no need for this and indicated that she should take
the time needed. Before she left Sister M. Theresa called the
Apostolic Delegate relative to the need for immediate response
and was again assured that this was not a problem.

Sister M. Theresa immediately informed Sister Agnes Mary,
Sister Helen Marie, and all provincial administrators of the letter
given her by the apostolic delegate's office. The general administrative team decided to keep this letter from the media in the
hope that the relative calm existing since the early March confirmation coverage would work to everyone's advantage. However,
an "official leak" from a Vatican source gave the media sufficient
lead to resurface the controversy.

The intervention of the Congregation for Religious and Secular
Institutes moved the discussion to the generalate level. This
thwarted attempts on the local level to arrange a meeting of the
conflicting parties in a broader, more objective gathering. The
provincial administrative team decided, however, to go ahead with
a plan to release to the Michigan bishops a chronology of the
events as experienced by the Sisters of Mercy, a statement of the
values the team perceived as central to the conflict, and a request
for the Bishop's judgment on the next steps to be taken. This
material was also to be submitted to the Congregation for Religious and Secular Institutes (CRIS) in order to provide a report
of the matter from the view of the religious congregation and its
legitimate authority. Sister M. Theresa agreed to enclose the
material with her response to the letter of March 23.

On April 4, 1983, Sister M. Theresa flew to Detroit to meet with Sisters Agnes Mary and Helen Marie to review the letter from the apostolic delegate and their individual recommendations. Responses to a request for consultation were also received from the provincial administrators and a host of interested parties. This extensive consultation signaled to the Mercy administrative team that significant values were in apparent conflict. The team received much encouragement to find a space/place for discussion and negotiation.

The Mercy administrative team met on April 6 to review all these consultations and to ascertain the most appropriate response to the March 23 letter. They determined to request a formal reconsideration of the decision. Accordingly, on April 11, 1983, Sister M. Theresa addressed a letter to Archbishop Laghi making this request. She asked that the request and documentation prepared by the Detroit provincial administrative team be submitted to the Holy See. The material also included a request from Sister Agnes Mary Mansour for a leave of absence from the Sisters of Mercy of the Union and the approval of that request by the Provincial administrative team and the Mercy administrative team. The leave of absence was effective April 20, 1983.

From a chronology made public by Bishop Anthony Bevilacqua in May 1983, the Sisters of Mercy now know the series of events that interacted with their own activities. A special courier carried the request for reconsideration of the decision to CRIS on April 12. On April 13, Archbishop Mayer, Secretary of CRIS, asked Bishop Anthony Bevilacqua of Brooklyn, New York, to serve as ad hoc delegate of the Holy See in the matter of Sister Agnes Mary Mansour. On the same day, Archbishop Laghi addressed a letter to Sister M. Theresa thanking her "for the sensitivity you showed in responding to my request for an early reply to the inquiry about action to be taken regarding Sister Agnes Mary Mansour" and indicating that the request and documentation of the Sisters of Mercy had been sent to Rome by special courier.

Bishop Bevilacqua met with Archbishop Mayer on April 15, 1983, to discuss the nature, scope, and content of a pontifical mandate under consideration in the matter of Sister Agnes Mary Mansour. On April 25, Bishop Bevilacqua received a letter which appointed him ad hoc delegate of the Holy See with the mandate to approach Sister Agnes Mary directly and to require, in the name of the Holy See and by virtue of her vow of obedience, that she immediately resign as Director of the Department of Social Services.

On April 26, Sister Agnes Mary received a call from a priest of the archdiocese of Detroit indicating a letter was in his possession which needed to be hand-delivered within forty-eight hours. After checking the authenticity of this messenger by a phone call to the apostolic delegate, Sister M. Theresa advised her to accept the letter. The letter stated that Bishop Bevilacqua had been appointed ad hoc delegate and that it was his responsibility to inform Sister Agnes Mary of the decision of the Holy See in her regard. The letter also discussed the date, time, and place of their meeting, with the suggestion that she "feel free to have with you two religious sisters from your province." On the same day, Sister M. Theresa received a letter from the apostolic delegate informing her that "in response to her request for an appointment to discuss the case of Sister Agnes Mary Mansour, the Cardinal Prefect of CRIS refers her to Bishop Bevilacqua who has been appointed the ad hoc delegate of CRIS for this entire matter." The letter further indicated that Bishop Bevilacqua would be "available to you after the initial interview with Sister Agnes Mary."

Understanding the meeting between Bishop Bevilacqua and Sister Agnes Mary (scheduled for May 9, 1983), to be a beginning point of the final phase of this matter, Sister M. Theresa and two members of the Mercy administrative team proceeded with their plans to attend the Assembly of the International Union of Superiors General held in Rome May 3-7, 1983. Immediately after her arrival in Rome on May 1, Sister M. Theresa requested through conversation with an official of CRIS to meet with Cardinal Pironio to discuss the Mansour case. No response was made to that request.

On May 9, 1983, Bishop Bevilacqua met with Sister Agnes Mary at the Provincial House of the Sisters of Mercy. She was accompanied by two companions: Sister Helen Marie Burns and Sister Emily George. Bishop Bevilacqua was accompanied by two companions: Monsignor Joseph Galante and Sister Sharon Holland,

IHM. Bishop Bevilacqua showed his mandate to all present and then read it. He then read the precept directed to Sister Agnes Mary, the final section of which communicated the decision of the Holy See: this decision required her in the name of the Holy See and by virtue of her vow of obedience to the Holy Father to immediately resign her position as Director of the Department of Social Services in the State of Michigan. It also informed her that, if she refused to resign, the ad hoc delegate would be compelled to initiate the canonical process subjecting her to imposed secularization and dismissal from the Sisters of Mercy.

After discussion, argumentation, reflection, and prayer, Sister Agnes Mary regretfully requested dispensation from vows. She had asked what alternatives were open to her and was offered none. She had stated that she did not wish to be in defiance of the Holy Father and did not wish to be dismissed. She asked for dispensation, then, as the only means possible to avoid resigning from a position she felt was in accord with the mission of the Sisters of Mercy and to avoid defiance of the Holy Father by forcing the Holy See to dismiss her from the Sisters of Mercy. Bishop Bevilacqua immediately processed the request for dispensation.

That evening, Sister Emily called Sister M. Theresa in Rome to apprise her of the Holy See's decision and Sister Agnes Mary's response. All parties involved — Sister Agnes Mary, Bishop Bevilacqua, the Mercy administrative team, and the provincial administrative team — prepared separate press releases with the agreement that confidentiality would be maintained until 11:00 a.m. on May 11. On that morning, Sister Agnes Mary held a press conference to accompany her press release stating her decision and its circumstances.

Media coverage again escalated. Various groups — within and without the Roman Catholic Church — offered public statements of dismay or support. Pentecost Sunday (May 22, 1983) was chosen as the time for many of these activities. Rallies were held in cities throughout the United States — Denver, Chicago, Washington, D.C., to name a few — to critique the process, to support Sister Agnes Mary, and to reflect on the issues involved. A spontaneous grouping of women in the Washington, D.C., area gathered for reflection several times and then asked one of their members to address an open letter "recalling the early Christian community who often responded to a particular situation in a local church by exchanging letters in an effort to come to a common agreement and purpose." Over 40,000 copies of this "First Epistle to the Church of the United States" were distributed throughout the United States. Newspapers, radio stations, and television networks sought interviews and statements from the principal actors in this most recent drama.

The Sisters of Mercy, vigorously attempted to redress what was perceived as a singular, grave injustice. On May 14, while still in Rome, Sister M. Theresa addressed a letter to Cardinal Pironio and Archbishop Mayer notifying them that a formal process to appeal the decision and the methods of CRIS regarding Sister Agnes Mary had been initiated at the office of the Apostolic Signatura. Subsequent canonical counsel advised that the appeal should be made first with CRIS and then, if redress was not obtained, with the Apostolic Signatura. Consequently, after her return to the States, Sister M. Theresa addressed a letter to Cardinal Pironio on May 18 registering *with* CRIS a formal appeal of the decision. During the rest of the month, letters were written 1) to Bishop Bevilacqua objecting to misrepresentations in his May 10 press release, requesting copies of the mandate given to him by CRIS and the minutes of the May 9 meeting, registering concern for Part I, Article 13, and Part I, Article 14, of the precept as well as the process leading to the request for dispensation; 2) to Archbishop John Roach, President of the National Conference of Catholic Bishops, informing him of the situation and expressing distress that this situation had occurred prior to any response from CRIS to the request for reconsideration; 3) to several persons seeking canonical advice relative to the process of appeal. In early June, the General Administrative Conference of the Sisters of Mercy of the Union sent a letter of support and regret to Sister Agnes Mary Mansour.

On June 6, 1983, CRIS informed Sister M. Theresa that "the Sacred Congregation cannot accept your request for an appeal not only because of the lack of foundation of your three affirmations but also because His Excellency, Bishop Anthony Bevilacqua

acted in the name of the Holy See under the direction of the Holy
Father." Eleven days later, Sister M. Theresa formally initiated
a process of appeal through the Apostolic Signatura. While this
request was under consideration in Rome, Bishop Bevilacqua replied at length to the concern addressed to him by Sister M.
Theresa in her May 23 letter and also submitted to NCCB members a chronology of the events in the Mansour case, as he saw
them, as well as answers to other questions relating to the case.
On July 11, Sister M. Theresa received a hand-delivered letter
from the Apostolic Signatura informing her "that the Signatura
Apostolica is unable to consider the recourse which you intend to
present because. . . Bishop Bevilacqua was acting under express
command of the Holy Father." On July 19, Sister M. Theresa
addressed a letter to Cardinal Sabattani of the Apostolic Signatura
requesting "to know what canonical recourse is possible in light
of the previous communication." On August 23, Sister M. Theresa
received a letter from the Apostolic Signatura reiterating its earlier position "that there is no possibility of recourse of any kind."

Even as closure was drawing near in the matter of Sister Agnes
Mary Mansour, *The Evening Bulletin* in Providence, Rhode Island,
signaled the next focal point for the issue of women religious in
public office. An August 3 story quoted Bishop Louis Gelineau as
saying "he had told Sister Arlene Violet she unquestionably will
be violating church law if she runs again for attorney general in
1984."

Meanwhile attempts to clarify and reflect on the Mansour case
continued. On August 1, Sister M. Theresa and Sister Emily spent
several hours in conversation with Archbishop Laghi and Bishop
Bevilacqua in an unsuccessful attempt to understand the events
surrounding the May 9 meeting. A group of Washingtonbased
theologians prepared an educational packet relative to the issue
of religious in public office for distribution to, among other parties,
the bishops of the United States. *Origins* and other publications
covered "the Mansour case" at length.

In early September, delegates of the second session of the
Eleventh General Chapter of the Sisters of Mercy of the Union
engaged in extended deliberations on events surrounding the dispensation from vows of Sister Agnes Mary Mansour. The end of

that deliberation was a lengthy resolution:

> . . . We speak because serious harm has been experienced by the Church, by our congregation, and by one of our members. We are deeply concerned for all involved.
>
> 1. That adequate dialogue between congregational and hierarchical authorities was lacking;
>
> 2. That responses to questions and sufficient information regarding the canonical processes to be used were not made available to congregational leadership or to Sister Agnes Mary Mansour;
>
> 3. That, at crucial points, legitimate authorities of the congregation were ignored;
>
> 4. That, prior to final action by Roman authorities, the congregation was not officially requested to represent its position, nor Sister Agnes Mary Mansour hers.
>
> We are even more seriously concerned that the above aspects of this event manifest what seem to us to be profound discrepancies between our understanding of the nature and role of religious congregations in the Church and the understanding which was operative in this enforcement of the law.
>
> We long to move from our deep sense of sorrow and our experience of powerlessness to a moment of hope and healing. We desire the development of processes which reflect greater mutuality within the community of believers. We call upon the Church to establish or activate procedures for due process which include appropriate appeal processes to deal with this case and other cases. Calling on the healing presence of God, we invite others to join us in prayer and in the discipline of dialogue within the Church.

On October 26, 1983, Sister M. Theresa received a letter from CRIS requesting a reply "as soon as possible" to their July 3, 1982, request for her position relative to the candidature of one of her sisters for the political office of attorney general of the State of

Rhode Island. The memo which Sister M. Theresa sent to provincial administrators informing them of this most recent inquiry from CRIS and seeking their consultation also conveyed her intent to request a papal audience regarding the Mansour case. The urgency for this audience became clear on November 26 when Sister M. Theresa received a letter from the apostolic delegate indicating he had received word "from the Holy See that the Holy Father. . . has made his mind clear on the application of certain provisions of the newly revised code with regard to Miss Agnes Mary Mansour. In her case, the provision of Canon 690 . . . does not apply." Canon 690 gives authority for the decision of re-admittance of a person who lawfully leaves the institute after profession to the major superior of the congregation, with the consent of her council. In effect, any request by Sister Agnes Mary for re-admission to the Sisters of Mercy would have to be approved by CRIS, Canon 690 notwithstanding.

Meanwhile, media coverage in Rhode Island and elsewhere began to escalate concerning the possible candidacy of Sister Arlene Violet for the office of attorney general of the state of Rhode Island. Extensive conversation took place in the internal forums of the Sisters of Mercy relative to its implications. On December 4, 1983, Sister Arlene Violet submitted a letter to Sister Mary Noel Blute and the provincial administrative team requesting a dispensation from her vows. She said she made the request with deep pain and with limited freedom of choice.

Sister M. Theresa's letter of December 21 in response to the CRIS inquiry (July 3, 1982) informed Archbishop Mayer that Sister Arlene Violet had decided to seek dispensation from her vows. She also recorded the continuing process of serious reflection and consultation regarding the complex issue raised in the July 3 letter. This included a recent General Chapter decision to set up a task force to study the appropriateness of political ministry in light of the charism of the Sisters of Mercy.

Unaware of Sister Arlene's decision, media coverage continued to escalate throughout the first weeks of January. This included a statement released by Bishop Gelineau on January 5 which presented his position regarding priests and religious in politics. He made specific reference to the candidacy of Sister Arlene Violet.

One day later, in the midst of this troubled scene, Sister M. Theresa sent a letter to Pope John Paul II seeking a private audience "in regard to the pastoral situation involving the administration of the Sisters of Mercy of the Union and Sister Agnes Mary Mansour."

By mid-January, Sister Arlene Violet had announced her candidacy for attorney general *and* her decision to request dispensation from vows. A letter from Archbishop Mayer sent with Sister Arlene Violet's dispensation papers, informed Sister M. Theresa that once again Canon 690.1 had been waived in regard to Sister Arlene Violet. The power given to the community in regard to re-admission of former members was rescinded relative to Sister Arlene. The letter also requested, again, Sister M. Theresa's personal position on sisters holding political office. The news articles in Rhode Island simultaneously linked the candidacy of Sister Elizabeth Morancy with Bishop Gelineau's stand on political office. On February 15, 1985, Sister Elizabeth Morancy addressed a letter to CRIS seeking clarification "as to what are my options in the present situation as a three-term state legislator, member of a religious order who wishes to run again but has been asked not to seek re-election by the bishop of the diocese."

On March 6, 1984, Sister M. Theresa received a letter acknowledging that the Holy Father had received Sister M. Theresa's request for an audience, but requested that she "outline in greater detail the scope of your proposal." Within the week, Sister Elizabeth Morancy also received a response to her inquiry: "given the clarity and importance of the prescriptions involved, a religious, who has freely vowed obedience in the church, should lovingly obey Church Law and with generous loyalty fulfill what is prescribed. If, unfortunately, a religious prefers to serve in an office not allowed by church law, he or she thereby chooses to resign from religious life."

The Twelfth General Chapter of the Sisters of Mercy of the Union convened in Cincinnati, Ohio, March 23-27, 1984. This was a chapter of elections as well as a chapter of business (the terms of service of Sister M. Theresa and her team would be completed July 1984). This chapter approved the following proposals:

1. That the 12th General Chapter request from the appropriate church authorities an indult granting Sister Elizabeth Morancy dispensation from Canons 672 and 285, Section 3, in order to permit her to continue in public office.

2. That the Twelfth General Chapter extend to Sister Arlene Violet our love and concern and pledge our continuing efforts to clarify the role of women religious in political ministry.

In April, Sister M. Theresa wrote to Archbishop Mayer again referring to her February 14 letter as her response to the inquiry regarding political ministry. She also wrote a letter to Pope John Paul II outlining her purpose in seeking a private audience. She facilitated the collation of materials sent to Rome to petition an indult granting a dispensation for Sister Elizabeth to continue in public office. On May 7, 1984, a letter from Archbishop Laghi informed Sister M. Theresa that this petition for indult had been denied.

The letter from CRIS recording this decision was received on May 9. In a separate letter on the same day, Archbishop Hamer* suggested that he did not find Sister M. Theresa's personal position on sisters holding political office in any correspondence: "If you had addressed this question with us, perhaps some of the difficulties involved in the Mansour, Violet, and Morancy cases could have been avoided."

On May 21, Sister M. Theresa notified Archbishop Laghi that Sister Elizabeth Morancy had requested a dispensation from her vows. In July, Sister M. Theresa Kane completed her term of office as general administrator for the Sisters of Mercy of the Union. One of her last letters was addressed to Archbishop Hamer in response to his letter of May 9. Once again she attempted to trace the record of her personal position on Sisters of Mercy holding political office. On August 3, 1984, she received word that her request for a private audience with John Paul II had been denied.

All our past and future rest in our present. Equally true, perhaps, is the statement that all our past and present rest in our future. Thus the story continues.

*Between April 1985 and May 1984, Archbishop Jerome Hamer replaced Archbishop Augustin Mayer as Pro Prefect of the Congregation for Religious and Secular Institutes.

II.
Task Force
Commentaries

Editor's Note:

Shortly after the events surrounding the swift dispensation of
Agnes Mary Mansour from her vows and, consequently, from her
membership in the Sisters of Mercy of the Union, a group of
theologians, ethicists, canonists, lay and religious scholars met
several times in Washington, DC, to explore ways of responding
to the handling of the case. The meetings, which began in May
of 1983, were chaired by Maria Riley, OP, of the Center of Concern,
and James Hug, SJ, of the Woodstock Theological Center. After
identifying the crucial issues in the case, several participants contributed commentaries for discussion and circulation to concerned
parties in the Catholic community.

Personal Morality and Public Policy

Charles E. Curran

Catholic theology has traditionally recognized the very important distinction between the realm of morality and the realm of legality or public policy. What is true in the personal moral order is not by that very fact necessarily to be incorporated into law.

Public statements in the case of Sister Agnes Mary Mansour unfortunatley have not always recognized this traditional distinction. The archbishop of Detroit claimed that Sister Mansour's refusal to state her opposition to Medicaid abortion payments for the poor was "contrary to the magisterium." Bishop Anthony Bevilacqua, ad hoc delegate of the Holy See in this matter, began his explanation of the Mansour case by stating: "There are two major issues. The basic and doctrinal issue is that of abortion. While Sister Agnes Mary Mansour stated that she was against abortion, she refused to make a public statement opposing public funding for abortions and, in fact, supported such funding. . . . The second major issue is a disciplinary one, that of disobedience."

All Catholics recognize the teaching function of the hierarchical magisterium in matters of faith and morals. In Catholic self-understanding, doctrine refers to a belief officially taught by the church. But the question of abortion legislation or the public funding of abortion does not come under these categories. Public policy in this matter involves many prudential judgments about which there can be no doctrine or magisterial teaching on faith and morals.

Respected Catholic theologians and philosophers such as John Courtney Murray and Jacques Maritain have tried to explain in a systematic way what is the basis for the difference between the personal moral order and the legal order. Murray develops his approach in the light of the position of many Protestant ethicists who are disturbed by the gap between public policy or the way the state behaves and personal morality. Murray firmly rejects the dichotomy between "moral man" and "immoral society" made famous by Reinhold Niebuhr. Morality in the Catholic tradition is determined by the ends and the relevant orders of political and individual morality. The end and order of political and social reality are different from the end and order of individual and personal reality.

Murray would certainly recognize an overlap between the two, but in his book he stresses the difference between public policy and private morality. "It follows, then, that the morality proper to the life and action of society and the state is not univocally the morality of personal life, or even of familial life. Therefore the effort to bring the organized action of politics and the practical art of statescraft directly under the control of the Christian values that govern personal and familial life is inherently fallacious. It makes wreckage not only of public policy but also of morality itself" (*We Hold These Truths*, p. 286).

Jacques Maritain spells out the same basic difference between political and individual ethics. The French philosopher seeks a middle ground between political hypermoralism and political amoralism. Politics is a branch of ethics, but as a branch it is specifically different from the other branches on the same stem. "For human life has two ultimate ends, the one subordinate to the other: an ultimate end *in a given order,* which is the terrestrial common good, or the *bonum vitae civilis;* and an *absolute* ultimate end, which is the transcendent, eternal common good. An individual ethics takes into account the subordinate ultimate end, but *directly* aims at the absolute ultimate one; whereas political ethics takes into account the absolute ultimate end, but its *direct aim* is the subordinate ultimate end, the good of the rational nature in its temporal achievement. Hence a specific difference of perspective between those two branches of ethics" *(Man and the State,* p. 62).

Thus Maritain morally justifies in political ethics the use of intelligence methods and coercive police measures; selfishness and self-assertion which would be blamed in individuals; a permanent distrust and suspicion; a cleverness not necessarily mischievous but yet not candid with regard to the other states; the toleration of certain evil deeds by the law; the recognition of the principle of the lesser evil and the *fait accompli* (the so-called "statute of limitations").

These two spokespersons of the Catholic theological and philosophical traditions thus indicate the differences between individual and political morality and trace them to the different ends and different orders involved. However, the Catholic tradition has not only recognized the differences between the two orders, but also tried to indicate more precisely what is the relationship between them.

Thomas Aquinas in his *Summa* attempts to show the relationship between the moral and the legal orders. Thomas poses the question primarily in terms of the relationship between natural law and positive or human civil law. Human civil law is ordered to the common good (note the emphasis on ends and ordering), but not all the acts of all the virtues are capable of being ordered to the common good (I-II, q. 96 a. 3). Thomas also recognizes the need for a realistic approach to civil law. Laws are to be applied according to the human condition. Civil laws should suppress only the more grievous vices from which the majority of human beings can abstain (I-II q. 97 a. 2).

Thomas mentions another important aspect of civil law when discussing the question of whether the religious rites of infidels should be tolerated in society. Thomas responds that human government is derived from divine government and should imitate it. Even though God is omnipotent, God still permits certain evils to occur in the world which the divine power could prohibit. God permits such evil lest greater goods would be impeded or greater evils would occur. Here Thomas cites Augustine's famous justification of the toleration of public prostitution (II-II, q. 10 a. 11). Thus Thomas indicates the importance of different prudential judgments in determining what is civil law.

The Second Vatican Council touches on the question of the relationship between law and morality in its discussion of religious liberty. Here the Thomistic approach of toleration is somewhat transformed in the light of a more systematic understanding of the role and function of law in a limited constitutional form of government. The *Declaration on Religious Liberty* accepts as its fundamental criterion for law that the freedom of human beings is to be respected as far as possible and curtailed only when and insofar as necessary. The end of the state is public order, and this order thus becomes the criterion justifying the need for law. Public order consists of an order of justice, which safeguards the rights of all individuals in society; an order of peace, which enables human beings to live harmoniously in society; and an order of public morality understood as the minimum of public morality necessary for people to live together in society. Note that the end of public order is more limited than the end of the common good. The common good is the end of society itself, but public order is the end of the limited constitutional state which is only a part of society.

In addition to the two criteria of as much freedom as possible and of public order to guide the coercive intervention of the state through law, in my judgment there are two other aspects that must also enter into the complete determination of what is good law. First of all the law as such must be equitable and enforceable. If a law cannot be equitably enforced, it is not good law. In addition, lawmaking involves a pragmatic aspect. Sometimes one will not be able to enact a law that one considers ideal but will have to settle for some type of compromise. At other times one might have to conclude that working for a particular law or piece of legislation is not feasible because there is no realistic chance for passing such a law.

The four criteria proposed here for the determination of civil law are by necessity somewhat broad and include a number of practical and prudential judgments about which people of good will can disagree.

In the matter of abortion law and public funding, there can be differing judgments which would result in different positions. One could readily maintain that a constitutional amendment is re-

quired to protect the rights of the fetus, since a primary aspect
of public order is to protect human rights, especially the rights
of those who are defenseless. Others might argue that in the light
of the difference of opinion within American society on the exact
status of the fetus, one should give the benefit of the doubt to the
freedom of the woman in this area or that attempts to change the
present abortion law will not be feasible or successful. On the
public funding question it is quite easy to see how those opposed
to abortion could be opposed to public funding of abortion. However, others could argue that poor people should not be discrimi-
nated against either in respect to more affluent people or in respect
to medical procedures which they might want for themselves.

My purpose is not to take sides on the issue of the public policy
and public funding of abortion. Rather, I am trying to explain the
relationship between morality and law to show that personal morality cannot be made directly into law. The four criteria and the
practical and prudential judgments involved in determining what
constitutes good law mean that even within the Catholic church
there will be different possible approaches. Yes, bishops and
church leaders can take a position on these issues, but they must
realize that they are not teaching here in the same way they teach
on faith and morals. They are dealing with the much more complex
case of law and public policy.

Two recent statements by American Catholic bishops are in
accord with the analysis just given. Recently the American Catholic bishops supported the proposed Hatch amendment to the
constitution which would give congress or the several states the
power to limit and prohibit abortions provided that a state law
which is more restrictive than a law of congress shall prevail.
Many "right to life" advocates and even some bishops objected to
supporting such an amendment that would not allow any direct
abortions. Apparently the American bishops made the prudential
judgment that a stronger amendment was not feasible and had
no chance of becoming law at the present time. (Others concluded
that even the Hatch amendment has no realistic chance of being
passed as an amendment to the constitution.)

In their pastoral letter on peace and war, *The Challenge of
Peace: God's Promise and our Response,* the American bishops

recognize that the application of principles involves different possible prudential judgments and interpretations by people of good will. The teaching in the pastoral letter condemning any first use of nuclear weapons falls into such a category in which other Catholics might disagree with the position taken by the bishops. These recent statements by the American bishops are in line with the traditional understanding of the complex relationships between law and morality and with the more systematic analysis of good law developed here.

Aspects of Justice

Barbara A. Cullom and Philip Land, SJ

The perception of justice and injustice in the case of Agnes Mary Mansour is a complex one, dependent on one's appreciation of various actions, and particularly, on one's cultural apprehension of whether "just" and "lawful" are coextensive. From the perspective of some American Catholics, several aspects of the case appear to be unjust: Mansour did not have a clear opportunity to present her case, to clarify incorrect information or interpretations; she and her community suffered from the lack of an agreed upon process for the resolution of a dispute involving the jurisdiction of the local ordinary and the religious community; the seriousness of the meeting between Bishop Bevilacqua and Mansour was not communicated to Mansour or to her superiors, and there was no opportunity for Mansour to have competent counsel present; Mansour did not know the specific charge made against her until the process was well advanced.

The perception of injustice, and the debate over whether what is claimed as lawful is also just, are particularly distressing to us in the local church of the United States. Our cultural bias is in favor of the type of public justice which our country offers. Certainly the protection of the accused, the right to trial before a jury of peers, the provision of a court appointed lawyer when the accused is unable to provide one for her/himself, give evidence of the care the civil government has in treating those accused of wrongdoing. It is sometimes argued that while such human rights are the object of concern for civil society, they are not the concern of the church because it is a society in a totally different order, that of grace. It is a divine society, exempt from norms binding human society, and so, when its own decree on religious freedom says "that the common welfare of society consists chiefly in the protection of human rights. . ." (*Declaration on Religious Liberty*, Article 3) and that "the person is to be kept from all manner of human coercion" (*Ibid.*, Article 13), this does not apply to the church.

Many members of the church abhor such immunization. But enough draw implicit, if not explicit support from the affirmation to warrant treatment here. In the first place the church, while it has its divine side, is equally a human society. Its tradition of natural theology has even defined itself as a perfect society equal in that respect to any civil authority. Persons entering the church through baptism do not thereby surrender any of their rights to be treated as humans or sacrifice any respect for their human dignity. The church may not demand such. This limits, but does not prohibit, church discipline which the baptized freely accept and are then subject to. The church, of course, acknowledges in principle that it must respect human rights (and indeed in principle desires to do so) in creating a code of canon law and in sketching a due process. It can be questioned whether the code is adequate and whether the fulfillment of it is sufficient for the doing of justice.

In the second place, the church should not only observe norms of human justice equally with the state, it should give exemplary witness to spontaneous, wholehearted and unreserved support of such rights. The church is called to this by its very foundations. The synod of 1971 said "the church has therefore a responsibility identified with her mission of giving witness . . . of the need for love and justice contained in the gospel message, a witness to be carried out in church institutions themselves." (*Justice in the World*, p. 14)

This principle of *a fortiori* witness draws roots from the very justification which is the life of the church and its members. For the *unica forma justificationis* by which the church is justified is the objective justice of God. It is nothing short of the totality of that order the creator proposes for human dwelling in the reign of God as initiated here, to be fulfilled beyond time. God, in short, cannot but want the divine order embodied in the kingdom. That order requires fullest realization of the human person and human dignity in whatever relationship, sacred or secular, gives it shape. It is unthinkable that the church, because of the order of grace, could be conceived as somehow being above the objective justice of God that justifies.

The justice of God is not the cut and dried justice of the *lex talionis,* but is the richer, more flexible and much more surprising justice of the gospel. Gospel justice pays to the worker hired last the same wages as the one who labored all day (Matthew 20:1-16), and offers a woman taken in adultery protection and forgiveness (John 8:1-11). This is a generous justice which is infectious: Zaccheus had only to experience Jesus' openness to him to respond with lavish restitution for any wrongs he had committed (Luke 19:1-10). In the gospel, God's good news is described as a searching out of the lost and the unloved, not to chide them, but to save them (Luke 15:4-10).

In Matthew's sermon on the mount, Jesus calls those who hunger and thirst for justice happy or blessed, and he assures us that their longing will be satisfied (Matthew 5:6). Further on comes the startling revelation that this justice is not a tidy proposal which deals only with the obvious — murder, adultery, love of neighbor — but with the subtleties of attitude and intention that take anger and sexual objectification and the enemy into consideration. How one treats others is as much a part of justice as what one does to/with them.

The gospels allude to Jesus as the Suffering Servant of Isaiah: "Behold my servant . . . I have put my Spirit upon him. He will bring forth justice to the nations. He will not cry out or raise his voice. . . . A bruised reed he will not break, a dimly burning wick he will not quench. He will faithfully bring forth justice." (Isaiah 42:1-4). The language of not breaking a bent reed or quenching a dim wick evokes language of Vatican II addressed to the church and the bishops: "The church encompasses with love all afflicted with human weakness," (*Lumen Gentium,* Article 9) and "Let him (the bishop) not refuse to listen to his subjects . . ." (Ibid Article 27). It evokes the language of John Paul II in January, 1982, at the time of promulgation of the new code of canon law: "The prime demand of justice is to respect people but above and beyond justice

. . . the (ecclesiastical) judge must tend toward equity and beyond that to charity."

Can the church move beyond a legal and restrictive sense of justice within its own dealings with its members to a more loving and gospel based justice? How can this local U.S. church, nurtured in a country with a rich tradition of protected public dissent and civil disobedience, learn to deal with reasonable dissent in church matters? Can the process of inculturation which has so enriched the North American church in its worship and religious images grow to include a style of communication and interaction between hierarchy and the people of God which is more egalitarian? Will the general perception of the church as speaking strongly to the state and acting weakly for itself in matters of justice and moral example undermine the powerful witness the church takes for justice in the world community?

These are hard questions, but unavoidable in the cultural milieu of the United States. Even more, they are challenges the church must face, perhaps not to resolve them once and for all, but to seek for the growth of the present moment. We are assured that one day our quest for justice will reach satisfaction, but with that assurance goes the responsibility that we will keep on with the quest, that we will hunger and thirst for justice in order to find that fullness in the reign of God.

Fair Process

James Coriden

". . . Anyone who ventures to speak to people about justice must first be just in their eyes. Hence we must undertake an examination of the modes of acting . . . found within the church herself. Within the church rights must be preserved. No one should be deprived of his or her ordinary rights because he or she is associated with the church in one way or another." (*Justice in the World,* nn. 40-41.)

In order to give credible witness to the cause of justice in the world, the church must not only act justly, but also appear to the wider community to be conducting itself justly, fairly and equitably. In the United States a sense of just treatment and fair play is deeply ingrained; it is one of the high expectations in our culture. That sense of fairness, the perception of what Bishop Bevilacqua terms "fair process," is precisely what was offended by the way Sister Agnes Mary Mansour was treated in the events and communications which led up to and culminated in the encounter of May 9, 1983.

Basic fairness or what lawyers call "procedural due process" means that every individual is accorded specific protections in administrative or judicial processes. Among these protections or procedural safeguards are often included:

— the right to be informed of proposed actions which might affect a person adversely;

— the right to be heard in defense of one's rights;

— the right to competent counsel;

— the right to know in advance the procedures to be followed;

— the right to normal and recognized avenues of authority.

32 Authority, Community and Conflict

When such rights are denied, when such procedures are disregarded, then the ordinary perception in our society is that the person was treated unfairly.

Based on the information which has been made public (e.g., in *Origins* 13:12 [September 1, 1983], pp. 197-206) it is easy to conclude, as many thousands of interested people have, that Sister Agnes Mary Mansour was in fact not fairly dealt with by the Holy See (specifically the Sacred Congregation for Religious and Secular Institutes and its ad hoc delegate, Bishop Bevilacqua.) The above-mentioned ordinary expectations of procedural fairness were lacking in the following ways:

1) Sister Agnes Mary was not informed in advance of the radical options which she would be asked to make on the occasion of the May 9 meeting. She was told that the purpose of the meeting was to be shown a mandate and to hear the decision of the Holy See. At the meeting she was required to resign her position at once or to be immediately subject to the process leading to the penalty of dismissal from her community and from religious life.

2) She was not given the opportunity to be fully heard in her own defense. She did not have the chance to prepare and to present her own side of the question, a complex, nuanced and sensitive set of issues, for objective consideration. That arguments were presented elsewhere by others on her behalf does not satisfy her own right to be heard in person.

3) The prior notice given to Sister Agnes Mary was entirely inadequate. It had the elements of suddenness and secrecy, but the more serious deficiency was the lack of candor about the nature of the confrontation: She was told that she was to receive the communication of a decision and she was presented with an ultimatum described in point one.

4) Sister Agnes Mary did not have competent legal counsel. She was told that she could have with her two sisters of her community; she had no one to inform her of her rights or to explain to her the implications of the procedures with which she was confronted. Common criminals are afforded better protection in our justice system than she was given in this respect.

5) The procedures to be followed in the meeting on May 9 and

those involved in the process subjecting her to imposed secularization were not explained to Sister Agnes Mary. She was not
informed of them, and had no reason to believe that she would
be given the opportunity to defend herself. Knowledge of the procedures is essential for justice, and the free choice of options cannot
be made without such knowledge.

6) The confrontation by a bishop-delegate of the Holy See, acting
at the direction of His Holiness, Pope John Paul II, accompanied
by two canon lawyers is an extraordinary intervention of the highest authority in our church. It is not only unusual and therefore
unpredictable, it is overwhelming and therefore intimidating to
the individual. It cuts across the normal lines of authority and
pierces through several levels of communication. Such agency is
intended to insure compliance, but the result is also to limit the
freedom of the person subject to it.

Other elements of this whole unhappy matter could be
scrutinized for further instances of what we in the United States
call "not playing fair," but the foregoing examples may suffice to
explain why the event is perceived as an injustice. Even when
canonical processes are scrupulously attended to, our sense of
"due process" can be gravely offended. This seems to have occurred
in the case of Sister Agnes Mary Mansour.

"The demand for due process of law is an exigence of Christian
dignity and freedom. It is to be satisfied as exactly in the church
as in civil society (one might indeed say, more exactly)." John
Courtney Murray, "Freedom, Authority, Community," *America*
115 (1966), p. 740.

The Magisterium
Richard McCormick, SJ

Agnes Mary Mansour repeatedly stated her moral opposition
to abortion. However, she also stated that, in the present circumstances, she favored Medicaid payments for abortion. Her
refusal to modify this judgment was responsible for her plight.
The ordinary of the archdiocese of Detroit stated that her position
was "contrary to the magisterium." There are two inaccuracies in
that statement. One is explicit, the other implicit. For the overall
health of the magisterium and the effectiveness of its functioning,
these should be spelled out.

For the sake of clarity in this discussion, "magisterium" refers
to the teaching authority of the Catholic hierarchy. Such teaching
is expressed in a "solemn" or "extraordinary" way when a doctrine
is *defined* by an ecumenical council, or by a pope speaking *ex
cathedra*. Any other exercise of the teaching authority of the
bishops or the pope is called "ordinary." Examples of such ordinary
magisterium are the teaching by bishops in their own diocese or
in regional synods, and the teaching by popes in their encyclical
letters (Cf. Francis Sullivan, SJ, *Magisterium: Teaching Authority
in the Catholic Church*, 1983, p. 121).

Explicit

There is a clear difference between "universally binding moral
principles" (*The Challenge of Peace: God's Promise and Our Response*, p. 4) and their application to concrete cases. Of these latter
the bishops' pastoral insists that they do not "carry the same
moral authority as our statement of universal and moral principles
and formal church teaching." Why? Because "when making application of these principles we realize — and we wish readers to
recognize — that prudential judgments are involved based on
specific circumstances which can change or which can be inter-

preted differently by people of good will."

Thus the pastoral, after citing *Gaudium et Spes* (article 43), clearly acknowledges that "on some complex social questions the church expects a certain diversity of views even though all hold the same universal moral principles."

Whether Medicaid should cover abortion or not is clearly not a "universal moral principle." Furthermore, the magisterium has never explicitly addressed this matter. Therefore, it is clear that the Medicaid question is an application where loyal Catholics will manifest "a certain diversity of views even though all hold the same universal moral principles." It is understandable that many, perhaps even most, will disagree with Mansour's judgment. But that does not alter the nature of the judgment — as an *application*. To say that such a judgment is "contrary to the magisterium" is to confuse universal moral principles with concrete applications. Such a confusion will only bring the magisterium into disrepute. As the editors of *America* noted: "To find her position on this issue unacceptable is vastly different from declaring her unfit for office or for religious life or unorthodox in Catholic doctrine" *(America,* May 18, 1983, 409).

Implicit

Implied in the phrase "contrary to the magisterium" is the notion that one may not, within the canons of Catholic loyalty, hold positions that diverge from those of the magisterium. This is both historically and theologically inaccurate. But more importantly it perpetuates a notion of the ordinary magisterium that can only harm the magisterium. It is the notion that the proper response to the magisterium's ordinary teaching is unquestioning and un-critical obedience.

Sound theology will not support such a notion. Yves Congar, OP, has shown that this understanding of the magisterium origi-nated in the first part of the 19th century. It reached its high point under Pius XII *(Human Humani Generis)*. Congar notes that the ordinary magisterium "has been almost assimilated, in current opinion, to the prerogatives of the extraordinary magis-terium." He then continues:

Besides, Pius XII, who carried it to its furthest point, expressed in the encyclical *Humani Generis* (1950) his opinion on two points of great importance: 1) The ordinary magisterium of the pope requires total obedience; "He who listens to you listens to me." When the Pope has expressed his *sententia* on a point previously controversial, there can no longer be any question of free discussion between theologians. 2) The (or a) role of theologians is to justify the declaration of the magisterium.

Congar concludes by asking: "Is this consonant with what 19 centuries of the church's life tell us about the function of *didascale* or doctor? No, not exactly" (*Readings in Moral Theology, No. 3,* ed. C. Curran and R. McCormick, SJ, p. 325). He refers to this development as "an unfitting inflation of encyclicals' authority (*Ibid.,* p. 326).

The text commonly used currently to reinforce this notion of the ordinary magisterium is *Lumen Gentium* article 25 ("religious submission of mind and will"). Yet the church's foremost theologian, Karl Rahner, has argued that this is an inadequate portrayal of the proper Catholic response. He states:

If, for example the statements of *Lumen gentium* (n. 25) on the matter were valid without qualification, then the worldwide dissent of Catholic moral theologians against *Humanae Vitae* would be a massive and global assault on the authority of the magisterium. But the fact that the magisterium tolerates this assult shows that the norm of *Lumen gentium* (and many other similar assertions of the past 100 years) does not express in sufficiently nuanced form a legitimate praxis of the relationship between the magisterium and theologians (*Stimmen der Zeit* 198, 1980, 373).

Similarly theologian Andre Naud, adverting to the wide rejection of Pius XXII's usage in *Humani Generis,* concluded that we must also advance beyond *Lumen Gentium.* "The thought of the church has, therefore, advanced in this matter. It must still advance. In my view, we should not repeat the text of *Lumen Gentium* (25), even less brandish it to condemn, without clarifying its sense" (*Science et Esprit* 32, 1980, 168-169).

If an uncritical obedience (the reading often given to "religious submission of mind and will") is not a theologically defensible understanding of a Catholic response to the ordinary magisterium, what is the proper response?

Writing in 1975, Bishop B.C. Butler stated the matter beautifully. He referred to the "respect that is due to the considered actions of those in positions of legitimate authority." More specifically, he stated that "the mood of the devout believer will be . . . a welcoming gratitude that goes along with the keen alertness of a critical mind, and with a good will concerned to play its part both in the purification and the development of the church's understanding of her inheritance. . ." (*Clergy Review* 60, 1975, 16).

Butler's "keen alertness of a critical mind" implies the possibility of disagreement, and precisely as part of that "good will concerned to play its part both in the purification and development. . . ." If such disagreement is experienced as a threat and treated as such, something is wrong. In other words, the effort to articulate our faith and its behavioral implications is a dialogical and processive one. Bernard Haring notes:

There is no doubt that for her own growth, for her abiding in the truth, and for the fruitful exercise of her pastoral magisterium, the church needs an atmosphere of freedom to examine the enduring validity of traditional norms, and the right of a sincere conscience humbly to doubt about norms which, in many or even most of the cases, are not accepted by sincere Christians (*Theological Studies,* 37, 1976, 85).

These healthy developments and/or statements, accepted by the vast majority of reputable theologians, are undermined by a onesided and heavily juridical notion of the magisterium — a notion implied in the action taken against Mansour on the grounds that her position was "contrary to the magisterium."

"Religious" and "Lay" as Statuses in the Church

Francine Cardman

One of the anomalies in the treatment of Sister Agnes Mary Mansour is the discrepancy between the demands made on her as a Roman Catholic sister and the striking absence of such demands on her three immediate predecessors in the office of director of social services for the state of Michigan, all of them Roman Catholic lay men. That Medicaid funding for abortions is made available through the Department of Social Services was judged by ecclesiastical authorities (and by some other Catholics, including some very vocal ones) to be an intolerable and insurmountable obstacle to Sister Mansour's service as its director.

In the case of her predecessors, however, that aspect of the department's operation evidently raised no serious difficulties in the Catholic community and their exercise of public office was not thought to compromise their good faith or to jeopardize their good standing in the Roman Catholic Church. What is even more striking in this situation is the fact that once she was dispensed from her vows as a Sister of Mercy, Agnes Mary Mansour, lay woman, was likewise free to continue in her government position without being subject to further ecclesiastical sanctions. Neither was she called upon by her bishop to recant publicly her position on the policy question of medicaid funding, a position she had arrived at by following traditional Roman Catholic norms for the formation of conscience.

In seeking to analyze some of the ways in which this case bears on the relationship between "lay" people and "religious" in the church (I use these terms relatively and reluctantly, for the sake of convenience and a certain clarity), several points must be addressed. The most obvious, perhaps, is the way in which her move from religious to lay status seems to have so thoroughly eradicated the problem that Sister Agnes Mary presented to the church as director of social services. What are the standards of faith and witness to which members of the church ought to be held? Is there a difference in the public and ecclesial character of Christians' lives, according to their status in the church? An equally important point has to do with the meaning of religious life, as members of religious communities experience it, as church authorities interpret and seek to regulate it, and as the "faithful" perceive it or expect it to be. At issue in this case, therefore, are some fundamental theological questions about the nature of the church and the variety of forms and expressions of Christian commitment within it.

At least since Vatican II Catholics have tried to think about such matters in a way that affirms the common Christian identity of all the baptized, their common call to holiness, and their common vocation to ministry. But because the council assumed a fundamental dichotomy between church and world, sacred and secular, it continued to divide the one people of God into two distinct groups, clerical and lay. By association religious were generally subsumed under the clerical portion, though in terms of both theology and canon law they are, strictly speaking, lay persons, since they are not (for the most part) clerics.

On the council's understanding, the so-called secular world is the particular sphere of the laity, while the sacred realm of church and sacraments is the province of the clergy. Where religious fall in this apportionment of reality is not entirely clear. As laity, it is to be expected that their lot would logically be with the secular; but because of the assimilation of religious to so many of the conditions of the clerical state, they tend to be regarded as belonging to the realm of the sacred. For all practical purposes, canon law pertaining to religious (in the new code of 1983 as well as in the 1917 Code) treats them more or less as clerics. The net result of this ambiguity is that religious are subject to most of the disadvantages of both states, while sharing few of the privileges of either.

The adequacy of this understanding of church and world, sacred and secular, clergy (or religious) and laity has met with increasing challenge in the years since Vatican II. The growing maturity of the laity and their consequent involvement in ministry and social action has been one source of challenge; the thoroughgoing renewal of religious life, especially among American communities of women has been another. As Catholics have heard anew the gospel call to the work of peace and justice, many of them — lay, cleric and religious alike — have responded by taking up political ministries of various sorts, including the holding of public office. Their experience has further highlighted the degree to which the council's dichotomy of church and world, sacred and secular has failed to account for the political nature of human existence — and of the gospel.

The events surrounding Sister Mansour's appointment as director of social services have underlined the inconsistencies of Vatican II's understanding of the church and its mission in the world. In her situation, therefore, we see not simply a confrontation between an individual and ecclesiastical authority, nor of one religious community and a Vatican congregation. Rather, we see a conflict about the very nature and integrity of religious life, the ecclesial identity of lay persons and members of religious communities, and the religious significance of political activity.

It is especially to the second of these issues that I want to attend in the rest of this essay, though it clearly touches on the other two. The question of ecclesial identity has two parts: To what extent do persons represent the church (that is, what is the public nature of their witness as Christians) and to what standards of accountability are they held?

The identification with Christ and the community that comes about through baptism pertains equally to all Christians. In this respect, all the baptized are representatives of Christ and the church. Beyond this, can it be said that some persons are more closely identified with or more representative of the church than others? Only, I would argue, in the strictly limited functional sense that some — namely the clergy — are designated as official representatives of the church. Their capacity to represent the church institutionally is a function of their office, that is, of their position in its structures of authority.

Because religious life is not primarily about this kind of office holding, it does not have the same sort of institutional function that the ordained ministry does. It is something of a truism to assert that official representatives of an institution have an obligation to present and interpret its teachings and beliefs responsibly (which is not the same as simply repeating them uncritically). It is quite another thing, however, to determine whether the rejection of Medicaid funding for abortion is an institutional position of the sort that those who hold office in the church ought to be expected to promote and defend.

What is clear from the statements of various parties representing the Detroit archdiocese and the Vatican is that it is acceptable for lay persons to hold a contrary position on this matter. But moral judgments deemed appropriate for lay persons are in this case considered so inappropriate for religious that they are not permitted to hold them in public. The assumptions behind this reasoning are worth examining. There is, in the first place, the assumption that members of religious communities are institutional representatives of the church whose moral judgments on matters of public policy such as the use of Medicaid funds ought to adhere to the strictest interpretation of the church's position on the subject.

Implicit in this assumption is another: that lay people ought not to be held to the same standards of faith, conscience and holiness of life as clergy or religious. Without at all wanting to imply that the laity should come under the same sort of scrutiny from the hierarchy as religious do — or even that religious should be directed and disciplined to the degree that they have been in this instance — I do think that the discrepancies between religious and laity are important to note. In terms of the Mansour case, they can be put this way: As a sister, Agnes Mary Mansour's exercise of conscience in reaching her position on Medicaid funding of abortion was not of sufficient weight to override what church officials thought to be her public role and the institution's self-interest; as a lay person, her public witness as a Christian was not of sufficient importance to evoke any pastoral concern on the part of these same officials.

What is missing in the reasoning that would permit such an anomaly is any sense of the public nature of every Christian's faith commitment. It is not just those who function in an official capacity as institutional representatives whose Christian witness is public. Nor is it those persons plus such others as have undertaken a "religious" rather than a "secular" life. Rather, Christian faith is public by its very nature. To commit oneself to Christ and to stand within Christ's church is to make a public choice that is political in its character and its consequences. For this reason, all Christians are accountable for the witness they bear.

To say this presumes, of course, that the matter under consideration rightly requires such accountability, that there are appropriate means of holding persons accountable, and that these means are applied consistently and justly. As the Mansour case makes glaringly evident, this simply is not so. Sister Mansour could be subjected to the discipline of obedience, not only within her religious community, but in spite of it. Because the 1983 code of canon law interprets the religious vow of obedience as referring ultimately to the pope (as the "highest superior," canon 590), she could also be subjected to the exercise of papal authority through the medium of the Sacred Congregation for Religious and Secular Institutes, as well as through a papal delegate.

It is perhaps fortunate that no comparable structures exist for lay people. For them, excommunication is the only real means of accountability at hand, and that is a penalty so severe that to incur it requires a matter of considerably more gravity — and a great deal more moral certainty — than one's position on Medicaid funding of abortion. In the long run, therefore, it is only the cogency of a moral position or doctrinal teaching, as well as the persuasiveness with which it is presented, that will command persons' attention and assent. Without that, even the most just structures and processes will be of little avail, and whatever other means might prove effective at removing or silencing offending individuals or groups will nevertheless fail to produce conversion of either mind or heart.

In the aftermath of Sister — now Ms. — Mansour's case, the most important theoretical work to be done, I would suggest, involves rethinking the church/world relationship as presented in the documents of Vatican II and developing in its place a view in which church and world are integrally related, so that the political is understood to be a constitutive dimension of the religious. In practical terms, it yet remains to give flesh to a church in which the ecclesial nature of all the baptized is recognized, in which the gifts of all are received, and is which the witness of all in acknowledged and valued.

As to the relationship of lay people and those in religious community, much of the tension and difficulty could be alleviated by the affirmation that they share an essentially similar vocation: to give witness to certain Christian values and charisms, both in the church and in the world. Which values and which charisms are specifically lifted up depends on the particular religious community or form of lay life, as well as on concrete historical circumstances. Regardless of the specifics, however, all members of both groups are representatives of Christ and the church by virtue of their baptism, and all are witnesses to the gospel by virtue of the public character of their religious commitment. Likewise, all share in the rights and responsibilities inherent in their baptismal incorporation into the one people of God. The freedom to be faithful in and to Christ includes, therefore, for lay and religious alike, the freedom to dissent when serious matters of conscience require it.

Toward Communal Empowerment

Mary E. Hunt and

Lora Ann Quiñonez, CDP

Decision-making in the Roman Catholic Church has come to be experienced and understood as an exercise of power by a few rather than as a work in which the Spirit is present among the many. Those with jurisdiction have sole power to decide fundamental issues of policy and discipline. The rest of the church is left to comply or not as their consciences dictate and to accept the sometimes severe consequences of choices into which they have had no input. The inadequacies of this exclusive model are emerging in many corners of the world church. The case of Sister Agnes Mary Mansour is one of the many instances in which the limitations of the present model are obvious. The Mansour case and others like it serve to precipitate a shift from the current exclusive model to an inclusive model of communal empowerment.

In the Mansour case the person, her community and the needs of the local church in Michigan were in conflict with the will of

the hierarchy. The current model favored ultimatums, stalemates, and either-or decisions in which many could not discern the presence and working of the Spirit. Rather, many faithful people were confused, scandalized, and alienated by the leadership of their own church. Likewise, the leadership was unable to fulfill its responsibility of active accompaniment of the people of God because it perceived itself and acted as if its role were circumscribed by law and dogma. Fortunately, perhaps providentially, creative alternatives are being envisioned and models of communal empowerment are beginning to emerge which invite all members of the church to assume the role of mature and mutual pilgrims.

This essay is an attempt to clarify some of the problems which many faithful Catholics have with the current model of decision-making. It does not deny the important role of the pope, councils, and bishops in the church but recognizes that these offices have been exercised variously in history. Further, it assumes that these important roles and the persons who fulfill them faithfully are part of the whole process of communal empowerment. It is an effort to show the difference between the exercise of jurisdiction and the emerging sense of empowerment. It is written as part of the constant process of renewal urged by Vatican II (*Lumen Gentium*, Article 9), which allows us to move from one model to another, contingent on the needs of the day and consistent with the values of the tradition.

The present institutional model of decision-making in which only a few persons engage in the process was not given by Jesus to the early church. Nor was it developed by the early church. Rather, it was a product of the Counter-Reformation, a response to criticisms of the hierarchy and of the papacy (cf. Avery Dulles, *Models of the Church*, 1974, especially chapter 2). Leaders in the late Middle Ages absolutized a rigid corporate pattern including little consultation with those who were not office holders.

The more fluid style of the early church, with its inclusion of many, was rejected further in the late 19th century by Vatican I. What Jesus had given were norms and values which apply to all evolving models of church in all moments in history. But these were often ignored by those who maintained that the monarchical

model was part of revelation rather than a product of the absolutiz-
ing of one model from a particular period of history. As a result
we have inherited an institutional model which is simply inadequate to respond to contemporary circumstances.

Among the inadequacies of the present model are some which
arose in the Mansour case. The inadequacies result in a model
which is at base exclusionary. First, authority is seen to reside
in one part of the community rather than in the community as a
whole. Thus decisions which are made without consultation are
met with surprise and resistance, not unexpected when those
involved have been left aside. In the long run they are decisions
more difficult to implement than those arrived at by communal
assent.

Second, there is an unfounded equation made between office
and power. Those who hold office, namely cardinals and bishops,
retain the power to decide everything from the next pope to diocesan budgetary matters. It is not clear that such a small group
can assess and evaluate the complex issues at stake in the modern
world. It is clear that competent authorities in specific areas are
needed for guidance and policy setting. The insights with which
the Spirit gifts different persons help to insure the integrity of
final choices.

Third, the limits placed on the *collegium* or the body of those
ordained are so constraining as to guarantee that the needs and
gifts of the many, particularly of the marginalized or outsider,
will never be a part of the decision making realm of the institutional church.

Finally, the present model relies heavily on secrecy. Processes
are often unclear and the persons deciding are often anonymous.
Accountability to the larger body is all but absent. These inadequacies add up to an exclusive model which keeps the church
from developing its full potential as a community committed to
and working together toward making love and justice visible.

The current model of authority is predicated on a limited notion
of apostolic succession. It passes over the fact that continuity with
the faith of the apostles is a charism of the entire church, not
simply of a small group. Apostolic succession understood in this

way helps us to value the whole community and to see the dignity
and worth of each individual. Persons are valued and respected
for who they are and not for the role that they play. This understanding helps us to see why the person and not the office is what
is compelling in contemporary leadership models. Many persons
of skill and compassion who act as servants of the entire church
are seen as leaders. Those vested with authority derived from
office are not necessarily perceived as leaders. Such sometimes
have only the power to compel which comes from their office, not
the power to enable, to invite, to accompany which effective servants possess.

This kind of empowering leadership is experienced by faithful
Catholics through many women leaders, nonordained ministers,
those who perform the diaconal tasks and those whose exemplary
lives and work outside of the institutional church mark them as
carriers of gospel values. Just as in the early church allegiance
to the community was generated through the life, death and resur-
rection of Jesus, so, in our time, care and respect are focused on
relationships. It is relationships with those who embody love and
justice that hint at new ways of being church.

Many sources are providing us with assistance in fleshing out
a relational, inclusive and thus empowering model of decision-
making. I will focus on three sources — feminist values, the specific character of the North American church and the contribution
of Latin American liberation theology. I invite readers to add their
own sources.

Feminist values are beginning to take root in the church via
the experience of Catholic women in the contemporary women's
movements. Among the commitments shared by such women is
an insistence on the importance of the process used in reaching
decisions, at times even its priority over the substance of the
decision reached. This does not mean that the content has become
unimportant. Rather, it means that how we interact with one
another, our right relations, is taken as sacred. It is in this way
that we mirror the divine.

Another value arising out of women's experience of marginali-
zation is inclusivity itself. Even though we know that it takes
longer to reach a decision with the inclusion of more people, we

choose to take the time rather than to leave the persons aside. A third shared value is our commitment to take a range of sources into consideration for decision making. This arises both from our realization that we have been excluded from many of the traditional sources (e.g. the formation of most theology until very recently) and from our awareness of the richness of sources which have been ignored. These include the arts, literature and the like.

These sources lead us to value more than the cognitive, rational mode and to take feelings, stories and prayer as important parts of integrated persons who make decisions. We have seen feminist values at play in many women's congregations as well as in the organizations and base communities of women seeking to share faith. We know how our lives have been enriched and our faith renewed when we embrace such values which flow from our Christian heritage. We recognize these as part of our contribution to a global church which seeks to be a community of empowerment.

The North American church as a whole, with the influence of committed women, brings other elements to the emerging model. As a relatively young church, its identity is less tied to a rigid way of being church. It is beginning to respond to the particular needs of a democratic country whose people understand the exercise of rights and responsibilities as inalienably linked to their dignity as human beings. It is finding that the richness of pluralism, while never easy to handle nor neat in its resolution, opens a range of new options for the church. For example it fosters interreligious dialogue, it allows for a diversity of opinion, and it respects the uniqueness of the individual.

The North American church community has taken Vatican II seriously in its effort to develop egalitarian relationships in the modern world. It has fostered the duty of citizens to engage responsibly in public life, seeing this not as alien but essential to being a religious person. The North American church shares with the diverse population of this country a willingness to experiment, to try new ways of being and acting, confident that it can incorporate what is consistent with the Christian tradition and disregard what is inconsistent.

A move in this direction was found in the process of wide consultation employed for the bishops' peace pastoral. Rather than erasing any sense of church, there is an upsurge in interest in religion, as well as a growing Catholic population. The North American church began as an immigrant group striving to imitate the many local churches from which it came. Now it is growing into another local church with its own clergy, religious and identity as well as its own contribution to make to the world church. This was the context out of which the Mansour case arose and it needs to be taken seriously.

The Latin American church has its own contribution to make to the evolving patterns of decision-making in the world church. Its heavy emphasis on context alerted it to the need to consider the particular person in the particular place at the particular time in history when evaluating a situation prior to making a decision. It has also stressed the importance of base communities, small groups of committed people in which actions, decisions and prayer can be shared so that everyone is a participant and no one is simply a spectator. This method on a small scale means major changes in the role of clergy and members of the hierarchy who find themselves joined by lay people in all of the work of the church.

The Latin American church has relied on the social sciences, especially sociology and economics, to analyze power structures. It is no surprise that the same analysis has been used on the church as an institution, resulting in a substantial critique of the allocation of ecclesial resources and especially of the limited participation in decision making. These insights are available to the North American church and have been taken seriously. They form part of the basis of the dissatisfaction with the official church's way of handling the difficult problems in the Mansour case.

These influences, and others which could be mentioned, combine to spell a new moment in the life of the world church. It is a moment when customary channels are expanding, when new voices are being heard, when suspicions are cast upon what limits and claims are made for what is included. There is a new stress on embracing the gospel but it is met with an equally strong expectation that we will be embraced, each of us, in our frailty and fullness. This was missing in the Mansour case, but need not be missing in the future when communities, aware of their own context as well as of their own limits, empower their members to take responsibility.

Lora Ann Quiñonez, CDP, contributed to the preparation of this article and was also a member of the Washington task force.

Analysis and Commentary on the Documents

Madonna Kolbenschlag, HM

Analysis

In an effort to clarify their respective positions, the principal actors in the Mansour case have each provided a "chronology" detailing their sense of what happened, when, and why. We have a chronology from the Mercy provincialate, a subsequent chronology by the papal delegate, Bishop Anthony Bevilacqua, and a statement and response by Agnes Mary Mansour (cf. *Origins*, vol. 13, September 1, 1983). It should be noted that in March, Archbishop Edmund Szoka also submitted a report to the Holy See through the apostolic delegate, Archbishop Pio Laghi. This report has not been made public.

As the various actors spin out their scripts, concerned onlookers who would attempt to unravel the complex skein inevitably experience a kind of "Rashomon-effect," finding themselves engaged as interpreters in a drama in which point of view seems to render facts and events relative, a context in which values such as truth and fidelity seem to mean different things to different people.

Two principal documents, the Mercy provincialate chronology and the Bevilacqua chronology (along with two interpretive documents), reveal some crucial discrepancies. The Mercy chronology indicates that Szoka's initial permission for Mansour's appointment did *not* include a reservation or stipulation that would require her to state publicly her opposition to Medicaid funding for abortions. Both Mansour and her provincial superior, who were the witnesses to these conversations, deny what Bevilacqua seems to assume, that Szoka's permission was premised on this condition. It is also evident that, at least in this portion of the chronology, Bevilacqua has used only Szoka's version as his source.

Szoka and Mansour disagree on the conclusions drawn from their conversation on December 29. Szoka says he gave Mansour permission to accept her appointment as director of social services on condition that she take a clear stand opposing Medicaid funding for abortions. She says that she made it clear that her position was a matter of conscience, that she could not oppose such funding, and that the archbishop's final admonition was to simply state that she was obliged to uphold the law and say as little as possible about it.

Judging by the archbishop's subsequent remarks to the media, this was his position on the matter in December. In an interview on December 31, Szoka said that he believed Mansour was in the same position as Catholic laymen appointed or elected to office: "they have to follow what the law is." He added, "(Sister Mansour) is a Catholic, she follows the teachings of the church, but she cannot control the laws of the state, and Medicaid funding is a matter of law. To make such a big issue out of this one thing seems a bit sensational" *(Detroit Free Press,* December 31, 1983).

Another substantive discrepancy is apparent in the description of the May 9 interview and in Bevilacqua's report that Mansour was "adamant in wanting secularization immediately" and that she stated she had "been thinking about it since the matter began." Both Mansour and her superiors, who were present and had been privy to her state of mind in preceding weeks, have objected to this as misrepresentation.

Mansour and her witnesses describe the interview in very stark terms. She and her superiors (she had been requested to bring two "companions") arrived at the meeting with no particulars of the nature of mandate to be presented to her, no preliminary description of the due process involved or of the rights and responsibilities of all those party to the discussion. Bevilacqua then read the eight page mandate and precept.

At the conclusion of the reading, Mansour inquired about her options. When she realized that there were only two proposed: "immediately resign or immediately be subject to a process of dismissal," she then expressed her concern about not being seen as "standing in defiance of the Holy Father," as she believed would be the implication of dismissal from her order. She then inquired whether a request for dispensation would be interpreted as an act of defiance. Bevilacqua replied that it would not. For Mansour, resignation from her office after four months on the job was not a viable option, since she felt obliged to continue her commitment to the people, and especially to the poor, of Michigan. She explained later, "I had never considered this option (dispensation) as an acceptable solution, but I had feared that this sacrifice might be required. This fear stemmed from the secretive way the current meeting had been arranged, the process to date which had continually bypassed my legitimate religious superiors and had never once allowed me to present my side for objective consideration."

In an explanatory note attached to his chronology, Bevilacqua says that Mansour, in requesting a dispensation, precluded the canonical process of dismissal, which would have given her the right to two opportunities to defend herself within a specified period of time. Mansour's response again highlights her state of mind at that time. "The canonical process in the explanatory note was never presented or discussed with me. I was never told the steps of the canonical process or that I would have been given the opportunity to defend myself. I had no reason to believe such would be the case. My fear was any delay on my part might well mean defiance and dismissal."

Another communication crucial to the turn of events took place on March 23 when Archbishop Pio Laghi, the apostolic delegate, informed Sister Theresa Kane, president of the Sisters of Mercy of the Union, and Sister Emily George, a member of the Mercy administrative team, that Kane must require Mansour to resign from her post. From Bevilacqua's report it seems clear that Laghi regarded the instruction given to Kane at that March 23 meeting as final. Yet the sisters did not perceive that the situation had reached an ultimate stage and subsequently requested a formal reconsideration because a "careful and deliberative study of all factors had not been taken into account." There was no reply to this request prior to the irrevocable events of May 9.

Commentary

These chronologies and appended commentaries have become the "briefs," or — depending on one's hermeneutic bias — the "scriptures" of the Mansour case. As I have noted, the major discrepancies between the two principal versions have serious implications for those concerned about justice and truth. But aside from these textual considerations, there are contextual elements which suggest that the values of justice and truth are being perceived and pursued differently.

Bishop Bevilacqua's report belabors the fact that the requirements of a fair canonical process and the protection of rights were "scrupulously attended to." Yet, it is obvious in the minds of many, including the objects of the process — Agnes Mary Mansour and the Sisters of Mercy — that "due process" was seriously flawed, if not ignored. Bishop Thomas Gumbleton of Detroit has expressed the common understanding of "due process" in the social context: "The minimum requirement for due process is that, in any dispute, both sides should be heard as completely and as fully as possible." It would seem that *canonical* truth and justice is of a different order than *social* truth and justice. Sister Emily George recounts another evidence of this that took place in the May 9 encounter with Bevilacqua. When she questioned the bishop about the accuracy of the "facts" contained in the precept he read to Mansour, Bevilacqua replied that her question was not relevant: what was important was that they had been presented and heard. Thus, on the one hand, one consciousness perceives truth as an *outcome* of a process of discovery and discernment, the other as *prerogative* of authority and obedience.

Ultimately the question of justice must also take into account the moral freedom of the individual and the imperatives of personal conscience. Mansour describes her decision to ask for a dispensation as one made "with limited freedom." One observer has described the action of the Vatican as a "cancellation of her moral freedom." This is indeed a serious question, and when issues of "obedience" and "magisterial teaching" are — as they inevitably will be — ameliorated and clarified with the passage of time, the injury to the spirit and social person of Agnes Mary Mansour will continue to demand acts of restitution and healing on the part of the institutional church.

Those who believe that she acted freely in requesting a dispensation point to the fact that she made her decision speedily and unequivocally, that she intentionally abrogated her right to a dismissal "process" and a hearing. Those who believe that her freedom was compromised point to her genuine commitment to her position as an extension of her commitment as a Sister of Mercy, to her unwillingness to stand in "defiance" of the Holy See, and to the fact that church authorities did not inform her, prior to the events of last spring, of her rights under canon law and the nature of the action to be taken against her.

Moral theologians distinguish between essential and effective freedom. Effective freedom can be compromised by external circumstances, one's psychological state, lack of knowledge and the unwillingness of the subject. Agnes Mary Mansour was, no doubt, essentially free on the evening of May 9, but many are convinced that her effective freedom to choose an acceptable option had been cancelled or at least gravely impaired.

Her conscience may have been violated in another way by the papal precept. In effect, in demanding an *immediate* resignation under threat of dismissal, it trivialized the significance of her sincere 30-year commitment as a Sister of Mercy in perpetual vows. The papal mandate chose to view her life-long commitment less seriously than the "scandal" of the moment caused by the publicity surrounding her appointment. Sadly, the church — which ought to stand for the essential — seemed to take the side of the ephemeral. A greater scandal may have been the result. Can one imagine a marriage or priestly celibacy being dissolved so quickly?

Other questions concerning authority and obedience remain. The new code of canon law carefully defines and guarantees the legitimate authority and autonomy of religious communities and local bishops. Were these provisions respected in the Mansour case? What procedures should be followed to insure justice when two legitimate authorities are in conflict? Should these procedures be incorporated into church law? What about the principles of subsidiarity and collegiality? What is the role and responsibility of the apostolic delegate in these matters. Is it one that is likely to protect and enhance the integrity and rights of the local church and the individual?

Beyond these considerations of how truth and a just resolution of conflict are arrived at and how legitimate authority as well as personal conscience are to be respected, the Mansour case leaves us with the impression that what we have witnessed in this sad spectacle is a clash of radically different perceptions of church — two conflicting ecclesiologies. Indeed the Mansour case seems to be a tragedy of expectations, acted out on the basis of a projected paradigm of church.

On the one hand, we see the familiar outline of the *societas perfecta* in the behavior of the church officials. This theological conception, which prevailed from the time of Pius IX to that of Pius XII, viewed the church as singularly true, hierarchical, monarchial society, a "perfect society" that was totally independent of every other society and endowed with everything necessary to attain its end of the supernatural sanctification and salvation of humanity. This notion fostered a juridical ecclesiology; it created ecumenical problems since it implied that all other Christian communities were "non-churches"; and it did not recognize or provide for a theology of the local church. The prevailing theology of Vatican II was markedly different. It preferred to speak of church as sacrament and mystery, the people of God and the Body of Christ, a pilgrim church in need of conversion, a prophetic, priestly, and eschatological community of disciples, an evangelized and evangelizing community. Above all, it recognized the principle of inculturation.

Religious communities, in the renewal period since Vatican II, have struggled to incorporate the ecclesiology of Vatican II in their own internal structures, particularly in their efforts to insure subsidiarity, collegiality, and fidelity to the spirit of their founders, to gospel rather than juridical norms. Clearly, Sister Agnes Mary Mansour and the Sisters of Mercy involved are a product of this second paradigm of church.

Thus, we see in their expectations and their ordinary *modus operandi* a consciousness, a perception of reality that is quite different from that of some church officials. We see "dialog" and directness as opposed to "fiat" and distancing by directive; "discernment" as opposed to "blind obedience"; openness as opposed to secrecy; a communal process as opposed to hierarchical decision-making. It is interesting to note that the papal mandate was precipitous, absolute, uncompromising, and came within days of Szoka's submission of a report to Rome. The official position of the Mercy General Chapter has come after months of internal discussion and discernment, phrased in the language of mutuality and reconciliation.

Thus the discrepancies in the different versions provided by the principal actors in the Mansour case reveal two disparate paradigms of consciousness and group behavior — men and women equally committed to the church and its mission, but perceiving and acting through distinctly different prisms.

Beyond questions of "what" and "how" the ultimate question of "why" remains. The particularities of time, place, publicity and psychology perhaps can provide more answers to that question than more universal considerations. Ultimately we must ask ourselves — hierarchy, laity, religious — how do *we* act as an authentic community of disciples of Jesus in the face of those very particularities?

III.
Theological Reflections

Redeeming Conflict

Thomas Clarke, SJ

My reflection on the case histories described in this volume aims to illustrate a method of theologizing which may assist others, besides bishops and professional theologians, to participate in dialogue and conflict resolution within the church. The past few decades have witnessed the emergence of what I would call a new way in theology, distinct from the characteristic ways in which the magisterium and academic theologians are accustomed to theologize. This third way goes by the name of theological reflection.[1] The most useful practical schema I have seen for its pursuit is the so-called pastoral circle or praxis cycle developed by Joe Holland and Peter Henriot of the Center of Concern.[2] After some introductory paragraphs describing in broad terms the three ways and their relationships, I will reflect on a particular facet of the Mercy case histories through four sets of comments which exemplify the four phases of the pastoral circle. My hope is that these observations will encourage readers to practice, in their own pastoral contexts, particularly conflictual ones, a similar kind of reflection.

History discloses that there is no single ideal way to theologize, that is, to seek and find a human understanding of life in the light of faith. From earliest times until the present, various theologies have been called into being by the needs of Christians in different cultural settings. Each of these theologies has had its principal agents or subjects, its primary locus within the church, its specific goals, its genre of discourse, and its shaping method. Augustine and Chrysostom theologized as pastoral bishops, Benedict and Bernard as monks, Thomas and Duns Scotus as medieval university doctors, Catherine and Teresa as mystics, Luther and Ignatius as Church reformers, Harnack and Newman and Barth and Lonergan from distinctive vantage points within the church and within culture. John of the Cross and George Herbert and Daniel Berrigan chose poetic forms of theologizing, Francois Mauriac and Graham Greene fictional forms, and T.S. Eliot the medium of drama to convey some distinctive understanding of faith. Some, especially academics, might prefer to call several of these forms theologal rather than theological. What seems beyond question is history's witness to the diversity of ways, agents, situations, goals, and methods, as different people have sought to articulate their faith.

In today's situation, one may distinguish three important and interdependent ways in theology:[3]

1) *Dogmatic* (or *magisterial*) theology has as its agents the bearers of church office and those who assist them or mediate their official teaching to others. The Tridentine seminary was the primary site for this way of theologizing, and the typical roman congregation still espouses it as a preferred way. Order and certitude were — and are — its chief preoccupations. Its method tends to center around the elucidation of dogma, particularly infallible dogma, as the solid doctrinal base for guaranteeing moral and disciplinary order and certitude within the church. This theology served the Tridentine church well as it reacted defensively to the reformation and subsequently to the various revolutions of modernity. Its conflicts with the second way have produced many of the headlines about Roman Catholicism in the Vatican II era. This way seems to provide the underlying theological assumptions behind the canonical, pastoral, and disciplinary behavior of church officials in the Mercy case histories.

2) *Academic* (or *professional*) theology as it emerged first, in Protestant and then, in Roman Catholic circles represented an accommodation of the church to modernity. Once the turn to sub-

jectivity and history, so characteristic of modern thought, was grudgingly accepted, and the passion for order and certitude mitigated, there emerged a way of theologizing marked by the passion for truth, or rather, for the detached pursuit of truth. The pluralism and cultivation of healthy doubt manifest in this way are in sharp contrast with the prevailing mood of magisterial theology. Methods and paradigms appropriate to this basic posture are continually constructed and revised by highly trained and specialized practitioners. As its exponents have gained confidence and have sought greater ecclesiastical tolerance and influence (sometimes resorting to an earlier language which spoke of the magisterium of theologians), tensions with the agents of the first way have heightened. The anonymous theologians and canonists with whom the Sisters of Mercy consulted were doubtless exponents of this second way. One drawback in the recurring quarrels between bishops and professionals has been the relegation of those who belong to neither of these elite groups to a passive spectator role. Fortunately this situation is changing, as a third force emerges in Roman Catholic theology. In the Michigan and Rhode Island conflicts, the Sisters of Mercy, along with supporting groups like Network and LCWR, were giving voice to this new way in theology.

3) *Theological reflection* is a way of naming this third force. It is interesting that, as this essay is being written, the Sisters of Mercy of the Union have embarked on an international project, "The Communal Search for Truth," which is designed to facilitate the practice of this way by their own membership and by others within the larger Mercy family. The primary agents of this new mode of theologizing are neither bearers of church office nor professional theologians but "ordinary Christians." This way appears strikingly post-modern in its disengagement from some principal postures of modernity. In the language of the three root metaphors, it seems to cultivate the artistic rather than the organic, or mechanistic root metaphors which prevail in magisterial and academic theology respectively.[4] That it should now be espoused by U.S. women religious who are, as I shall later claim, lay members of the church, is fitting in view of the current need to give both women and lay people their due place in shaping the life of the church. Far more than academic theology, where the

individual theologian, however collaboratively, remains the primary agent, this third way is predominantly a communal exercise. Its goals and methods are focused neither on certitude nor on speculative truth but rather on action or praxis, on the decisional shaping of faith experience. With greater immediacy in its concern for the integration of belief and lived faith, it aims not merely at defining or interpreting human life but at transforming it.

Elsewhere, in a reflection on tradition and teaching within the church, I have elaborated a simple understanding of how these three ways are related to one another.[5] Basically the relationship is one of mutual dependence, challenge and support, i.e., complementarity. All three include the transcendent elements which are to be found in every version of theology: recourse to scripture and tradition, to human experience, to history and cultural ambience, to rational reflection aided by a philosophical outlook, and to practical implications for the faith life of believers and the fulfillment of the church's mission. But the guiding paradigms and inner dynamisms will be different. In the process of employing the pastoral circle for reflection on the Mercy case histories, some of these major differences will be manifest.

Finally, it needs to be said that the three ways not infrequently intersect. The U.S. bishops, for example, have begun to develop in the pastorals on peace and the economic system a mode of magisterial theologizing which draws extensively on the theological posture of the second way.[6]

With the foregoing as introduction, let me now make some observations on the case histories within the framework of the pastoral circle. A few preliminary remarks will indicate the character and modest scope of what I am doing.

First, the pastoral circle may be described as an holistic exercise of faith in search of pastoral understanding. It engages in several kinds of theological behavior, all of which are informed by faith and, therefore, dependent for their quality on the quality of the faith which informs them. At the same time, their excellence will be conditioned by the skill of the agents in exercising each of the several theological behaviors; in integrating them all into a wholeness; and in making the total process relevant and effective in the transformation of consciousness and structures in a given situation.

Second, the four phases are identified as: 1) *Experience* (or "insertion", as Holland/Henriot now designate it); 2) *social analysis;* 3) *theological reflection* (from which the entire process gets its name), which I would further differentiate into *evaluational* and *recommendational* components; 4) *pastoral decision* (or *discernment)*.

Third, given the complexities of the case histories as well as the modest limits of this study, I must select one or two important aspects for treatment. The various participants have given assorted listings of the important issues, most notably obedience, cooperation in the grave sin of abortion and the accompanying scandal of the faithful, and due process. My reflection will focus on underlying issues: to some extent on the autonomy of communities of women religious in relationship to hierarchical authority, but more directly on the place of women religious, as compared with clerics and other laity, within the church, and hence on the issue of their appropriate participation in political life. Obviously these issues could not be integrally dealt with except in connection with others such as collegiality, subsidiarity, the role of representation and dissent in the church, etc. But my concern is not so much to make an overall evaluation about the cases as to illustrate a particular way of theologizing about them. Finally, it is important to add that I am not directly concerned with canonical evaluation but with a reflective theological response to the case histories.

I. *Experience*

"I have a story to share this evening." That is how Helen Marie Burns, Agnes Mary Mansour's provincial superior, began her presentation to the 900 people who had gathered on Pentecost evening in 1983 to express their solidarity with Agnes Mary. The sentence epitomizes the first kind of theological behavior constitutive of the pastoral circle. Before the analysis and the reflection, and the moment of decision and action, must first come the sharing of the story. Helen Marie went on to give a chronology of events, and it was no accident that this chronology differed from the account rendered by Bishop Bevilacqua and by the SCRIS *praeceptum*. Stories are more than the listing of facts. They are spoken by persons, standing in particular places, and carrying the memories of the heart, not just of the head. The way the story is told is already a powerful shaper of the judgments and decisions which are to follow.

Similarly, the first question proposed to participants in "The Communal Search for Truth" project reads: "How did you *feel* as a Sister of Mercy and as a U.S. woman religious when each situation (the Mansour case and the appointment of the Quinn commission) became public?"

For agents of the first two ways in theology this kind of experiential question is at best pre-theological and extrinsically dispositive of the theological agent; in no way is it constitutive of the theological process itself. In the third genre, however, the retrieval and sharing of experience already mediates, in story form, an understanding of faith. The articulation in speech of memories of the heart (as contrasted with a merely empirical listing of objective data) already points to the final praxis-word that will terminate the journey around the circle. Such a "narrative theology" affects each of the other phases. Where academic and dogmatic theologies bracket personal experience as irrelevant or even as hindering the detachment or clarity of their theological pursuit of truth or certitude, the third way's theological goals are realizable only if the personal story of each participant and the communal story of the group grounds the rest of the process.

As a belated participant in the reflection on the Mercy experience, I begin by retrieving and sharing some relevant aspects of my own story. I am a U.S. Catholic, Jesuit priest, erstwhile professional theologian, and friend and collaborator of the Sisters of Mercy. So, when I set my feet to journey around this particular circle, I have to ask myself about my own feelings in the various stages of the unfolding drama. And my affective memory recalls a rich variety of pertinent earlier experiences: how I had my very first contact with the Sisters of Mercy in 1938, in a little farmhouse outside of Saranac Lake where I was recovering from TB, and where my Jesuit vocation began to present itself; then, how I felt through my years as a Jesuit, as I personally experienced or learned about a whole series of episodes in which individual Jesuits or the whole Society of Jesus were constrained in their apostolic initiatives by actions of the official church. The string of memories includes John Courtney Murray, Pierre Teilhard de Chardin, Henri de Lubac, Robert Drinan, Fernando Cardenal, the entire 32nd General Congregation of 236 Jesuits in 1975, and the leadership of our community in the months consequent upon the sudden illness of our beloved Pedro Arrupe.

What feelings appear as I engage, in present context, in this exercise? They are varied: compassion for those afflicted, together with a certain comfort that my religious community also has experienced the ecclesiastical institution as repressive; at the same time, a sense of being challenged as I ask whether my response and that of my community has had the courage and authenticity which I see in the response of the Sisters of Mercy. I experience horror at seeing institutional repression happening within the same church which I have experienced as deeply loving and nurturing of my life. I feel spontaneous anger at the personal agents and instruments of the repression, and a more deliberate anger at the structures, language, and procedures which have facilitated it. I also am in touch with my fears: fear that I may have to risk involvement, fear that involvement may direct the displeasure of others against me; fear of making a fool of myself, especially if both anger and fear cloud my theological judgments or make my speech incoherent; and the dread that, despite all valiant efforts, we may all be helpless to overcome what appears as a fated recurrence: holy church simultaneously nourishing and devouring its children.

Right now I am apprehensive that some professional colleagues, at once sympathetic and impatient, may be saying, "For God's sake, get into the theology, if that's what you're doing. You haven't really said anything theological." But I think I have. I have already tipped my hand, disclosed my value base, expressed a bias, and pointed towards areas of interest and kinds of analytical and reflective questions which I can now go on to ask. Also, in having to deal with my fear and anger, I increase the likelihood that my theological reflection will be graced with courage and hope, both of which are impossible unless the rather dangerous gifts of anger and fear are permitted to make their contribution.

Here I would suggest that participants in a theological reflection process dealing with conflict and the resulting emotional turbulence need to build into the process ways of dealing with the psychological projection that constitutes a frequent form of social and dialogical violence. One helpful vehicle for coping with this kind of intrusion may be found in the "Intensive Journal" technique of Ira Progoff.[7] This is an exercise of imagination in which, in written form and in solitude, we dialogue with another person who is in an adversarial relation with us. Already in touch with the "stepping stones" of our own history, we enter sympathetically into the outlook of the other by constructing, from our own perspective, similar "stepping stones" in their history. The technique is not a substitute for but can be either a complement or an alternative to actual dialogue with someone in whose eye we think we have detected a mote or two. This recourse implies no backing down from perceptions and convictions born of our awareness and freedom. But it does remind us that there is more in the adversarial "other" than we, in our fear and anger, might be inclined to see, as well as more, hidden within ourselves, of the dark attitudes and behaviors that we are all too prone to attribute to those with whom we are in conflict. When a group engaged in conflictual dialogue has available and becomes practiced in such spiritual techniques, the chances are greater that the ensuing phases of the pastoral circle will engage the energies of faith in a creative, life-giving way.

II. *Social Analysis*

The shift from the first to the second phase of the process is like a dramatic change between the first and second movements of a symphony. If the heart, its memories, and the feelings and values that such memories lay bare are crucial in the retrieval and sharing of experience, social analysis calls for a cool, empirical, dispassionate, and critical gaze. Here is where the communal character of the process is an advantage. Behaviors which a single individual rarely can practice in a highly skilled way become available to a group when it knows how to call upon different types of individuals who can model for the group the appropriate theological behavior. Let the story-teller step back a bit now, so that with the help of more analytical types the whole group may be able to situate the experience more rationally.

It is the role of social analysis not merely to bring data from the social sciences to bear on conflictual issues, but, more importantly, to let faith values guide the group to objectivize, contextualize, analyze, and order the elements of the conflict. I have already indicated that the following venture into social analysis is no more than a sampling. It focuses on a few closely related questions touching charism and autonomy, the situation of women religious in the church, and the appropriateness of their involvement in political life in the U.S. scene.

Here are some of the pertinent facts of both the Michigan and the Rhode Island conflicts:

1) There was question of *women* religious, hence of a group excluded by law from the ecclesiastical offices held solely by male clerics. This fact constitutes an important analytical point of contrast with the Drinan and Cardenal cases.

2) The Michigan and Rhode Island cases differ notably because of the presence and absence, respectively, of the abortion issue in constituting the conflict. The large differences between the positions of Archbishop Szoka and Bishop Gelineau should not be overlooked. The latter's posture appears as far more restrictive and rigid.

3) The grave scandal perceived by Szoka and SCRIS and what church officials claim to be formal cooperation in the grave sin of abortion, implicit in their view of the Mansour case, has never been an issue in the case of thousands of Roman Catholic laity in Michigan and elsewhere who are charged with implementing the legal provisions for the funding of abortions for the poor. The Sisters of Mercy several times called attention to this notable difference. The hierarchical response to this difficulty was for the most part implicit. The language employed by representatives of the magisterium, from John Paul II down, quite consistently couples "priests

and religious" when there is question of political involvement and of permission needed for it. However
Bishop Bevilacqua did make the explicit statement, important for analysis, that Agnes Mary, as a religious,
was a public figure in the church, so that her actions
would be a source of greater scandal.

4) This coupling of priest and religious is clearly present in the code of 1917, in the new law promulgated
in 1983, in "Religious Life and Human Promotion" and
other Vatican documents.

5) The *Constitution on the Church* of Vatican II, on
which the new law of the church and many other post-
Vatican II documents are selectively based, actually
speaks ambivalently of the place of non-clerical religious in the church. Where there is question of the distinctive role of the laity within the secular, religious are
not included, and in fact are spoken of as being, along
with clerics, a distinct group. But in two formal statements which reflect a different longstanding view, it
seems clear that, as non-clerical religious, women religious belong to the laity of the church.[8] This ambiguity
has, to my knowledge, never been resolved, even though
Vatican agencies have selectively followed the view
which dissociates women religious from the laity where
there is question of engagement in the secular.

6) Immediately pertinent to what has just been noted
is the fact that the new law of the church, as well as
the "Essential Elements" document, refer to all apostolic religious as separated from the world (canon
607, 3; "Essential Elements" nn. 9ff.).

These several facts appear to reflect, for the most part, the
canonical and theological assumptions from which church officials
were working in their handling of the Michigan and Rhode Island
cases. I will not attempt here to establish what seems very likely,
namely, that the Sisters of Mercy were working from very different
theological assumptions regarding their place in the church and
hence regarding what was for themselves appropriate involve-

ment in politics. A fuller and more careful analysis would be needed to establish that here indeed was a major element in the conflicts: radically different *theological* views on the relationship of apostolic women religious to the world and on the appropriateness of some specific involvements in politics on their part.

Although I will not engage here in further analysis, I would propose that the *cultural* analysis of the church's response to modernity developed by Joe Holland might be helpful at this point.[9] In essays written under LCWR and CMSM auspices, I have, in fact, offered a framework based upon his schema which might assist such an analysis.[10] There I have suggested that today's ecclesiastical conflicts regarding religious life stem in great part from the fact that three culturally conditioned paradigms, corresponding respectively to the organic, mechanistic, and artistic root metaphors described by Gibson Winter and Joe Holland, are in contention. Without applying the framework of the three root metaphors to the present cases, my analysis would suggest that in Michigan and Rhode Island there was a conflict between, on the one hand, an organic, pre-modern, sacral, and hierarchical mentality applied to the life of these U.S. women religious, and, on the other hand, an inchoate post-modern mentality, rooted partly in the U.S. civil and Christian experience and partly in the post-Vatican II renewal process as experienced by U.S. women religious. I would see both of these mentalities as containing also some of the distinctive ingredients of the second or mechanistic metaphor. The hierarchical outlook does so concessively, for the most part, while the inchoate post-modern mentality does so with a view to incorporating some of the meanings and values gained through modernity into a post-modern vision of life, a vision whose language and corresponding structures are still in the making.

In broad outline, then, I am suggesting that an analysis which is especially cultural, in attending to the place of nonclerical apostolic religious in the church and the appropriateness of their engagement in the secular political process, would helpfully attend to the ideological and cultural assumptions carried into the conflict by the respective parties. Without excluding other important facets of the situation which call for analysis, this approach might eventually provide an ordered state of the question for the third phase of the circle.

III. *Theological Reflection*

I have already indicated that I understand this third phase to comprise two quite diverse theological behaviors, one *evaluative* and the other *recommendational* (or, if you will, *futuristic*). How would each of these steps be pursued in a fuller endeavor?

1. The theological evaluation of the experienced and analyzed situation takes place on the basis of "the gospel." This is a broad term, to be sure, within which one would have to distinguish and characterize several elements: for example, recourse to scripture (not, obviously, for "proof texts" but rather for the disclosure of values, themes, and accents which would then be dealt with hermeneutically); recourse to the relevant basic teaching of the church through the ages, also handled hermeneutically in a careful differentiation of what is culturally conditioned; the basic history of charismatic communities from the beginning of the life of the church, including the recurring conflicts between charism and institution which adorn that history; the principles contained in the church's social teaching in the past century; the canonical heritage touching religious life; some coherent ecclesiological constructs from systematic theology; and, not least, the revelatory experience of present day religious as they attempt to respond faithfully to the signs of the times.

From such a complex recourse to "the gospel" as basis for evaluating the Mercy situations, here are some possible statements to be applied to the situations:

1) A sound ecclesiology needs to reduce radically the claims of some traditional ecclesiologies regarding what is essential for the structural identity of the church as founded by Christ.

2) A similar reduction is needed with respect to what is required for the essentials of religious life. In fact, the language of "essentials" is too prone to abstraction and inflation, and it seems preferable to speak of the historical identity of communities founded and developed under the charismatic guidance of the Spirit.[11]

3) The priority of the church as communion over the church as hierarchical institution, with the needs of the former conceived as normative for the appropriate behavior of the latter, is to be

emphasized (see Vatican II's *Constitution on the Church,* n. 8).

4) The applicability of the great social principles of the church to the inner life of the church is to be affirmed. Human dignity, participation, subsidiarity, the equality of the baptized, human and Christian rights, need not only to be generally stated in church law (as they are in the new law) but held high in consciousness when conflicts occur. More specifically, the profound observations of the future John Paul II characterizing solidarity and opposition as authentic forms of participation in community, and conformism and non-involvement as inauthentic forms, are to be applied (*a fortiori,* as Gregory Baum has said) to the church.[12]

5) A real authority and autonomy, in an anthropological and theological sense, are to be affirmed as residing in the membership of Christian charismatic communities prior to ecclesiastical recognition of such communities. And canonical recognition, however valuable in itself, should not be seen as carrying with it the same degree of control of such communities as is appropriately exercised towards deacons, priests and all who, because they bear church office, speak and act in the name of the church.

6) Religious life is not a middle state between the life of the clergy and that of the laity. Non-clerical religious are best seen as belonging to the laity of the church, life does not belong to the hierarchical structure of the church, that is, they have not changed their position in respect to the hierarchical church by the fact of their profession. The public nature of the religious state should not be used by church authority to impede the charismatic freedom and due autonomy of religious communities.

7) In the face of longstanding and still operative tendencies to monasticize the life of apostolic religious, especially women, the notion of separation from the world, whatever its validity for the church as a whole and for those called to monastic forms of life, seems today to be theologically and pastorally inappropriate for speaking of the life and ministry of apostolic women religious in the United States.

8) The very real risks inherent in political ministry, especially within government (risks never denied by the Sisters of Mercy, including the three who found themselves called to public office),

need to be evaluated within the concrete contexts of each nation and its culture. We also need to acknowledge a major difference in such participation on the part of religious who are clerics and those who are not. The former by their ordination are called in a formal and official sense to speak and act on behalf of the church; the latter do not have this call, whatever the popular perception may be.

On the basis of such principles as these I would then seek an evaluation of the situation described in our case histories. The following statement is less a considered conclusion from careful argumentation than a bare indication of what might result from the argumentation. I would say then that the ecclesiological assumptions behind the decisions of Archbishop Szoka, Bishop Gelineau, and SCRIS, and also, for the most part, behind relevant portions of Vatican II and of the old and new laws of the church and several subsequent documents of the Holy See, are rooted in a cultural mentality unsuited to the challenge confronting the U.S. church today. Whatever flaws may have been present in the language employed by the Sisters of Mercy, I believe that they have been working from ecclesiological assumptions which are basically congruous with the gospel, and especially with the movement of the spirit challenging the U.S. church to the fulfillment of its mission within the present cultural context. If I may indulge in a bit of shorthand jargon, the case histories disclose a need for both declericalization and demonasticization in the prevailing church understanding of the status and ministry of apostolic women religious in the United States.

If this statement appears either simplistic or arrogant or both, I need to reaffirm that I do not conceive myself to have established the case for it, but only to have sketched out the broad lines of the process of evaluating the experienced and analyzed pastoral situation on the basis of the gospel.

2. The *recommendational* or *futuristic* component in the third step of the pastoral circle calls for an exercise of theological imagination, and hence, for an activation of dreaming hope of a distinctively Christian kind. Such anticipations of future deliverance, it has been often noted, radically differ from a rational optimism based upon detached analysis of favorable present trends. Fre-

quently, there appears to be an inverse proportion between grounds for optimism and wellsprings of hope. Without suggesting that the present situation is totally bleak, I am inclined, however, to accent the need for hope. Given the strong convictions and personal involvement of the present pope, given also the fact that, twenty years after Vatican II, the new law of the church regarding apostolic religious still speaks in large part a sacral, monasticizing, clericalizing, and hierarchalizing language, and given that the new assertiveness of the U.S. hierarchy in other contexts was not effectively brought to bear on the disposition of these cases, it is truly time to exercise some dreaming hope.

Here is a sampling of one participant's dreams:

1) I dream of a fuller and more consistent implementation of what Vatican II declared regarding episcopal collegiality and the role of local churches in the universal church. This would entail a more equitable distribution of power as between the Roman dikasteries and the episcopal leadership of the U.S. Church. More concretely, the U.S. church would possess within itself more adequate structural resources for resolving conflicts, so that movement to Roman adjudication would be in reality a last recourse.

2) I dream of a deeper awareness in all of us of the importance of cultural assumptions in our approach to the inevitable conflicts of pastoral life. This entails a greater freedom on the part of all, whether designated as conservative, liberal, or radical, in disengaging from cultural blind spots and fixations, and in engaging in new and unfamiliar linkages between faith and culture.

3) I dream of the day of common recognition of the lay, non-clerical, apostolic, and world-oriented character of the vocation of apostolic communities of religious sisters and brothers.

4) I dream of the continuing decline of hierarchalism in the church, so that the energies of voluntarism, a major feature in the U.S. ethos, may be more available for the mission of the church in our culture.

5) Closer to home, I dream of a more conscious effort by myself and my Jesuit brothers at the grassroots to deal honestly with the risks (notably of cynicism and conformism) inherent in our special relationship to the Roman pontiff.[13]

6) More concretely, in the context of the Mercy case histories, I dream of equal treatment for apostolic women religious and for other lay persons where there is question both of their aptitude for holding public office and of any possible grave scandal given by them in public office;[14] and of full freedom exercised by every U.S. bishop in exercising his power to dispense from ecclesiastical laws without undue regard for whether the Roman pontiff is dispensing; and, finally, of strenuous effort on the part of every skilled canonist who also bears the power of episcopal office to modify the workings of due process in the church when, in fact, they impede justice and charity, particularly toward the weak.

Such dreams might appear to make me more partisan than participant, and I might reasonably be asked whether I have any comparable recommendations for the Sisters of Mercy. To this I would make two responses. First, a discreet love makes us slow to make gratuitous recommendations to the gravely afflicted. And second, the Sisters of Mercy have already embarked in their "Search for Truth" project, on the very kind of alternative behavior which I might be inclined to recommend.

IV. *Pastoral Decision*

Together with the conviction that the retrieval and sharing of story are constitutive elements in the theological process, this fourth phase helps to distinguish the third way from dogmatic and academic theologies. Originating in conflictual experience, and aimed ultimately at the salutary resolution of conflict, the process now returns to experience as something to be shaped and directed through significant choices made by individuals but more importantly by groups. Once more I would point to the "Search for Truth" project, now as an example of a concrete discerning choice made within a carefully designed process of reflection on a deep and traumatic ecclesial experience. Let me make several observations which may assist others to understand and practice this phase of the circle.

First, there is question of a decisional process. Hence, in the U.S. scene, so rich in psychosocial and organizational techniques, we are dealing with the need to choose strategies and tactics, to set goals and objectives, to provide for implementation, responsibility, accountability, further evaluation and revision, budget, and all the rest.

But, second, because we are involved in a faith process, the renewal during the past few decades of the insights and techniques of the Christian discernment of spirits offers a rich resource for structuring the process of pastoral decision.[15]

Third, let me recall what I said under the first phase of the circle about dealing with fear and anger, which inevitably surface in the story phase of retrieving and sharing the experience of conflict. Here again, when a group reaches the stage of responsive decision making, there is frequently need again to deal with the same dangerous gifts of fear and anger, and in such a fashion that they may be energizing forces in the courage and hope required for persevering Christian action. From my own experience of how the hierarchical church has dealt in recent years with the Society of Jesus, and from the vicarious experience, through reading many documents in which the proper canonical language concealed the most intense underlying feelings, of the trauma of the Sisters of Mercy, I am convinced that such decisional processes need to give full weight to grieving and to the airing of grievances. The language of reconciliation, especially when used by one who has not been oppressed, can represent a bland evasion of truth. Far more difficult is the costly grace of a peaceful and non-violent response to violence. In the discernment process, it normally comes when God is permitted, in contemplative prayer, to comfort those who mourn and to lift up the lowly.

Fourth, along with peace there is another sign of true discernment: *freedom.* God, who always does what he wants to do, invites us, created and redeemed in his image, to grow in doing the same. To the degree that we become our true selves under the guidance of the Spirit, God invites us to do what we really want, without letting our behavior be dictated either by inner resentment or by repressive forces from without. In this connection, Paul's contrast in chapters seven and eight of *Romans* between the before and after of the redemptive process is capital: as sinner, I find myself doing what I don't really want to do; as redeemed, I am set free by the Spirit to do what I truly desire. One of the inspiring features of the conflict of the Sisters of Mercy with opposing Church structures and policies was the freedom and "revolutionary patience" shown by the Mercy leadership at both provincial and general levels. The path led through labyrinthian ways of juridical procedures, right up to the final request — and final refusal — of an audience with the pope. Notable in this patient exercise of freedom and truth was the seemingly deliberate insistence on the part of Theresa Kane, as president of the Sisters of Mercy of the Union, on dealing with church authorities only in solidarity with her own council, with the general chapter, and with the provincials. The irony that this happened to be the same U.S. woman who, as president of LCWR in 1979, publicly laid before the pope some of the grievances of American women, has surely escaped no one. God's humor, like his mercy, is without limits.

Finally, a crucial aspect of the freedom bestowed by the Spirit in Christian discernment is the freedom to fail. On the surface, the extraordinary expenditure of energy of the Mercy leadership these past several years has failed. They have "lost" three outstanding women from their formal membership (the final blow being a suspension in their regard of the ecclesiastical law which would have permitted their subsequent canonical readmission to the community). The Mercy initiatives on the tubal ligation issue have been thwarted. Their repeated efforts to meet with the pope have been fruitless.

No small support for my own hope comes from the fact that, like Jesus, and like the saints in history, they have not been wedded to success, but rather to fidelity to truth and justice and mercy as they have perceived them. To this extent, when historians in a calmer time review the lights and shadows of this strange history, I hope they will appreciate that they have been, as we are today, witnesses to one more actualization of the paschal mystery. Many tend to evaluate the courage of afflicted Church members by whether or not they "take a stand." I would suggest that the very early history of Catherine McAuley and her companions offers a different metaphor. In those days, before they were pressured into canonical status by nervous ecclesiastics, their visits to the homes of the poor won for them the description of "the walking sisters." The lesson of the courage of our sisters in these Mercy case histories is that courage is exercised just by continuing to walk in the way that we are given to see.

1. See James Hug, SJ (ed.) *Tracing the Spirit: Communities, Social Action, and Theological Reflection.* New York: Paulist, 1983.

2. See Joe Holland and Peter Henriot, SJ, *Social Analysis: Linking Faith and Justice.* 2nd edition. Maryknoll, NY: Orbis, 1983.

3. David Tracy in *The Analogical Imagination: Christian Theology and the Culture of Pluralism.* New York: Crossroad, 1981; and Edward Braxton, *The Wisdom Community.* New York: Paulist, 1980, have suggested triadic schemas for differentiating various theological approaches.

4. See below, note 9.

5. "The Shepherd and the Tradition: Bishops as Teachers," *The Way,* April, 1981, pp. 103-112.

6. Patricia Wolf, RSM, has called my attention to the very different teaching style still maintained by the U.S. bishops on matters touching human sexuality; here they come closer to the Roman dogmatic style, and are less influenced by professional currents. The reasons, undoubtedly complex, would be worth exploring.

7. See his *At a Journal Workshop.* New York: Dialogue House, 1975, pp. 158-177.

8. "From the point of view of the divine and hierarchical structure of the church, the religious state of life is not an intermediate one between the clerical and lay states. Rather the faithful of Christ are called by God from both these latter states of life . . .(n.43)."
"Although the religious state constituted by the profession of the evangelical counsels does not belong to the hierarchical structure of the Church, nevertheless it does belong inseparably to her life and holiness. (n.44); trans. from W. Abbot and J. Gallagher, *The Documents of Vatican II,* New York: Guild Press, 1966.

9. See Holland and Henriot, pp. 31-40, 64-88; and Holland's essay in Hug,pp.170-191.

10. See LCWR, *Religious Congregations Within the Church,* Washington, DC, LCWR, 1982,pp.1-13. The other essay, "Religious Leadership in a Time of Cultural Change," is for a CMSM volume to be published later this year.

11. See my volume of essays, *New Pentecost or New Passion?.* New York: Paulist, 1973,pp.5-13.

12. See K. Wotyla, *The Acting Person.*

13. See K. Rahner, "The Society of Jesus and Devotion to the Sacred Heart."

14. A NETWORK statement of May 15, 1983 asserts that the demand made on Agnes Mary Mansour and not on other Catholics in the same or similar political roles "perpetuates inequality of membership in the Roman Catholic Church." In an unpublished essay, "Religious and Lay Statuses in the Church," Francine Cardman has dealt with this inequity in a penetrating analysis.

15. See my observations of the application of discernment principles and techniques to public life in J. Haughey (ed.), *Personal Values and Public Policy*. New York: Paulist, 1979, pp. 212-231.

Ecclesiastical Intervention

David F. O'Connor, ST

The church strives to promote unity, not division, among its members. However, as holy scripture (see, for example, 1 Cor. 1:12) and our 2,000-year history indicate, the church is no stranger to internal conflicts, factions, dissensions and misunderstandings. The recent interventions of ecclesiastical authority into the cases of some American religious assuming civil offices is just one modern example of such internal disputes. The recent conflicts between these dedicated "church-people" seem to be based on different visions of church, ministry, authority and religious life.

The thinking, reasons, expectations and practices of the church have to be examined in order to understand what is behind the disputes and what implications they hold for the future. After all, the church does have some official positions about the role and place of men and women religious and their institutes. It has a direct interest in how they live and what activities they undertake because it considers religious communities to be public institutions established, sponsored and supervised by ecclesiastical authority. As the Vatican Council II documents stated:

> Church authority has the duty, under the inspiration of the Holy Spirit, of interpreting these evangelical counsels, of regulating their practice, and finally of establishing stable forms of living according to them.[1]

The canons of the Code of Canon Law of the Roman Catholic Church are the practical implementation of the church's official theological and policy positions. The canons of the 1983 Code can only be understood against the background of the positions established in the conciliar and post-conciliar documents. The Code is the instrument the Church uses to insure some order in the life of its members and its institutions. It is an attempt "to translate the same conciliar doctrine and ecclesiology into canonical language."[2]

The new Code takes a more rigid position than the former one in the matter of the clergy and religious being involved in politics and civil public office. The 1917 Code (canons 139 and 592) permitted local bishops a certain amount of discretion in granting permission to clergy and religious. However, the 1983 Code (canons 285, 3 and 672) states a flat prohibition against priests and religious assuming public offices which entail a participation in the exercise of civil power. It no longer addresses the issues of a dispensation. It appears that any dispensations will truly be rare and exceptional.[3]

Why has the position of the church become stricter in these matters? Why does the hierarchy expect immediate acquiescence by religious to cease and desist when commanded to do so? What about "due process" and the rights of the people involved? An answer to these legitimate questions must be found essentially in an examination of the church's official theological positions as expressed in the Vatican II conciliar and post-conciliar documents, and in the thinking, convictions and expectations of John Paul II. Also, it requires an appreciation of the juridic heritage and practices of the Roman Catholic Church.

As stated above, religious and their institutes, unlike the members of other church groups and organizations, are considered to be "church-people" and "church-institutions." They come into existence as church sponsored organizations when they are chartered by church authority. It is the bishops who establish groups of the faithful as ecclesial institutes. Once established, they are regulated in their life and activities by the laws of the church and their own charter or constitutions, which must be approved by the bishop at the local or diocesan level or by the Sacred Congregation of Religious and Secular Institutes (SCRIS), at the Roman or pontifical level. Religious are presented to the world by the church as public witnesses to gospel values. But it is church authority which sponsors, supervises and governs them through its laws, rules and regulations.

The church acknowledges that the historical appearance of a particular form of the religious life is a movement of the Spirit. Religious institutes belong to the church even though these institutes are not part of its hierarchical structure. Charisms are given for the building up of the community of the faithful and for the benefit of the people of God. It is, therefore, necessary and reasonable that the bishops should make some judgment on every religious institute and oversee its life and activities.

All approved religious institutes enjoy a certain institutional autonomy which must be exercised in accordance with their own charter or constitutions and the other regulations of church law.[4] Institutes are not free to make changes in their way of life or their activities which conflict with those things approved by Rome.[5] However, hierarchical interference in the internal life of an institute is an unusual and extraordinary occurrence. The bishops are not inclined to be concerned about religious men or women as they go about their day-to-day life and activities. Such intervention only occurs when something is judged a serious matter and spills over on to other people in the church community. If the religious superiors — internal authority — cannot effectively deal with the matter, then hierarchical intervention may take place.[6] If a local bishop does not have authority directly over the religious involved, then he will usually appeal to SCRIS, that branch of the Roman curia or Vatican bureaucracy which supervises and regulates religious institutes throughout the Catholic Church in the name of the pope. This is what happened in the recent cases in this country when American religious assumed public civil offices.

What is behind the hierarchy's intervention and the canon law which now prohibits religious from these activities? Essentially, it is the role which religious have in the church as public witnesses to gospel values, especially the evangelical counsels of chastity, poverty and obedience. Religious are presented by the church as public, visibly dedicated, servants of God and the Catholic Church.[7] Identity is the key issue. They are not permitted to assume roles and positions which becloud their identity as "church-people." Religious are to represent the visible church in its efforts to reach out to and minister to people in a myriad of ways appropriate to the charism and approved charter of each institute. Secular and political spheres of activity are considered to be proper to others in the church, not the clergy and religious. Vatican Council II stated that secular responsibilities and activities belong properly, but not exclusively, to the laity.[8] It compared the distinct vocations of the clergy, the religious and the laity, in these words:

> It is true that those in holy orders can at times be engaged in secular activities, and even have a secular profession. But they are, by reason of their particular vocation, expressly and principally ordained to the sacred ministry.
>
> Similarly, by their state of life, religious give outstanding and striking testimony that the world cannot be transformed and offered to God without the spirit of the beatitudes.
>
> But the laity, by their special vocation, seek the kingdom of God by engaging in temporal affairs and by ordering them according to the plan of God. They live in the world, that is, in each and all secular professions and occupations. They live in the ordinary circumstances of family and social life, from which the very web of their existence is woven. Today they are called by God, that by exercising their proper function, and led by the spirit of the gospel, they may work for the sanctification of the world from within as a leaven. In this way they make Christ known to others, especially by the testimony of a life resplendent in faith, hope and charity.[9]

Therefore, efforts to bring about a more just society through the assumption of public office and through political activity are meant to be the work of lay men and women. Traditionally, mainstream Catholic social theory has always considered the promotion of social justice, especially through political activity, to be the special contribution of the laity who are engaged daily in the market place and in their own professional and occupational milieu. Dedicated lay women and men bring their experience, competency and political experience into the efforts of the church to help bring about a more just society and promote human development.

The "Chicago Declaration of Christian Concern," signed by many lay veterans with long experience in Catholic social action, criticized the clergy and religious for overlooking the proper role of the laity in ministry in the United States in recent years. It called attention to a new "clericalism on the left" evident in the actions of those religious and clergy who act as if the primary responsibility in the church for promoting justice, ending wars and defending human rights rested on them. The "Declaration" accuses them of by-passing the laity and imposing their own agenda for the world upon the laity. The signers presupposed a developed laity and lamented the loss of priests who saw their ministry as enabling, arousing and serving the laity without manipulating them. They state:

> In the last analysis the Church speaks to and acts upon the world through her laity. Without a dynamic laity, conscious of its personal ministry to the world, the Church, in effect, does not speak or act. No amount of social action by priests or religious can ever be an adequate substitute for enhancing lay responsibility. The absence of lay initiative can only take us down the road to clericalism.[10]

The ecclesiology expressed in the Vatican II documents ought not to be overdrawn. There is a danger that the distinctions between the various ministries of clergy, religious and laity can be too sharply and narrowly categorized. The sacred and the secular cannot always be easily limited, distinguished or delineated. Since the II Vatican Council, there has developed a greater sense of the common Christian vocation. Yet, the history of clericalism on the part of the clergy and Catholic religious has shown their adeptness at arrogating to themselves the most prominent places in the current relevant ministry.

Now that social involvement is in the forefront, to

> oust the layman and take his place is a temptation not
> all clerics and religious will find easy to resist. For
> centuries, religious have benignly given the laity advice,
> material aid, education, development schemes, and so
> forth. It now comes most natural to offer socio-political
> solutions.[11]

Therefore, while zeal for justice and social reform is admirable,
Catholic religious and priests must remind themselves that they
do not have all the answers to the complicated problems of this
world. Likewise, there is no small danger that in the lives of some
priests and religious, the priesthood and the religious life can
become mere appendages to socio-political activity.

In 1980 the Sacred Congregation of Religious and Secular Institutes (SCRIS) conducted a study on the specific role of religious
in the mission of the church for the integral promotion of the
human person. It gave special attention to the socio-political involvement of religious. The study, "Religious Life and Human
Development," was published in conjunction with a companion
document, "The Contemplative Dimension of Religious Life."[12] It
acknowledged the link between the church's mission, its wide-
spread commitment to the advancement of people and the better-
ment of society, and the important role religious play in this ministry. It noted, sympathetically, the particular problems and difficulties which have faced religious when they have tried to intervene
more decisively in the areas of injustice and oppression, attempting to express solidarity with the poor and underprivileged, compelling them, at times, "to become actively involved, sometimes
in the working world and in politics."[13] However, the document
reminds religious that "they are bearers of human and Christian
values which will oblige them to repudiate certain methods of
trade union action or of political maneuverings which do not respond to the exact demands of justice, which alone is the reason
for their involvement."[14] The document expressed concern that
certain types of involvement carry with them "risk of a loss of
identity proper to religious life and to the church's mission. . ."[15]
Therefore, religious were warned not to let themselves become
directly involved in politics and should "not be deluded into thinking that they will have greater influence on the development of

persons and people by substituting a political involvement, in the strict sense, for their own tasks·"[16] They "should stand apart from certain political options, being seen not as men and women who take sides, but as agents of peace and fraternal solidarity."[17] Unlike the laity and lay members of secular institutes, religious have committed themselves to obedience to the common purpose of the religious community and to their religious superiors. Therefore, states the document, the presence of religious should "always be as consecrated persons who seek the full conversion of people and society to the ways of the gospel through witness and service."[18]

Pope John Paul II has insisted that the distinctive roles of the priest, the religious and laity, as stated in the Vatican II documents, be maintained in the socio-political arena. Religious and priests should be conscious of their own vocation to preach God's word by their actions. While this certainly includes a concern for justice, priests and religious must always appear as agents of reconciliation and not division. Their primary role as servants of God and of his church, the pope asserts, does not permit them normally to be directly involved in partisan politics where divisions are inevitable. The priest and religious are called to inspire, motivate, educate and exhort and witness. The task of renewing the temporal and secular order is the responsibility of the laity. The Christian vocation to public ministry and service in the name of the church belongs to priests and religious. The vocations are distinct from, but complemented by, other Christian vocations. Therefore, in his February 17, 1981 address to men religious in Manila, he stated:

> At the same time I ask you to observe this guideline: that each apostolic endeavor should be in harmony with the teachings of the church, with the apostolic purpose of your individual institutes. May I also remind you of my words at Guadalupe: "You are priests and religious; you are not social or political figures or officials of a temporal power . . . let us not be under the illusion that we are serving the gospel if we 'dilute' our charism through an exaggerated interest in the wide field of temporal problems." It is important for people to see you as "servants of Christ and stewards of the mysteries of God."[19]

While the pope does not confuse politics with religion, courageously he has condemned the violation of human rights, the lack
of religious freedom where it occurs, consumerism, self-in-
dulgence, unconcern for the poor, bias, and moral chaos. While
he argues for personal and religious values, he opposes moral
laxity and totalitarianism. Likewise, while he tells politicians that
they ought to aid the poor and ban weapons, he clearly expects
priests and religious to stay out of politics.

With this as a background, it may help explain why the bishops
have reacted so decisively and directly in the cases of American
religious assuming public civil office. Church authorities, pope
and bishops, do not want religious and clergy engaging in those
activities which are considered appropriate to the vocation of the
laity.[20] Also, it should be noted, religious women and men, even
if not ordained, are considered to be in a special ecclesial category
of public dedication, witness and service in the name of the church.
They are not treated simply as members of the laity because of
their own distinctive vocation and life-style in the church community.[21] Moreover, there is no religious institute which has been
established which has as one of its purposes the engagement in
political activities. Nor, it is safe to assert, do the bishops seem
even remotely about to permit such activities by religious.

While, in the immediate past, the hierarchy did grant permission, by way of exception, or, at least, tolerated individual clergy-
men and religious engaging in such activities, today, the bishops
have taken their cue from John Paul II. While the laity are encouraged to engage in the secular sphere and in the give-and-take of
political life to bring about a more just society, the bishops have
become adamant that the diminishing numbers of clergy and religious keep out of these activities. As James Burtchaell has
stated:

> The church's labors for the public good require two
> somewhat distinct services. Some must work within
> the give-and-take of the political order, trying to make
> the best of it, rescuing the best options available. Others
> must work outside that order, complaining that the
> best of all options available still falls short — far short
> — of what Jesus requires. On the whole these two ser-

vices work best in different hands, and while neither is better, both are needed.[22]

What can be said about the emphatic and decisive manner in which church authority has intervened in these cases? The interventions have been criticized, at times bitterly, as being shamefully lacking in a respect for the rights of those involved and with no procedure for "due process." The interventions are considered by some critics to have been arbitrary and based on unfounded church discipline with destructive consequences.[23]

One major consideration is that the interventions were directed at members of religious institutes. This is important because religious men and women are treated differently in ecclesial relationships. They are "church-people" and there are different ecclesial expectations made of them. All religious profess the evangelical counsels. One of them is obedience. Canon 601 of the 1983 Code of Canon Law states:

> The evangelical counsel of obedience, undertaken in a spirit of faith and love in the following of Christ, who was obedient even unto death, requires a submission of the will to legitimate superiors, who stand in the place of God when they command according to the proper constitutions.

The profession of obedience is made by vow, a promise made to God, to obey commands given them by their superiors. In fact, commands or precepts based on the vow are restricted, usually, to assignments and appointments to ministry and residence. Rarely are superiors required to command by the vow of obedience in other serious matters, although they may do so. Generally, such commands are given with certain formalities. That is, they are given in writing or before witnesses. There should never be any doubt on the part of the religious that she or he is being obliged to obey by the vow which was professed as a member of the institute. Today, while not required to do so, but certainly expected by modern religious, new assignments and appointments are preceded by discernment, discussion, dialogue and prayer. Then, afterwards, the formalities of the command or "obedience" are observed. Years may pass between invocations of the vow of obedience in the lives of men and women religious.

What is extraordinary, as already mentioned, is that the vow
be invoked by church authority outside the religious institute. It
is quite unusual to have Rome intervene, as it has done in some
of the recent cases under consideration. The Code of Canon Law
in Canon 590 does state:

> 1. Institutes of consecrated life, inasmuch as they are
> dedicated in a special way to the service of God and of
> the entire church, are subject to the supreme authority
> of this same church in a special manner.

> 2. Individual members are also bound to obey the su-
> preme pontiff as their highest superior by reason of
> their sacred bond of obedience.

The Holy Father supervises religious and their institutes
through SCRIS. When it appears that some intervention should
be made, SCRIS may do so in the name of authority of the pope.
In the case of Sister Mansour, Bishop Bevilacqua was given a
special mandate by SCRIS at the direction of Pope John Paul II.
The bishop gave her a formal precept, in the name of the Holy
See and in virtue of her vow of obedience, to resign immediately
her position as Director of Social Services in the State of Michigan.[24] She was presented with a formal command to obey a decision which had been made at the highest level of authority in the
Catholic Church. There is no recourse or appeal to an authority
beyond the pope.[25] When she judged that she could not obey, she
requested to be released from her vows and leave her religious
institute. This was granted by Bishop Bevilacqua that same day,
May 9, 1983.

Church authorities would not consider this as a violation of
Sister Mansour's rights. They would view it as an extraordinary,
unusual and unfortunate action taken by legitimate authority in
the case of a scandalous situation which was not being resolved
to the satisfaction of Rome at the local level.[26] This was a judgment
call, a prudential decision. It was one made in a situation aggra-
vated by the influence of the media and of pressure groups. Such
decisions, obviously, can be judged as arbitrary. But that, too, is
a judgment call. Religious may not agree with decisions that are
made in their regard when they receive a command in virtue of

the vow of obedience. Nevertheless, because they have taken the vow, the expectation is that they will obey, because they promised to do so knowing that the possibility existed that they would be required to do something someday which they might not want to do.

What about "due process?"[27] Due process is part of the procedural law of those countries, such as the United States, which have a common law tradition. It means that the administration of the law is in accordance with established and sanctioned legal principles and procedures along with safeguards for the protection of individual rights. At the procedural heart of the legal system there stands a series of rights for a person accused of a serious crime.

If "due process" simply meant that there is a legal procedure and that this procedure was followed, then the church has due process. However, the church does not have a "due process" similar to that of the Anglo-American legal system which is primarily concerned with the criminal process where life, liberty or property are in jeopardy. The reason is that church law comes out of another legal tradition and that relationships in the church are not the same as those in civil society. The ecclesial community is meant to be a "graced community" and any type of legal restraint or due process would be intended to promote ecclesial communion. The Canon Law Society of America has been working on the promotion of some type of due process plan for resolving administrative conflicts.[28] Over ninety-four dioceses and many religious institutes have developed some form of "due process" by establishing boards of arbitration and conciliation and a number of others plan to initiate similar boards:

> Conciliation is the most distinctly Christian aspect of the structure . . . Christian notions of forgiveness, peacemaking and fraternal charity argue that the primary process for resolving disputes in the church should involve a conciliation of people rather than the assertion of legal rights.[29]

The intention is to resolve conflicts fairly and equitably before disciplinary action or before the imposition of a sanction. However, there is still much to be desired because of the slowness in the development of such despite the great advances made in the last twenty years.

Another point of view is that there remains some question that "due process" is the issue when it concerns a case of a legitimate superior ordering religious to do something in accordance with that which they have vowed. The right to command by virtue of the religious vow of obedience is something that should not be inhibited by an appeal to "due process." The legal issue, if it came to that, would be: does the superior have a right to command this man or this woman in this matter? (The wisdom or the prudence of a decision made by a legitimate superior is something else entirely.) Likewise, it is presumed and expected that Christian men and women intend to treat each other charitably, equitably and justly. Yet, as we know, this is not always the case. Unfortunately, the sinfulness, weaknesses and limitations of church-people are, at times, all too evident.

What we also see manifested in the examination of these cases is two quite different but legitimate styles of exercising authority. Most American religious have developed organizational structures within their institutes that are intended to recognize and implement the values of consensus, subsidiarity and a collegial-style of operating. The recognition of these values by religious is due to the influence of Vatican II and is also a reaction to an often excessively authoritiarian, maternalistic or paternalistic, style of exercising authority on the part of many religious superiors in pre-Vatican II religious life. Most religious institutes have moved dramatically away from a style of life that was highly controlled and often quite rigid and inhibiting. At times, it seemed, little concern was manifested for the individual religious man or woman; for his or her preferences, talents or personhood. Religious were taught "not to reason why, but to do or die." I think many would agree that this is not an exaggeration or a caricature of that time.

So, today, religious place great stress on dialogue, discernment, prayerful reflection, consensus-seeking, personalism or respect for the individual, and what is called "a collegial-style" of operating. It is obvious in some instances that it is most difficult to bring things to a quick conclusion if such participative structures are overly dominant. In some cases, the personal authority of superiors, so clear in pre-Vatican II religious life, has all but been done away with and replaced by committees and group decisions. It may seem to some observers that things might have gone from one extreme to another in some institutes. In fact, SCRIS has been insisting for many years that the personal authority of religious superiors should be retained in the organizational structures of religious institutes while it has, at the same time, encouraged the retention and development of participative structures.[30] SCRIS will not approve the revised charters or constitututions of institutes which do not give recognition to the role and personal authority of religious superiors as required by church law.[31]

However, even when the institute does have religious superiors with personal authority, some of those who hold that office may be personally reluctant to exercise it in many instances, or they may find themselves in a position where community expectations or structures actually inhibit their doing so.

Ecclesiastical authority, on the other hand, appears to some observers to be exercised in many instances, even today, in a more bureaucratic, direct and impersonal style, even though there have been many participative structures which have been developed since Vatican Council II on the parish, diocesan, provincial, national and Roman levels of church life.

In those instances when the local hierarchy have failed to bring about the desired results in their dealing with religious institutes, they have had recourse to the Apostolic Delegate (now, the Apostolic Pronuncio) in Washington, or to SCRIS in Rome. When this happens, there may not be as much dialogue, consensus-seeking and discernment as the religious desire.[32] Religious may interpret this quite legal intervention on the part of the hierarchy as being disrespectful of the internal authority of the institute, lacking in acknowledgement of subsidiarity and respect for the rights of the individual and the institute. Part of this is due to the fact that religious may not experience this style of exercising authority in their own institutional lives too frequently these days. But it adds to the frustration and anger of those who are involved. For some, it is just another example of what they would refer to as the high-handedness of the exclusively male, authoritarian church bureaucracy.[33] For others, it is judged as a welcome exercise of church authority against the aberrations of a disorganized and disobedient group of religious. Both assessments seem extreme and tend to employ the rhetoric and hyperbole of the movements or mindsets they represent. For there appear to be no real villains. The conflicts are between dedicated people who desire to build up the body of Christ. The tragedy is that so much time, pain and frustration have been involved in this clash of church people with very strong, but conflicting visions of church, ministry and religious life. I think that it is safe to state that in this world of increasing complexity and strong feelings, disagreements will continue, even among very dedicated servants of the people of God.

Special attention should be given in these recent cases to the pervasive presence of the media, which thrive on conflict, and the publicity intentionally given by well-organized and highly critical pressure groups.[34] The principals involved were often under the glare of the public eye and were robbed of the time and conditions for quiet dialogue. They had to be concerned about their every action and word and how these would be interpreted. None of this aided in reaching a peaceful solution to the matter. It is an unfortunate part of modern life that church-people who find themselves in disagreement will also find the dispute being aired in the eyes of the public.

Finally, the history of the church manifests the extraordinary dangers which beset it when it becomes too closely identified with the ruling class, the state, government or a political faction. It is all too easy to be seduced by secular power, even when it is intended to be used for good. A number of prominent churchmen in history immediately come to mind as witnesses of this, such as a Richelieu or a Wolsey. Loyalties can be compromised and roles and identities confused. The experience of Catholics in the United States has seemed to demonstrate the wisdom involved in keeping their clergy and religious independent of the state, of public office and of partisan politics so that they can speak freely and unhesitatingly as witnesses of the gospel. The author of 2 Timothy (2:4) seems to have recognized this when he directed a public servant and leader of the early church to: "Put up with your share of difficulties, like a good soldier of Jesus Christ. In the army, no soldier gets himself mixed up in civilian affairs because he must be at the disposal of his commanding officer."

1. *"Gaudium et spes."*,par. 43. Walter Abbot, ed., *Documents of Vatican II* (New York: American Press, 1966).

2. *Sacrae Disciplinae Leges,* Apostolic Constitution of John Paul II, January 25, 1983. Official Promulgation of the 1983 Code of Canon Law. *Code of Canon Law, Latin-English Edition* (Canon Law Society of America, Washington, D.C., 1983).

3. *The Code of Canon Law: A Text and Commentary,* ed., Coriden et al., pages 223-225, Paulist Press, New York (1985).

4. Canon 586

5. Canon 583

6. Communication to the Provincial Administrators by Sr. Theresa Kane (May 18, 1983): "Archbishop Mayer indicated that we had been uncooperative and had refused to require the resignation of Sr. Agnes Mary Mansour);" Meeting of Srs. Theresa Kane, Betty Barrett, Mary Ellen Quinn and Emily George, RSM, with Archbishop Pio Laghi and Bishop Beviliacqua, August 1, 1983, at the Apostolic Delegation, pages 2 and 6. (The Apostolic Delegate indicated the interventions took place because neither the Detroit Provincial nor the Mercy General would ask Sr. Agnes M. Mansour to resign.)

7. "Essential Elements In The Church's Teaching On Religious Life As Applied To Institutes Dedicated To Works Of The Apostolate," SCRIS, May 31, 1983, ##4, 10 and 34.

8. *Gaudium et spes,* par. 43

9. *Lumen gentium,* par. 31

10. *Origins,* 7, December 29, 1977, pages 440-442

11. Anthony Malaviaratchi, C.SS.R., "Religious and Their Commitment to the Poor," *Review for Religious,* 41, n. 2, 1982, page 249.

12. *Canon Law Digest,* vol. 9, pages 379-410. James I. O'Connor, S.J., ed., (Mundelein, Illinois: St. Mary of the Lake Seminary, 1983).

13. Ibid., page 384

14. Ibid., page 394

15. Ibid.

16. Ibid., page 395

17. Ibid., page 396

18. Ibid., page 407

19. *L'Osservatore Romano,* English Edition, February 23, 1981, page 6.

20. Letter of SCRIS to Sr. Theresa Kane, RSM, concerning the candidacy of Sr. Arlene Violet, RSM, for the political office of Attorney General of the State of Rhode Island, July 3, 1982, Prot. N. 51772/82; Meeting of Sisters M. Theresa Kane and Emily George with the Apostolic Delegate, Pio Laghi, March 23, 1983, at the Apostolic Delegation, Washington, D.C.; Comment of Bishop Louis Gelineau of Providence, R.I., January 4, 1984, on Sr. Arlene Violet's candidacy for Attorney General, *Origins,* 2 February, 1984, pages 570-571; Letter of Apostolic Pro-Nuncio, Pio Laghi, to Sr. M. Theresa Kane, RSM, May 7, 1984, indicating the refusal of the Holy See to dispense Sr. Elizabeth Morancy, RSM, from the restrictions of C. 672 and 285, #3. Prot. N. 1756/84/2

21. *"Gaudium et spes,"* par. 31

22. *Commonweal,* 6 November 1981, pages 626

23. Madonna Kolbenschlag, "Sister Mansour is not alone," *Commonweal,* 17 June 1983, pages 359-364; Letter of Sr. M. Theresa Kane, RSM to the Most Rev. Eduardo Cardinal Pironio, Prefect of SCRIS, May 18, 1983.

24. Press Statement by Agnes M. Mansour, May 11, 1983; Chronology of events surrounding Sr. Agnes M. Mansour's appointment as Director of Social Services — Sisters of Mercy — Province of Detroit (May 12, 1983) page 4; Letter of Bishop Anthony J. Bevilacqua, Ad Hoc Delegate of the Holy See to Sr. M. Theresa Kane, June 6, 1983.

25. Letter of Eduardo Card. Pironio, Prefect of SCRIS (June 6, 1983) Prot. N. 35271/83, to Sr. M. Theresa Kane: The letter indicates that there is no recourse or appeal because Bishop Bevilacqua acted in the name of the Holy See at the direction of the Holy Father; Letter to Sr. M. Theresa Kane, RSM, from the Supreme Tribunal of the Signatura Apostolica (4 July 1983) Prot. N. 15363/83 CA:" . . . the Signatura Apostolica is unable to consider the recourse which you intend to present, because (of) . . . your intention to impugn the decision taken by His Excellency, Monsignor Anthony Bevilacqua, who was acting under the express command of the Holy Father."

26. Letter of SCRIS to Sr. Theresa Kane, RSM, concerning the candidacy of Sr. Arlene Violet, RSM, for the political office of Attorney General of the State of Rhode Island, July 3, 1982, Prot. N. 51772/82; Meeting of Sisters M. Theresa Kane and Emily George with the Apostolic

Delegate, Pio Laghi (March 23, 1983) at the Apostolic Delegation in Washington, D.C.

27. Letter of Sr. Mary Theresa Kane, RSM, to Bishop Anthony J. Bevilacqua, May 23, 1983. (On page 2, she writes: "As president of this religious institute, I am profoundly disturbed about the manner in which this matter has been handled.")

28. *Proceedings* of the Canon Law Society of America, 41st Annual Convention October 15-18, 1979, pages 19-23 and 60-67.

29. *Origins,* May 21, 1981, pages 1-8.

30. *Canon Law Digest,* vol. 7, pages 484-485 (See SCRIS, Plenary Assembly, February 2, 1972.)

31. Canons 617-630

32. Letter of the Mercy administration team members to Archbishop Laghi and Bishop Bevilacqua, October 17, 1983, in which they complain of "the inadequate dialogue between congregational and hierarchical authorities. . ."

33. Madonna Kolbenschlag, *Commonweal,* 17 June 1983, pages 359-364; Letter sent to the bishops of Michigan by the Sisters of Mercy of the Detroit Province, April 12, 1983.

34. "Szoka Doesn't Object To Nun's Overseeing Abortion Payments" — a headline article in the *Detroit Free Press,* December 31, 1982; Report of the Sisters of Mercy of the Province of Detroit Relative to the Appointment of Sr. Agnes Mary Mansour, RSM (April 11, 1983) page 3; An advertisement which appeared in the *Wall Street Journal* and other newspapers paid for by the Center for Documentation of the American Holocaust and highly critical of the hierarchy and Mercy Sisters for permitting Sr. Agnes Mansour to become Director of Social Services in Michigan; Meeting of Sisters Theresa Kane, Betty Barrett and Mary Ellen Quinn with Archbishop Pio Laghi and Bishop Bevilacqua, August 1, 1983 at the Apostolic Delegation: page 2 ". . . the media most likely have taken advantage of the entire situation."

Differing Views of the Church

Rosemary Radford Ruether

Recent confrontations between the Vatican and the Sisters of Mercy, as well as with other groups of women religious, particularly with Americans, reveal a fundamentally different understanding of the relationship of church and state, the sacred and the secular, held by the nuns, on the one hand, and the Vatican on the other. Current Vatican policy assumes a rigid line between church and state which makes any office-holding, either elected or appointed, in government, by either a priest or a nun (or monk?), incompatible with the religious vocation. Although the first conflict between the Vatican and Sister Mansour of the Sisters of Mercy appeared to be primarily over differing interpretations of the relationship between personal morality and public policy in the specific case of payments for abortion, subsequent conflicts with the Sisters of Mercy over other nun-office holders went beyond specific differences over church teachings on moral issues. The holding of any public office was defined as out of bounds for priests or religious.

A similar line has been taken in the case of the four priests who hold public office in the Nicaraguan revolutionary government. In each case, the resolution of the conflict has been to force the persons involved either to resign the public office or else be removed from their religious orders.

This decision by the Vatican has been forced, not only on the individual without due process, but upon the religious order itself. Religious obedience is regarded as obedience to the pope, mediated through the religious superiors of the order. The religious superiors are not allowed to have an independent voice in relation either to the Vatican or the individual concerned. Their sole role is seen by the Vatican as one of passing on orders to the individual. Thus the concept of subsidiarity is violated in favor of a military concept of the church as a chain of command.

There are many questions that can be asked both about the appropriateness of such a concept of church organization and also about such a concept of church-state relationships. A historical overview of concepts of church-state relations in various periods of church history will readily reveal that such a dichotomy between the holding of political office and religious vocation has hardly been typical of Roman Catholicism. One has only to think of the bishops of medieval times who were regarded simultaneously as heads of dioceses and the temporal heads of ecclesiastical states. The pope himself continues to combine these two roles as bishop of Rome, and religious head of the Catholic Church and also political head of the Vatican state as an internationally recognized political entity. Before the unification of Italy in 1870, the territorial holdings of the Vatican extended to much of central Italy.

In the development of European parliaments in the medieval and early modern periods, the bishops and higher clergy were regarded as one of the three estates represented by the parliaments. Such a concept of the three estates made the upper clergy one of the three constituencies represented by parliaments, the other two being the nobility and the bourgeois or "commons". At the time of the French revolution, Catholic bishops continued to be regular members of the Estates General, while the lower clergy found their place among revolutionary members of the "third estate". Bishops continue to be members of the House of Lords in England which preserves the dual definition of lords as both lords spiritual (bishops) and lords temporal (nobility). Cardinals of the church regularly held top positions of state in pre-revolutionary France; for example, Cardinal Richelieu and Cardinal Mazarin who successively held the post of secretary of state and were, effectively, the political rulers of France between 1619 and 1661.

This history, and much more that could be cited in the same vein, make it apparent that no such line between religious vocation and political office was recognized in the Catholic Church prior to the French revolution. Indeed the opposite was the case. Catholicism presupposed a unity of church and state in which the ecclesiastical predominated over the political. In this theocratic understanding of church-state relations, for churchmen to combine ecclesiastical with political office was the norm, not the exception. The present understanding of separation of political office and ecclesiastical office is, in fact, a product of the church's reaction to the French revolution and other modern revolutions which displaced the church from its earlier role as arbiter of state affairs in a theocratic concept of society. Ecclesiastics expelled from their earlier power, in what now became secularized parliaments, not only forbade their own members to participate in such secular parliaments, but even attempted to prevent lay Catholics from voting for or becoming members of them. In the first forty years of the unified Italian state, the pope remained a "prisoner in the Vatican", protesting the confiscation of the papal states that was carried out in order to unify Italy as a state. The pope ordered Catholics not to participate in political activity, either by voting or by political office, in the new state.

In the twentieth century this attempt by the Vatican to boycott the modern secular state has been modified into a concept of separation of spheres between the church as an ecclesiastical institution and secular states. This line of demarcation between the spheres of jurisdiction of the two social institutions is interpreted as a distinction between the "sacred" and the "secular". A hierarchical relationship between the two is still maintained. But now the Catholic liberal mode of relationship between the two demands that ecclesiastical personnel be employed solely by the ecclesiastical institution. Their job as priests and nuns is seen as forming the spiritual life of the laity through the sacraments and moral teaching. The laity are, in effect, to submit their personal consciences to the clergy within the sphere of church authority. Thus, armed with rights, teachings and spirituality, the laity venture out into the world to shape secular institutions to conform to church teachings. Secular institutions become the proper sphere of lay activity. The clergy are no longer to participate in that political world defined as "secular" directly, although they do so indirectly through their control of the personal lives of laity. The laity are seen as the delegates of the church in the world.

In the 19th century, Catholicism created a variety of Catholic social institutions to shape the laity to do the job of properly representing the church in the world. Catholic workingmen's associations and Catholic political parties were created to prevent Catholics from becoming secular liberals or communists and to shape vehicles of social influence and control by the church. Priest chaplains would control such movements from behind the scenes by shaping the private consciences of the workers or party members who would then be prepared to act on the instructions of these clerical advisors in their social and political activity. The close association between the Italian Catholic hierarchy and the Christian Democratic Party in Italy is evidence of the continuation of this dual model of collaboration between ecclesiastical and political power. Thus the liberal Catholic doctrine of separation of spheres between church and state by no means indicates an abdication of the historical claims of the church to exercise influence over the state, but rather is a reshaping of that claim under the new conditions of secular states and churches disestablished from direct relationship to the state.

From this perspective it becomes evident that the objection of the Vatican to priests and nuns in political life does not derive from a theory in which the church is considered to be apolitical. Rather it derives from a view of how the church is to exercise political power. The church is understood as a corporation of clergy and religious under vows, who are seen as the official representatives of the church as an institution. In a way, this means that the laity are not really members of the church at all, in the sense in which the church is an official corporation. They are the subjects of the church who are to be taught by it, but are not official representatives of it. All official representatives of the church should operate within systems of institutional life directly controlled by the church. They cannot hold offices in secular government because such secular systems of power are not directly under the control of the church.

This means that there is no objection at all to ecclesiastics intervening in political affairs, negotiating treaties between states, influencing policies of states through both suasion of public opinion and the exercise of the power wielded by the church itself as an institution, as long as they do it as part of their ecclesiastical office. What is out of line is for members of the church corporation (priests and religious) to exercise political power as a representative of the secular state itself. The objection to such a role is not because the role is political, but because it is political in a way that is not controlled by the ecclesiastical institution directly. This is the real basis of the objection of the Vatican to members of the Sisters of Mercy of the Union exercising political office, either as elected or appointed officials of the state.

The correspondence between the superiors of the Sisters of Mercy and the Vatican officials shows a continued miscommunication on this issue. The Sisters of Mercy operate out of a post-liberal or liberationist concept of the world which regards all creation as the sphere of God's redemptive activity. Although the church exists as a social organization in society, its mission is to serve this redemptive activity of God throughout creation. Such a view cannot make a strict separation between sacred and secular, church and world. Although service within church structures may be part of the vocation of the committed Christian, it does not exhaust that vocation. Those who understand their vows in this larger sense, as special dedication to this general mission of redemption of the world, regard themselves as legitimately serving that vocation by serving human needs in a variety of social settings. The key distinction is humanitarian. Is political office primarily the selfish pursuit of power or is it primarily to serve the human and hence the redemptive needs of society? Any social role can be regarded as redemptive if it is exercised in this latter fashion.

Such a view of the mission of the church in the world also breaks down the strict separation between the mission of the clergy and the mission of the laity. Particularly for religious women, who are canonically defined as laity, no such line can be drawn. Religious women see themselves as specially dedicated and committed Christians who devote their lives to this general redemptive mission to the world.

This theological perspective on the relationship of Christian vocation to human needs, constantly reiterated in the correspondence of the sisters with Rome, is simply ignored by the Vatican leaders. The Vatican leaders think in another language and operate out of another world view. But the actual meaning of the Vatican world view is concealed behind a rhetoric about the proper vocation of religious to the church that baffles and mystifies the sisters.

When the women religious finally try to clarify the situation by declaring that they and the Vatican have different "ecclesiologies", this evokes the immediate reply from the Vatican that the nuns have no right to hold any other ecclesiology than that held by the papacy. For the Vatican officials, ecclesiologies are not a legitimate area of difference of theological world view. There is only one ecclesiology and that is the one held by the Vatican. To hold any other ecclesiology from this is heresy and rank disobedience.

Thus the sisters never quite discern that the real issue is the separation of two mutually exclusive spheres of political power, that of ecclesiastical government and that of secular government, and not a separation of political and "spiritual" (although everything the ecclesiastical government does is simply labeled "spiritual"). Nor is the issue a definition of religious vocation, in a theological sense. It is not exercising political power *per se,* but exercising it in a secular government which is not under the jurisdiction of the ecclesiastical government, which is the real basis of the Vatican objection.

Logically, these same strictures should be applied to all employment by priests or religious that is not part of the ecclesiastical institution. If one were consistent in this view, it would be no more appropriate for a nun to be a teacher in the public school system or a welfare worker paid by the public welfare department, than it is for a nun to be an elected or appointed official of the state. In fact, one may well ask at what point ecclesiastical institutions themselves are no longer ecclesiastical. When a Catholic college is incorporated under a lay board, and the religious order that founded it no longer has controlling power, is it still a church institution? Similarly, if a hospital is incorporated under a lay board, is it still an ecclesiastical corporation? What about autonomous newspapers, publishing houses or peace and justice centers which are not under ecclesiastical control? Do these similarly become inappropriate jobs for a priest or a nun?

Although there is no consistent policy here, there have already been instances of the ordering of nuns and priests out of jobs in such non-official "Catholic" organizations. This occurs usually when such organizations are seen as promoting positions contrary to the teachings of the hierarchy, such as the ordination of women or the acceptance of homosexuality. But the reality is that the line between the church as an institution and the secular world is much fuzzier than the Vatican would like, or even realizes, and so a consistent application of the principle that nuns and priests should not serve in "secular" political life is impossible. The rule, in fact, is applied selectively. It falls heavily on those nuns and priests holding political office with a liberal or left perspective, particularly when there is a conflict over the church's sexual teachings (the key area of church control over the life of the laity). It is much less likely to be applied to those holding office who promote conservative teachings of the church on these matters.

A second important area of conflict between the nuns and the Vatican has to do with different perceptions about the nature and organizational structure of the church itself. The Vatican view of the church is centralized and hierarchical. It sees the church normatively as a top-down chain of command. The pope passes the orders to the Vatican secretariats, who pass the orders to nuns, who pass the orders to the laity. At no point is independent conscience or decision-making to be exercised. Each level obeys the level above it without question. There can be no negotiation between superiors and inferiors. Those below have no "rights" before their superiors. This is the clear message of the Vatican correspondence with the nuns. Efforts at appeal of decisions made by one authority to a "higher court," familiar to American jurisprudence, is simply regarded as an impertinence of the nuns by the Vatican officials, further evidence of their lack of "obedience".

This concept of the church is not only not accepted, it is not even fully recognized by the nuns. They have another view of the church that comes from contemporary post-Vatican II theology.

Not only is there no rigid line between church and secular society, when creation itself is seen as the subject of God's liberating action and the arena of God's presence, but the nuns take it for granted that the church should be a collegial institution which puts human relationships above coercive power. (Following Carol Gilligan's pioneering work, we may have here a key expression of the difference in moral formation and values between women and men as well). Following the Vatican Council, the nuns define the church, first of all, as the people of God. The church finds its primary and foundational reality in the baptized community, not in the apex of the ecclesiastical hierarchy. The task of ordained and vowed religious personnel is to be the servants of the church as the community of the baptized, helping shape a redemptive community that will witness to the truth of the gospel and help heal the wounds of the world.

Although this view of the church does not necessarily imply congregationalism, it does assume a principle of subsidiarity. Hierarchical levels of organization on the regional, national and international level are appropriate to network communication and resources. But the primary locus of decision-making should be at the level where the service is actually being carried out. Personal conscience is to be respected. And so when there are differences between a person's understanding of their ministry and those with responsibility for larger networks of organization, it should be resolved by full and open discussion whereby the "superior" listens carefully to the self-understanding of the person whose life is most intimately affected. That person is presumed to be both a responsible adult and also possessed of the best information about her own basis for decisions.

Although the Vatican leaders assume that there can be no legitimate disagreements about what line of ecclesiastical authority one should espouse, in fact, such disagreements have profound historical and theological bases. One needs to ask, in the most basic sense, which view of the church has the greatest legitimacy? Which has the most legitimacy historically? Which has the most legitimacy theologically? Historically, it is not difficult to establish the fact that the present kind of centralized hierarchical power, taken as normative by the Vatican, is the product of a long historical struggle of the papacy against contrary traditions of ecclesiastical organization, based on congregational, presbyterial and national church models. These alternative models are not simply options "invented" by different Protestant churches in the reformation. Each has deep historical roots in the formation of the church from the beginning.

Historically, it would be more appropriate to see the church as an institution as having been constructed from the bottom up, rather than from a papal apex down. Congregational autonomy was the earliest pattern of the church, even though this was modified by "letters between churches". Gradually local congregations developed into clusters of congregations based on cities, tied together by the bishop and his presbyters. Bishops, in turn, formed councils, who met together on what roughly corresponded to a regional, provincial or national basis. In the fourth century this began to be tied together by an international council of bishops that met for major decisions, called together by the Roman emperor. This world organizational pattern was, in fact, only made possible because of the legitimization of Christianity as the official imperial religion by the Emperor Constantine, making it possible for bishops to travel by imperial post to world meetings.

In this patristic development, the bishop of Rome was seen as holding a primacy of honor for Western or Latin Christianity, but hardly a primacy of jurisdiction over the whole church. The Roman church notion of a world primacy of jurisdiction by the bishop of Rome was basically modeled after the role played by the Roman emperor and his imperial bureaucracy. It was never accepted by Eastern Christianity and was never fully successful against more autonomous patterns in the West during the middle ages although it was increasingly asserted by medieval popes. In a sense, only when the Roman Catholic Church became disestablished from national state power in the 19th century, was it possible to carry through a thoroughgoing ecclesiastical centralization. The First Vatican Council was intended to be a council to abolish the need for all further church councils by establishing the pope as the sole legitimate authority in the church from which all other authority derives.

The Second Vatican Council, however, revived ancient and more recent understandings of a more collegiate church, in which national episcopacies, the diocesan presbyterate and, finally, the local parish have a certain appropriate autonomy and collegiality. But this revival of collegial concepts of the church remained primarily ideological. The council did not succeed in creating a new structure that corresponded to their redefinition of the church. And so, as soon as the Council was over, the Vatican curia set about trying to abolish its effects by reasserting centralized control. But the vision of a new church radiated out so quickly to the "provinces" that all sorts of groups embarked on new ways of thinking and patterns of life without permission from those "above". They simply assumed that the council itself had given them permission to carry out its vision in practice.

American nuns were among the most forward in appropriating the new vision of the church of the council and translating it into a new pattern of thought and organization in their religious orders. It is this development which now finds Vatican officials and American nuns on opposite sides of what has become different worlds of ecclesiology and Christian self-perception. The Vatican, in attempting to reestablish the Vatican I pattern of ecclesiology, finds these renewed women's orders particularly threatening to its concept of a hierarchical church. To repress such autonomy among nuns is seen as a key element in the reestablishment of hierarchical power over the church generally.

Thus it is impossible to establish that the Vatican I concept of a monarchical church has been normative historically. Such a concept of the Church is even less verifiable as the intention of Christ. Since Jesus established a movement rather than an institution, all patterns of church polity are relative and historically developed, patterned after political and social patterns in the culture. Thus the more relevant question is not whether Jesus explicitly founded a church with this or that polity but what pattern of ecclesiastical organization seems most congruent with the theological vision of the church? If that vision is seen as one of a redemptive community that witnesses to a community of love *vis á vis* the power systems of the world, the manner of exercising power claimed by the Vatican would be remote from the authentic nature of the church indeed! Patterns of church life which model respect for the conscience of each person within a community of mutual responsibility would seem the most appropriate to the vision of the church. It is this pattern which the nuns have been trying to model in their renewed constitutions and redefinitions of religious vocation.

Since Vatican absolutism can be justified neither historically nor theologically, what recourse do Catholics have for changing it to one more suitable to their understanding of the nature and mission of the church? It is clear that a non-democratic or monarchical institution with no structures of accountability to the people cannot be changed by appeal to its own legal processes, since, in fact, it is bound by no legal processes and follows the arbitary will to power of those in control. Moral appeals and efforts to enter into dialogue on different visions of Christian good-will fall on deaf ears before such will-to-power.

Thus it seems that the only real recourse of Catholics is one of systematic subversion of hierarchical power. I use the word *subversion* here precisely in its sense of "turning things around from below". How is this possible? Hierarchical power, although claiming that all power comes from above, is, in fact, dependent on assent to its power and economic support from below. It is precisely at this point of assent and economic support that Catholics need to subvert hierarchical power.

Each organizational level of the church needs to disassociate its automatic assent and economic support from the level above it. Most particularly, such assent needs to be disassociated from the Vatican in order to begin to construct a more organic sense of local church, diocesan and national churches. Religious orders also need to disassociate themselves from Vatican power by appropriating control over their own property and perhaps by defining themselves as noncanonical communities. This would imply also the forging of a new sense of international networking among themselves as an order. As assent to authority and economic support falls away from the hierarchical apex and is funneled to the local levels, where the actual ministry of the church is being carried on, hierarchical power, as ability to coerce, will wither on the vine. The networks that hold the church together on local, diocesan, national and international levels will begin to be redefined in a way that must take into account the integrity of the base. Perhaps, out of this process, arbitrary monarchical authority will be reshaped into constitutional government, elected by and accountable to the people.

An Historical Perspective

David J. O'Brien

In the 1890's, a major controversy between the American church and Rome led to the condemnation of "Americanism" by Pope Leo XIII. One point of discussion was church law. Dennis O'Connell, one of the leaders of the liberal party in the American church, argued that canon law was derived from Roman law and was a conception of law as promulgated by a sovereign. It was based on rational principles and stated as an ideal to which many exemptions may be granted. Common law, which informed American practice, was, in contrast, grounded in experience and set forth minimum requirements whch all were expected to obey. Law came from below rather than from above and rested on the will of the people, expressed in constitutions or legislative enactments.

Some European Catholics attacked O'Connell's argument that common law was more appropriate to modern conditions. When some Americans also argued in favor of religious liberty, church-state separation, and reliance upon personal faith rather than on power, authority and cultural isolation, Rome intervened. The "suspicion" had arisen "that there are some among you who conceive of and desire a church in America different from that which is in the rest of the world", Leo XIII wrote, adding immediately: "One in the unity of doctrine, as in the unity of government, such is the Catholic Church and, since God has established its center and foundation in the chair of Peter, one which is rightly called Roman, for where Peter is, there is the church."

We live in another age when, as one of the documents central to this case puts it, "human promotion" must be "genuinely adaptable to the cultures, sensibilities and specific problems of the localities" in which the church finds itself. So we can adapt to the United States it seems, but it also still appears that "where Peter is, there is the Church." In the case of the Mercy sisters, multiple Peters appear upholding canon law, and so do angry Americans, asking not for exceptions but for dignity and participation. The Americanism problem, it appears, is unresolved.

Authority, for example, is still a problem. Twenty years ago Hans Küng toured the United States delivering a lecture entitled "Freedom in the Church." Soon phrases like human dignity, the people of God, shared responsibility, and due process indicated that the days of arbitrary, irresponsible authority in the church were numbered.

Roman actions regarding the Mercy sisters indicate that this presumption was premature at best. All too evident, is one of the most damaging features of pre-Vatican II use of authority, the tendency to move any issue of substance as quickly as possible to an issue of obedience. Church authorities challenged dissenters, not on the truth of their position, but on the scandal they gave by dissent itself. They were charged with lack of respect for the welfare of the church by their defiance of legitimate superiors. In the disputes recorded in the documents in this volume, church officials do not discuss Medicaid funding for abortion or political responsibility. Instead, the only issue is obedience. Archbishop Laghi says "every bishop is the vicar of Christ"; he himself is "the Holy See here"; Bevilacqua is the pope's personal representative, so: submit or leave! Such an attitude, unjust in itself, also damages the church by limiting discussion and demeaning persons of conscience who attempt to address substantive issues.

This approach portrays three basic assumptions. First, the organized church is of such importance that there is, in fact, only one substantive issue, the well-being of the church. Second, the church is so fragile that its unity, solidarity and discipline are of far greater importance than personal freedom, shared responsibility or fruitless efforts to change the world from within. Third, God, perhaps anticipating such situations, placed the pope in charge of the church; he established a monarchy. Now if these assumptions are valid, then there really is only one option — solidarity with the church and submission to the vicar of Christ and such sub-vicars as he may appoint. Take away any of those assumptions, by suggesting that the church is responsible for the state of the world outside itself, or by questioning monarchy as the only divinely authorized mode of ecclesiastical government, and the structure loses legitimacy; redefinition is necessary. For the three Sisters of Mercy all three assumptions became questionable, in part, because none is compatible with the gospel. For the bishops, apparently, gospel and church — monarchical church — are identical. As Archbishop Laghi put it, expressing surprise at the sisters' anger: "Is this the gospel, the church of Peter?"

Sister Theresa Kane pointed out to the papal legate and apostolic delegate that their dispute reflected differences in ecclesiology. The contrast between the ministry paradigm and the hierarchy paradigm, in John Coleman's useful terms, is evident in the terms each side sets for the problem. These are not abstract matters, as if the sisters or the bishops have simply been listening to the wrong theologians. Rather, the individuals involved have a very large personal investment in their "models" of the church.

For Sister Theresa and the three political sisters, words like discernment, ministry, dialogue, mutuality, and shared responsibility come easily. They have a taken-for-granted, self-evident quality, as if their value is indisputable. One suspects this is so because for almost two decades they have in their community engaged in dialogue with superiors, small group discussions, innumerable meetings, regular processes of corporate and individual reflection. Through it all they have been pursuing a concrete program of reorganization redefining their lives and vocations in very personal ways.

Such deep renewal goes beyond workshops and theological retooling to the most profound and personal questions of identity, Christian commitment, and vocation: who am I? what do I believe? why am I a Catholic? why am I a religious? Those who remain in religious life have forged their vocation anew out of this often painful process of personal reconversion carried out in the context of close and supportive community relationships. Thus, at stake in the new language used to explain and legitimate their vocation is an enormous personal investment and a powerful commitment of sisters to each other and to the community.

The evidence suggests that Sisters Mansour, Violet and Morancy did not make their decisions about political action alone but in the context of this kind of personal self-examination and community renewal. To have another person, one who has not participated in the process, who even seems uninterested in finding out about it, and whose language suggests profound lack of respect for the symbols that give it meaning, to have such a person intervene and impose a decision on a member of the community thus seems a violation so profound that it perhaps explains the odd references in several letters to the need to resolve problems in a "nonviolent" way.

One hopes the words at the end of episcopal and Roman letters about prayer and compassion are evidence of some appreciation of this investment. The sisters, for the most part, seem a bit more understanding of the personal investment their male hierarchical superiors have in the hierarchical model of church. We learn less of these men from the documents, but clearly neither the members of the Sacred Congregation nor Bishop Bevilacqua can conceive of a church without the kind of authority they represent. Their training and formation has been different; their vocation has been different; to use different symbols to explain and legitimate their decisions. To use the sisters' words of dialogue and discernment would be less than honest, for few priests have shared the experience of deep community renewal. Further, the sisters' language, in fact, undermines the bishops' understanding of the episcopal office; if they accepted the sisters' idea of the church, they might find themselves in opposition to the source of meaning and identity in their ecclesiastical life, the pope.

Interestingly, when Laghi and Bevilacqua respond to Sister Theresa's comments about ecclesiology, they remark that "our understanding of the one holy, Catholic and apostolic church" must "be in accord with the documents of Vatican II taken in their entirety so that one model of church does not exclude the other." But the hierarchical organizational model they represent reserves to one party the right to declare "the dialogue is over," whether or not it even began. Such a view of church and of authority does indeed exclude other models. Community, discernment and dialogue, as the sisters understand these things, are acceptable only so long as permitted by that pope and bishop by grant of the sovereign.

Thus, again, the raw nerve of renewal is exposed, for if the model operative in the action of these bishops is one which all must hold, the game is indeed lost — at least for priests and religious, for whom Andrew Greeley's option of "do it yourself Catholicism" is not available. In practice, if not in theory, authority today rests with the hierarchy. Other models are only partially organized and are not yet fully legitimate. They exist within the structure, but do not touch it except by permission of those who consider themselves responsible for that structure. The laity in a renewed parish who lose their pastor and find his successor opposed to participation and shared responsibility learn that hard lesson. So do these sisters, who have given flesh in their lives to models of community and service, but learn that, when the chips are down, these models, and those who hold them, remain subordinate to the only model which has power behind it. They can, of course, leave, as the three sisters did, but those who remain behind, including the bishops, are diminished by their departure. That the larger communities they serve are enriched simply adds more evidence to their ecclesial case.

In such a situation, mediation is needed within the system. Unfortunately, the bishops of the United States have been notable by their absence from these conflicts. Those who did get into the picture do not come off very well. The Archbishop of Detroit, on the surface at least, made a decision and called on Rome to back him up, which it did with a vengeance. Curiously, he did not turn to his fellow bishops of the province, all with a stake in the immediate issue, or to the episcopal conference, but to Rome, like a royal governor summoning in the imperial forces to discipline an unruly civil service. In Rhode Island, the bishop first tolerated and even encouraged a sister in office. Then, when the pressure came, he declined permission in a statement filled with references to canon law and the will of the pope, like another royal governor following instructions prepared in the colonial office. Most distressing is Bishop Bevilacqua, an authentic imperial legate. Armed with the authority of the sovereign, he arrives on the scene to receive submission. Local bishops, the royal governors, are to step aside; the apostolic delegate, the viceroy, defers to the special legate, who is "his superior because the Holy Father is aware of the case." Faithful service to the crown is rewarded, as the legate later gets assigned to a diocese which turns out to be America's most liveable city.

Lost in all this is the Quinn Commission, assigned the task of straightening out relations between Rome, the bishops and religious orders — its efforts at dialogue and collaboration undoubtedly badly damaged by these Roman interventions. Both sides try to inform the body of bishops and the officials of the episcopal conference, but the bishops take no action. There may be some rewards for them, for sisters diverted to battles with Rome will have less time and energy to bother bishops. More likely, they head for cover, hoping Rome will leave them alone. One suspects that such localism and denial of responsibility for what happens in Detroit or Rhode Island proved an added benefit to Roman officials, who seem to have little use for collegiality.

The events recorded here dramatically indicate the importance for the American church of a strong episcopal conference. In the local parish the pastor is caught between the awakening of ministry, community and participation among his people and the demands of the hierarchical structure. He must be a mediator giving his people enough space to grow, to discuss their differences and to explore new forms of church life. He must, at the same time, maintain those links to the hierarchy which can insure that, in the end, they remain Catholics and not Congregationalists.

So, too, no one quite knows yet how the development of a "world church," indigenous within the many cultures of the world, will remain united in faith and witness. To preserve the unity and integrity of the church in the face of the dramatic tendency toward decentralization which has followed the council is a problem, one in which the bishops are the key actors. As Archbishop Roach argued in stepping down as president of the American bishops' conference, the bishops must guide the development of collegiality by carefully explaining and interpreting church teaching and discipline and, at the same time, articulating to Rome and to sister churches the pastoral experience and needs of the American church. Laity, religious, even individual bishops alone cannot expect to win a hearing in Rome, particularly if their "call" or experience sharply differs from the direction of Roman policy. Nor can they alone do much to limit dangerous or misguided Roman actions toward the members of the church in the United States. To give the American church space to grow, while making sure it stays Catholic, is the responsibility of the bishops.

Roman interventions damaging to the development of the American church have punctuated American history. Between 1829 and 1884 Rome's authority was mediated by a body of bishops who met regularly in council and recognized the informal primacy of the archbishop of Baltimore. They were able to keep the increasing conservatism of Rome at a distance, as when James Cardinal prevented condemnation of the Knights of Labor in 1886. They more or less controlled the appointment of new bishops and secured their own authority over sometimes restive clergy and laity by maintaining a united front. After the appointment of the Apostolic Delegate in 1893 and the condemnation of Americanism in 1899, the American church became a "states rights" church, with each bishop supreme in his diocese, accountable to and dependent upon Rome. After Vatican II it became clear that Roman centralization and episcopal independence could make renewal difficult, for renewal required adaptation to American circumstances. The need to refer every decision to Rome hampered a more pastoral approach to annulments, for example, while diocesan autonomy could lead to a sometimes embarrassing contrast between dioceses that some called "geographic morality" or "geographic renewal." As a result, the bishops have struggled to define the role of the episcopal conference. While most Catholics remain indifferent to this body, episodes like the one outlined in these documents show how important it is, if we are to be both an American church and a Catholic church. A strong episcopal conference can prevent or divert divisive Roman interventions and, at the same time, communicate effectively to Rome the circumstances and experiences of the American church.

In this sequence of events, the Sisters of Mercy and the Vatican were like trains passing in the night. As I write, Rome is demanding that religious communities dismiss members who signed a *New York Times* ad on abortion. Only the decisive intervention and mediation of the American bishops, accepting their shared responsibility in matters of vital interest to the American church, can prevent such actions which are unjust and damage the American church as a whole.

The greatest scandal in the events recorded here is not sisters holding office or bishops enforcing arbitrary papal authority, but the controversy itself. Whatever good it might do in exposing long avoided internal issues, it trivializes substantial questions about abortion and political responsibility and makes church authorities look ridiculous. On the collision course that lies between Rome and loyal religious, and between the American bishops and extremists from the right and left, only a strong episcopal conference can insure that dialogue and legitimate authority based on consultation and shared responsibility provide a framework for resolution.

Another problem raised by arbitrary and irresponsible authority is that it prevents, not unorthodox thought, but thought itself. The only person presented in these documents who seems to have *thought* about the problem of Medicaid funded abortion is Agnes Mary Mansour. Her position, grounded in clear-cut opposition to all abortions, is balanced and carefully stated. Going well beyond the simplistic argument that she is personally opposed to abortion but cannot impose her views on the majority, she argues that precisely by occupying the role of state director of social services she can make a positive contribution by strengthening alternatives to abortion, combating poverty and other conditions which breed abortion, and helping to shape the public moral consensus.

The bishops, for their part, refuse to discuss the issue with her; they merely issue orders. They charge that by occupying the office, she is in formal cooperation with abortion, and therefore in opposition to church teaching. This is simply not true. It is true that the church has fairly consistently opposed priests or sisters who support public funding. As Richard McCormick has shown, the Medicaid issue involves a series of complex prudential judgments, but support for funding does not necessarily involve formal cooperation. Voters who support the policy, legislators who vote for it, or lay persons who administer it may make imperfect applications, but they do not violate church teaching. So far, bishops have not refused to pay a portion of their taxes; nor have they recalled their lobbyists seeking funds from legislatures or assistance from state social service offices. Catholic charities has not turned its back on the money that comes from offices like those Sister Mansour administers.

Escalation of opposition to public funding to the level of "church teaching" is confusing, for it clearly occupies a place in the spectrum of teaching more ambiguous than opposition to abortion itself, on which Sister Agnes Mary's position was clear and unequivocal. If toleration of Medicaid funding is as serious an evil as Bishop Szoka and Bevilacqua suggest, then they should be equally adamant in condemning voters, legislators and officials who tolerate the evil in the way Mansour suggests. Bishops who really believe the arguments made against Sister Agnes Mary should not retreat from the single issue approach upheld by some of their number during the recent campaign. If most agreed with the bishops' conference statement placing abortion within a spectrum of issues, or with Archbishop Bernardin's "seamless garment" approach, they undoubtedly do so on the basis of arguments indistinguishable from those made by Sister Agnes Mary. Yet none came to her defense because, after all, the real issue was obedience.

Sister Theresa and the Mercy Sisters use the phrase "political ministry" to describe the problem discussed in these letters. Nowhere is there a reasonable argument about the matter from church officials. Bishop Gelineau, who tolerated Sister Morancy's presence in the legislature and gave her an award during the first term, takes his stand in a statement which simply cites canon law and the well known position of the Holy Father. Quoting the words of canon law, he says that religious are specially consecrated "to seek the perfection of charity." Nowhere does anyone respond to the argument that perfect charity brings with it a priority for the poor and needy and, in this country, the most important vehicle for relieving the needy is the state. As the national conference of bishops and its leaders have regularly argued, the pursuit of justice and peace must, inevitably, lead to the public policy process.

Perhaps in other countries (Poland, Chile) the political system is under the exclusive control of a party hostile to the church and thus participation of priests and religious would, in fact, be a kind of collaboration with the enemy. But here the sisters believe, along with the overwhelming majority of their fellow Catholics and their bishops, that the political system is open to Catholic participation. If government acts improperly, that is as much the fault of Catholics as anyone else. Catholics, therefore, have a high degree of responsibility for the quality of public life. Whatever the wisdom of priests and sisters running for office or occupying positions of responsibility in government, American Catholics surely believe that the church should not undercut the policy process or the political system. Rather it should encourage the widest possible participation and the fullest acceptance of political responsibility.

Unfortunately, the language of canon law does demean politics by setting it against the "gospel witness" and "apostolic initiatives" of religious. Following Christ "more clearly" and seeking "the perfection of charity" are said to be incompatible with public office. One can only surmise the attitude this reflects. While tolerating the participation in politics of mere lay persons, the hierarchy must lack real respect for politicians and even for citizens, whose engagement in the messy, ambiguous, morally dangerous field of politics is less valuable, less a sign of the kingdom than the detached, separate — one might suggest irresponsible — position occupied by clergy and religious. One might also suggest that by avoiding office and standing outside politics, the leaders of the church may do little good, but at least they will not do evil. When things go badly, when the worst of times come, they who have refused to engage in politics can say it is not their fault. The pure, unsoiled church will be there, awaiting our return.

Behind the issue of priests and sisters in politics lie several other theoretical issues of great importance. One is the language of the church and the world. The ecclesiastical argument is that religious are vowed to a way of life marked by its distance from the world. "The public witness which religious are to give to Christ and the church involves that separation from the world which is proper to the character and purposes of each institute." This suggests that the church itself is most church when it is most distinct from the world in which it lives. Church activity, to which religious have pledged their lives, is religious activity; the sign that the religious provides is a sign of the kingdom standing apart form and in judgment upon the world. Joseph Komonchak and others have noted that this conceptualization of church and world rests on shaky foundations. There is no church in history apart from the world. The church does not constitute itself over and against the world and then, removed to a cave or mountain top, decide how it will re-enter a world it has at least temporarily escaped. Rather, the very process by which the church constitutes itself is carried on within this world, for there is no other. Prayer and worship, hermeneutics and theology, all religious activities are also worldly activities, carried out by a particular people in a particular culture at a particular time.

These documents hardly reflect a church other than worldly. Well meaning people with different understandings of responsibility struggle to understand each other and to contribute to the life of an organization which they love and to which they have given their lives. The basic questions are about who is in charge, how decisions are made, what kinds of work people will do, who is accountable to whom, what do symbols and language mean in specific contexts. The sisters are a bit naive, trusting that the "desired outcome" of "common discernment is consensus." The bishops have a touch of that patient cynicism so characteristic of the Roman Catholic Church. There are very worldly human emotions involved as well. The sisters admit to anger. They are offended by the paternalistic prodding of Sister Theresa Kane by SCRIS. They seem weary of the long struggle to be treated fairly. Bishop Bevilacqua responds with touching defensiveness when he thinks the sisters suggest he needed the help of canon lawyers, or when he hears charges of cruelty and injustice. Politics injects its soiled presence as well. Both sides try to inform the press, to command the support of the hierarchy, to secure the unity and support of their own camp, to infiltrate the ranks of the other. The latter is seen in the sisters' claim to secret support from Michigan bishops and the apostolic delegate's delight at a letter of support from a Mercy sister — he even asks to share her letter with the press! Sister Theresa Kane regularly tells SCRIS that the question of political ministry is under study, but she wrote to her sisters on August 2, 1982 asking for their help "toward the development of a well-reasoned statement, an apologia, if you will, for the inclusion of political ministry among the works appropriate to contemporary women religious." As Rome suspected, the question had more or less been resolved. On the other hand, episcopal velvet gloves hardly hid another problem that had been resolved: the decision about appropriate ministries would not be made by the sisters. According to Bevilacqua's press release there was only one "relevant" question: "Does a religious have a right to determine the nature of his or her ministry and occupation in the face of a specific determination by church authorities? The church's answer has been and remains — no." These are, one would suggest, worldly activities, worthy of the best denizens of city halls and state houses. There are no caves and mountain tops to which the Christian can flee to cease being worldly, there is only the church, as worldly a refuge from the world as one can find.

When all this is said, there still is the sad truth that in this struggle there are no winners. On many scores of equity and charity the sisters were surely right, the Roman officials surely wrong. Those who avoided substance and rested on their role as representatives of the sovereign suffer a loss of dignity; such royalism is less evil than sad.

On the other hand, the sisters do not emerge unscarred. If all decisions must be based on dialogue, mutuality, and discernment, does a time come when decisions are made and people submit to them for the sake of the shared commitment to the organized entity, the church? Does the vow of obedience dissolve when it is completely encased in the new language? Is obedience incompatible with human dignity? Does the use of the words "political ministry" enlighten or obscure the serious problems that arise when priests or religious enter public office?

Still, it is the sisters, not the pope or his delegates who display superior comitment to and concern for the church. In the press release issued by the Sisters of Mercy after the humiliating resolution of the Mansour case, they promise to "work for reconciliation" by countering "processes" which, as they experienced them, reflected "neither respect nor mutuality." Throughout, the Sisters seek that reconciliation, not by rejecting canon law or due process, but by insisting that personal dignity, corporate rights, and considerations of mission and service be given proper attention. In every instance recorded in these documents, the Sisters were met with attitudes that unequivocally express a definition of reconciliation best stated by the late Saul Alinsky: "reconciliation means we have the power and you must reconcile yourself to it." In this case such arrogance is made worse by the conviction that the power possessed by human beings has been given them by God.

In a press statement Agnes Mary Mansour points out that, as a Mercy Sister, she must balance her vow of obedience with her equally compelling vows of poverty and chastity and her special Mercy vow of service to the poor, sick and oppressed. Most important, to be faithful to her vows she "must be free to be faithful." The bishops are surely within their rights to insist that, at some point, Sister Agnes Mary must respond to the question whether her use of her freedom, and her decisions about fidelity, are in accord with the church to which she has vowed her obedience. But she is surely even more correct to insist that, for such a question to be legitimate, there must be respect for her as a person and willingness to dialogue about the process of discernment she has experienced. On the two issues of substance, political office and Medicaid funding of abortion, she received no response to her argument but escalation immediately to the level of obedience. Given the evidence of her thirty years of ministry and of the seriousness with which she examined these issues, particularly that of abortion, she had a right to much more; so did her sisters in Rhode Island. They were right to refuse and their refusal constitutes a positive contribution to the life of the church and should be recognized as such.

For the rest of us, who are neither bishops nor priests nor women religious, the problems are even more severe. The only specific mention of the laity as laity comes in Archbishop Szoka's claim that "the good, sensible Catholic people are confused, disturbed and dismayed by the spectacle" of Sister Agnes Mary accepting her post in state government; "confusing the faithful" again. By each of the tests above, the laity are marginalized within the church. They have second class citizenship by the presumptions embodied in the canon law cited and the attitudes expressed by the bishops involved. They have even less access to the struc-

ture than the sisters, but few have access to the kinds of communities of shared faith, mutual affirmation, discernment and
support which characterize the Mercy Sisters. If the basic question
is how the church is best served, might it not occur to sisters
entering public office or to bishops challenging their right to do
so that somehow they might ask the rest of the church what they
think? Did Bishop Szoka or Bishop Gelineau consult with their
dicoesan pastoral council before making their decisions? Do the
Sisters of Mercy bring representative Catholics into their discussion of political ministry? In the absence of open and honest consultation with lay people, does Rome listen to self-appointed lay
representatives like Catholics United for the Faith? Do individual
bishops respond to the pressure of organized lay groups while
ignoring the need for fair and open advice from the whole church?
Until such questions are asked, and answered, until those who
hold office in the church and those who engage in its public ministries do so in responsible relationship with the people of the
church, there will be no creative resolution of problems such as
those recounted in these documents. Church reform remains essential if the life and mission of the church is to become appropriate to the world in which we live and the future we wish to create.

In the 19th century controversy, Rome was determined to bring
the American church in line with the centralization confirmed at
Vatican I. Ideas of freedom and independence were to be decisively
rejected. Roman officials and most European conservatives saw
the United States as a profoundly materialistic culture whose
people were intoxicated with a liberty destructive of all institutions and all authority and they feared that such attitudes were
infecting the American church. Recent events suggest that some
European churchmen, including the Holy Father, still believe the
American chruch has surrendered to a permissive culture. The
Vatican treats religious women with special harshness because
they most clearly represent that American emphasis on personal
autonomy which Rome seems persuaded is an expression of selfish
materialism and irresponsible freedom. The Americanists lost in
the 1890's because they accepted the terms of the argument set
by Rome. Political liberty and economic advancement, they insisted, were perfectly compatible with loyalty to the pope and
docility before the religious authority of the church. In other words,

American Catholics could live quite comfortably with an authoritarian church in a free society, and, in fact, they did.

Both the church and American culture paid a heavy price for this surrencder to an ecclesiastical imperialism. It led to complicity with some of the greatest tragedies of modern history. We should never forget the manner in which the Roman Catholic Church disdained liberal democracy, manipulated and abandoned responsible Catholic political parties in Germany and Italy, encouraged the triumph of fascism in Australia, Portugal and Spain, and struck deals which helped legitimate the governments of Mussolini and Hitler. The defeat of liberal Catholicism in the church universal, of which the condemnation of Americanism was a part, had consequences both in the church and in modern history.

Today, when the church claims to take a different stand toward the world, to be a sign and safeguard of the dignity of the human person, a similar surrender of integrity is again being demanded. For the sake of the church as organization, many bishops seem prepared to accept that demand — again at a great price — far beyond the loss of the sisters' services. In more ways than we usually suspect, our personal relationship with God and the church is profoundly influenced by the quality of the church's public presence in the world. Its claim to be the Body of Christ is compromised, if not contradicted, by the treatment it metes out to its most dedicated servants, the possibility of preaching the word and witnessing to the gospel in anything other than marginal ways is rendered impossible. If all we can do is await the return of the Lord to rule like Caesar over a mindless and spiritless flock, so be it. But if the kingdom is to be one in which free people might wish to live, we had best not permit its living witness to be blasphemed by the abuse of power.

The ultramontanes of the 19th century who created the monarchical church, still served by the male actors in this drama, wanted to render the pope infallible in his every utterance. They wanted a daily papal pronouncement to read with their morning newspaper. They made an idol of the church and clothed the papal office with a power which reflected only their own fears. If we wish to have a church which identifies with the "joys and hopes" as well as the "griefs and anxieties" of real men and women, we will have to choose the church in which Theresa Kane and Agnes Mary Mansour are our sisters and pray that the bishops who shared in these events will someday want to join us.

From Across the Canonical Fence

Arlene Swidler

Religious communities are complicated organisms; tampering with them can be dangerous. Especially since the years of the Second Vatican Council, we have been reminded over and over that changing the patterns of people's lives forcibly from without may have unexpected results.

Yet within the Catholic Church, it is more often the opposite truth which remains unrecognized. When restraints are clamped on a living movement within the church, the results are equally unpredictable. The Catholic women's movement, because of its size, its amazing energies, and its scope, provides some of the most useful illustrations.

The exclusion of women from holy orders and even from the role of acolyte, for example, has made many women question whether the mass is really such a central and important part of Catholic piety after all, and they have begun to devise their own liturgies and symbols — certainly an unintended and unexpected result. The Vatican declaration that women could not image Jesus encouraged them in focusing less on a Christocentric piety and more on a relationship with a creator God in whom they could see both feminine and masculine. Here, too, the results were unforeseen, although, because in both cases we have seen growth in women's sense of responsibility and worth, theology as a whole will perhaps be richer for these developments. The long-term results of a continued limitation on nuns' creative energies by Vatican-imposed rules and pressures are unimaginable. If the details and extent of this repression are widely recognized and pondered, laywomen will more and more reach out in solidarity to their sisters in religious orders. Because the goal of the Vatican is to differentiate and even isolate women in religious orders from the rest of the laity, a joining together of all women, and perhaps all laity, in common cause would come as one more surprise.

The divisions between sisters and laywomen are long standing. Since Vatican II we have begun to analyze and talk about them more openly. The subject has not been fully explored, but any even vaguely feminist Catholic group is aware of tensions vibrating just beneath the surface.

Two articles of some years back suggest the issues. The first is a full-page letter in *America* of February 7, 1976 from Georgia M. Keightley, then chair of a laywomen's caucus in Virginia. Keightley — and her point of view was typical of many women — was highly critical of *America's* coverage of the first Women's Ordination Conference in Detroit the previous November, which assumed that women religious were leaders in and largely responsible for the Catholic feminist movements although, as Keightley pointed out, the questions had first been posed by laywomen. "I do find it somewhat puzzling," she wrote, "that this entire subject of the status of women has suddenly been given new credibility and respectability now that the leaders of the women religious have associated themselves with this cause." Sisters themselves have not always been entirely innocent of projecting this view, she noted.

The second source is a paper which canon lawyer Clara Maria Henning — one of the pioneer laywomen cited by Keightley — delivered at a general assembly of the LCWR in 1972 and which was then reprinted as "The One Sisterhood" in *The Catholic Mind* of November 1973. Henning told the leaders, "Let us not kid ourselves. There exists an incredible amount of animosity between nuns and laywomen, especially on the part of laywomen toward nuns." But Henning, here and elsewhere, was immensely optimistic. Laywomen are unorganized, in diaspora, but religious women have all the tools the movement needs, according to Henning,

control of the church's educational system, huge buildings, access
to the news media. Perhaps at a later date, she would have seen
these buildings serving the women's movement as child care centers, and even more recently she might have imagined them as
shelters for battered women.

Keightley and Henning both recognized that the barriers between women religious and laywomen were not entirely of their
own making. It was the embracing of a potentially divisive position
by a clerically-controlled journal that triggered Keightley's response. Henning reported that in her years in the canon law school
in Washington she saw that priests were far more open to the
idea of a diaconate for sisters than for laywomen.

Almost anyone involved in the Catholic women's movement
learned that lesson early. Doing research in Europe in the late
fifties, I was constantly annoyed at having to sit in vestibules
while my husband was taken into the monastery libraries. When
one monk sympathized, I told him not to worry, we were visiting
a convent the following week, and this time it would be I who got
the favored treatment and my husband who would sit outside
looking at the scrapbooks. Not so, I soon learned. In women's
convents no one at all enters the cloisters — except, of course,
clergy. That rule, I knew instinctively, had been imposed on
women by men.

The gulf, the class system, the inequities all remain, at times
a source of anger, at times forgotten. They serve the purposes of
an ecclesiastical system which believes it can function best when
directing static categories. The recent Vatican initiatives, however, may unwittingly help to break down some of the distinctions.

One major way in which the spotlight on sisters is revealing
possibilities for a new solidarity of nuns and laywomen is in our
common understanding of proper ministries or, in less ecclesiastical language, professional roles. Laywomen and sisters discovered early that they were traveling much the same road, along
which neither had yet come far. The styles of two or three decades
ago in which laywomen at marriage and women religious at profession both changed their names and suffered some loss in identity were seen as symbolic. All women, religious and lay, were
expected to be mothers of a sort and to limit themselves to work

which could be understood as an extension of their feminine maternal spirituality. Sisters were, for the most part, confined to such roles as teacher, nurse, and social worker, all jobs in which they were to be responsive to the immediate needs of others rather than responsible in the sense of planning, analyzing the problems and their causes, and speaking out.

Seeing the limitations imposed on us laywomen mirrored in those imposed on our sisters across the canonical fence evoked sympathy, of course, but also, especially in the beginning, some disparagement of nuns' work. Still, we soon discovered that not many of us had any real desire to climb mountains, study oceanography or take up chess after all. What did seem inviting to many Catholic women were issues like environment, hunger, justice, health legislation — all authentic extensions and expressions of a spirituality of motherhood, but now, more often, seen as concern for God's creation and commitment to the future.

Laywomen were aware that nuns too were seeing themselves charged with broader tasks and ministries. At times sisters began to serve as models for laywomen as they succeeded in secular structures with no loss of simplicity. Yet today we see some of them discouraged or even prevented from walking further along the road with us. The civil offices in which they have served are obviously extensions and expressions of our shared commitment to God's creation and its future, and the tasks undertaken are often those in which many women — and nuns in particular — have proved their competence. Sister Elizabeth Morancy, a member of the state legislature of Rhode Island, for example, received a diocesan award from Bishop Gelineau for her work which included sponsoring two bills providing subsidy programs for parents of handicapped children. A number of sisters around the country have served as elected members of school boards.

The decision of the Eleventh General Chapter of the Sisters of Mercy of the Union on September 1-6, 1983 "That the Mercy Administrative Team authorize a task force to undertake a study of political ministry as an appropriate expression of the charism of the Sisters of Mercy" strikes many laywomen as a call to reflect more profoundly on what is already clear. The fact that the Sacred Congregation for Religious and for Secular Institutes (SCRIS) in its 1980 "Religious Life and Human Promotion" labeled public office a "substitution" for religious mission is seen as a setback for all dedicated Catholic women who seek to assume a greater responsibility for the world. Once again women are seen as heart, not head. Once again we may apply bandages but not speak out in the councils of war.

Much of the division between women religious and laywomen stems from schooldays, when sister was the implementer of the clerical system of intellectual and moral discipline. Looking back on their days with the sisters, many women today acknowledge that they were unwilling and, therefore, somewhat ungrateful recipients of the nuns' ministry. Parents too were not always eager to send their children to parochial schools, as impassioned Sunday sermons and interrogations in the confessional attested. Of course many nuns, when given a chance to choose their ministry, moved out of the school system quickly. Neither the ministers nor those ministered to had accepted their roles freely; both were being coerced by the hierarchical system. But attitudes die slowly, and many a laywoman is still somewhat cynical today about being ministered to by nuns.

The news that the Sisters of Mercy had seriously concerned themselves with tubal ligation, — a procedure specific to lay women, — as early as 1977 would have been welcomed with surprise by many laywomen had they known of it. The sisters themselves felt the need to pursue their review and consultation in private, though their confidentiality was violated. As it is, the news has trickled out only to a comparative few, and most Catholics are completely unaware of the enormous amount of work undertaken — the study and review, consultation, surveys and interviews with personnel in the many Mercy hospitals.

The sisters' emphasis on "wholistic" health care reveals a view of married women as more than physical mothers. Their stress on insuring the full and informed consent on the patient's part through the provision of pastoral and ethical counseling acknowledges and supports the good will and autonomous conscience of the individual laywoman. Inasmuch as many Catholic women do not consider abortion an option in the case of unwanted or dangerous pregnancies, and contraception is repugnant for moral, medical or practical reasons, tubal ligation is seen by them as a positive step toward responsible sexuality and parenthood.

That religious women have long been aware of and concerned about the specific needs of laywomen, that they have invested much thought, time and care in looking for solutions enabling women to act freely and responsibly, and that they have been willing to take risks for laywomen is truly inspiring. Here is a ministry to laywomen which has remained for the most part unknown and unacknowledged.

Most laywomen have considered nuns a part of the hierarchical system. Truth, as children perceived it, flowed down from God to pope, pope to bishop, bishop to pastor, and thence, via the good sisters, to the junior laity. Sister spoke for and represented the clergy, though she may have been painfully deferential when father appeared in the classroom. It is interesting that sister's place in the great chain was repudiated by girls when they grew up. Women's groups, for example, did not seek nuns out for chaplains or even for consultants to any great extent.

The old confusion of status and power can be seen here. Sisters, like many women of the upper classes, had status — were deferred to and mentioned with reverence — simply because they were outside the power elite and the public eye, serenely beyond mundane power struggles. In short, their status was a function of their powerlessness, their dependence. Sisters were a tool of, not a part of, ecclesiastical power.

The recent clashes of nuns with the Vatican illustrate that they, like the rest of the laity, are powerless. This is not a matter of their being subject to alien rules. One could argue that they accepted obedience to church law willingly, knowing that it is a jurisdiction which they, like all non-clerics, have never had any voice in forming. The problem here is rather the lack of principle, the inconsistency in practice, which, when found in an ecclesiastical arena, is genuinely scandalous.

A brief example can be found in a February 29, 1984 letter from SCRIS' Archbishop Mayer to Sister Theresa Kane, stating that Arlene Violet, a sister seeking dispensation from vows because she was a candidate for attorney general of Rhode Island, should be informed that "any future readmission by her to a religious institute will require the special permission of the Holy See, canon 690, 1 notwithstanding." In issuing this prohibition, the Vatican was "waiving" or overriding a provision specifically granted to major superiors in the new code. Canon law, so often invoked in restricting nuns, can be ignored from above at will.

The case of Archbishop Edmund Szoka of Detroit and Sister Agnes Mary Mansour is more widely known. On February 23, 1983, Szoka wrote to Sister Helen Marie Burns, Mansour's superior, reviewing the dialogue between his chancery and the Sisters of Mercy in regard to Mansour, and stating his position. The letter speaks of

"the absolute necessity for (Mansour) to take a clear stand against Medicaid payments for abortion . . . because of the teaching of our church and also because of the moral obligation of opposing anything that encourages abortion. I'm sure you can also appreciate the moral problem of cooperation. There is the further moral consideration of the genuine scandal that anything but a strong position against medicaid abortions would produce." All of this, according to Szoka's letter, he had already communicated to Mansour on December 20, 1982. Yet in an article in the Detroit *Free Press* on December 31, Szoka is quoted as saying, Mansour "is a Catholic, she follows the teachings of the church, but she cannot control the laws of the state . . . and Medicaid funding is a matter of law." He also said, "To make such a big issue of this one thing seems a bit sensational."

Between December 31 and February 23 had come the organized opposition and advertisements in several newspapers, including the *Wall Street Journal*. The "genuine scandal" referred to by Szoka was simply a matter of organized public pressure. Reasoned positions were shouted down, "sensationalized." Mansour was powerless against such moral anarchy.

The cohesion of the episcopal fraternity made discussion even more difficult. Sisters meeting with Bishop Bevilacqua, representating the Vatican on this matter, and the apostolic delegate in August asked why Szoka's earlier position in the *Detroit News* had not been included in Bevilacqua's chronology of the affair.

Bevilacqua's response, according to Sister Emily George's records, was that he did not take his information from the newspapers but from official reports.

Mansour found herself in this position because she was a nun. Until Geraldine Ferraro's campaign for the vice-presidency of this country, it had been assumed that lay people had more autonomy in political judgments. Now it is doubtful whether anyone can take much hope from Szoka's assertion in the *Free Press* interview that "he feels Sister Mansour is in the same position as Catholic laymen appointed or elected to office — '(they) have to follow what the law is.' " But for the laity the sanctions are fewer.

Finally, there is the collegial style of women religious contrasted with that of the official church. Women's groups in general have tended to proceed in what is often somewhat unfairly claimed as a "feminist" model over against a "male" hierarchical model. Even casual readers of religious periodicals know the same consensual process — with its slowness, ambiguities and underlying commitment — has been developing in religious orders. Laywomen seeing the archives of congregations of nuns are likely not only to see their own ideas and policies reflected, but to see them in action in a way the laity have not yet been able to implement — and to see sisters as unexpected role models.

The style is less valued in hierarchical circles. Consider this abridged version of the volleying between Sister Theresa Kane and SCRIS. On July 3, 1982, SCRIS asks Kane to state her "position concerning Sister Arlene's candidature (for public office), especially in the light of Canons 139 and 592. . . ." On August 2, Kane writes to the provincial administrators and Church/Institute Committee of her order, "The team and I think it advisable to consult with you on this matter."

On December 21, 1983, Kane writes to SCRIS' Archbishop Mayer and Father Heiser, "Having consulted with select knowledgeable persons in the U.S.A. Catholic community, I also considered it advisable to bring your request before our Chapter of Affairs scheduled for this year," noting that Arlene Violet has in any case withdrawn from the order. The reply, dated January 9, 1984, says, "We appreciate the procedure of consultation that you

have initiated. However, we wish to receive your own decision in
your responsibility as supreme moderator of a religious institute
bound by the common law of the church."

As the question of a dispensation from perpetual vows for Arlene
Violet continues, a February 29, 1984 letter from SCRIS once
again asks for a response "concerning your personal position on
Sisters of your Institute holding political office. . . ." And once
again on May 9, SCRIS writes thanking Kane for her report on
the vote of the council concerning Violet's dispensation, but adding
— this time with underlinings — that "we do not find in the
aforesaid letter . . . or in any of your other correspondence . . .
your *personal* position on sisters of your institute holding political
office. . . . We now understand from your letter of May 5 that
you do not wish to honor our request at this time and state your
personal position until a study of political ministry, authorized
by the general chapter of your institute, has been promulgated.
When this study is promulgated, we wish to have a copy of it,
along with your *personal* opinion on the subject."

A broadly consultative process has clear disadvantages for both
sides. First, there is the inefficiency and slow pace which under-
standably irritated the Vatican officials, who perhaps forget the
many years lay people used to wait for decisions on annulments
and clerics still await release from the active priesthood. On the
other side, there is the difficulty of maintaining limits to the scope
and participation of the process. In the case of tubal ligation, for
example, preliminary study papers and confidential correspondence found their way to church officials who then intitiated action
unilaterally.

The real problem, though — here as throughout the recent
struggle between the Vatican and women religious — is one of
obedience and accountability. A decision made after long, broad,
and in-depth consultation is a decision of conscience, not to be
changed unless new facts or relevant insights are brought forward.
Such a process must necessarily appear "defiant" to authoritarian
minds.

This issue of collegiality really includes many other issues
within itself. It makes room for open sincere discussion of topics
like the nature of the religious vocation. It allows for a system of

due process in which authority is accountable for its decisions. It provides channels for broad in-put in decision-making.

Collegiality does work, as not only religious orders, but also lay associations and priests' groups demonstrate. The challenge is to nourish it, support one another, and become a light to the Vatican.

A Theological Perspective

Monika K. Hellwig

The events recounted in this volume raise the most serious questions because they seem to represent not only a clash of different ecclesiologies but also, and more urgently, a clash of two very different theologies. At issue are the content and manner of revelation, the relationship between creation and redemption, the nature of sin, the content and process of the redemption, the understanding of grace, the nature and function of the church, and the guiding principles for the structure of the church and for the exercise of authority within it. This may seem, at first glance, to be an overstatement, but further reflection will show that the "hidden agenda" in the conflicts chronicled in this volume is indeed as complex and as far-reaching as this.

An exercise of authority, such as that demonstrated here on the part of those acting in the name of Rome, assumes that revelation is not a continuing reality in the lives of all who are open to God's presence and call, but rather a finite reality that has been captured and codified and entrusted to certain office-holders to be taught and applied to others. This is evident from the fact that the officials in these cases steadfastly refused to enter into dialogue with those involved in the issues more immediately. Such refusal could only be justified if nothing in the concrete situation could be expected to open new questions or throw a new light on our understanding of God's grace in human history and our place within that history. Such a refusal can only be based on the understanding that our knowledge of God's grace and call to us has reached a timeless completion and certainty in the past and need now only be applied without further critical reflection to any and all situations. It might be objected that this over-simplifies the events because serious reflection has been devoted to the matter by the Holy See. The objection cannot be upheld, however, because the documentation in this volume shows that any testimony on the situations from those who were in dialogue with them, was not admitted and, therefore, could not have been taken into consideration.

For many of us today this is puzzling in the light of the theology of revelation because the self-revelation of God is understood to be continuing everywhere and at all times, so that faith consists of alert attention to God in the unfolding of history. Christian faith consists of doing this with the person of Jesus as the constant reference and criterion of God's self-manifestation. It assumes that no institution and no formulation of precepts can ever really capture or exhaust the divine self-revelation and its implications for human lives and relationships.

Also at stake as a kind of "hidden agenda" is the understanding of the relationship between creation and redemption. We have come to see ever more clearly that in public affairs as in private, grace does not destroy or ignore nature but restores and enhances it. Creation is distorted by a history of sin but not destroyed. Redemption is restoration of all things in Christ. Redemption takes place within the limitations of our situation within a sinful history. To participate in the restoration is necessarily to participate in the ambivalent situations, in structures that are not morally and spiritually perfect, in organizations in which others also make decisions and do not always do so according to Christian principles. If redemption were only concerned with lifting souls, so to speak, out of the world, keeping them uncontaminated until death made the isolation permanent, then, perhaps, apostolically committed Christians could refrain entirely from political involvement and could confine themselves to sacramental and catechetical ministries and solacing of individual victims of sinful structures. But if redemption is concerned with the world, with all creation and history, then apostolic endeavors must address the structures that embody human selfishness and ambiguity. There is no way to do this except by participating in the structures and becoming, at least in the broad sense of the term, politically active. This is, of course, what the popes have encouraged and practiced since the 19th century in the social encyclicals. It is what the U.S. bishops have been about in their recent pastoral letters.

Such a fuller understanding of the relation between creation and redemption and of the very nature of redemption in the world has its correlate in a fuller understanding of sin. It rests upon a definition of sin that goes beyond transgressions of explicit commandments. It sees sin as essentially disorientation of creatures from the creator and the purposes and harmony of creation. Indeed, it sees sin as the uncentering of God by self-centeredness in which creation falls apart because in its many competing centers it no longer has a center strong enough to hold everything together and to hold it in balance. The result is chaos and suffering, untold depths of unnecessary suffering. Conversion means reorientation of the world with all its social structures and personal relationships toward God. It means reintegration not only of individual lives but of human society and of all creation. This is a task not for individuals alone, but also for society at all levels of organization and complexity. Any Christian who seriously recognizes and acknowledges the complexity of sin and the stranglehold it has through the structures of society, knows that the task of redemption is one that means entering into the complexity and ambiguity of the structures in order to make whatever provisional change is possible at this time and from this position. It will not change the whole instantly, nor will it enable such Christians to remain devoutly insulated from the ambiguity of the structures in which they work. That, of course, is why sin is so intractable, so oppressive, so pervasive and elusive.

This, in turn, carries further implications for the fuller understanding of grace. It assumes that grace is operative not only in individuals but also in social situations. The church itself is clearly intended to be the anticipation of eschatological grace in the world, a restructuring of human history and society from within. Church, when it is most truly itself, is seed of unity and hope and rescue from disaster for the whole human race, in all its apparently secular activities and dilemmas. If there are structures of sin, then there are also structures of grace: those structures that move toward the overcoming of cultural, racial and political barriers and discriminations among peoples, that challenge and overcome oppression and greed, that redress the balance of power and resources in favor of the poor and the excluded. To participate in such structures is to cooperate with grace. But these structures are often part of a larger and more ambivalent complex. They are often under the auspices of the state, implementing those values that are agreed upon in the public forum of a pluralistic society. If Christians are not willing to participate under those conditions in those positions in which they can do most good and make most difference, then they are not really willing to cooperate with healing grace where the opportunities open up, but are demanding of God some ideal situation for cooperation which does not, in fact, exist in our history. It seems that we must act where we can in the real world and not dither around helplessly waiting for an ideal and unambiguous situation to turn up, before we are willing to get involved.

Such an understanding suggests that evaluation of particular situations in the light of all the circumstances is a necessary and permanent aspect of church life. In other words, it implies that church authority cannot be exercised in a mode in which all the communication is downward in the hierarchic structure and all the obedient attention is turned upward. Nor can it be exercised in a mode in which all the decisions concerning the apostolic life and work of women are made by men who do not listen to the women's testimony concerning the particular situations and the issues involved in them. Authority cannot appropriately be exercised in this way because it blocks the process of discernment and of sensitive, adaptable responses to the grace of God wherever it breaks through. A heavy-handed reassertion of authority with no further justification than its simple claim by those who have long held the power, does not logically answer the objection because it does not address the soteriological and ecclesiological problems inherent in some of the customary uses of power which are themselves modelled upon secular governmental structures of an earlier age.

From the foregoing it is clear that the issues raised by the case histories set forth in this volume go far beyond the rights and wrongs of the particular actions of authority in these cases. The issues raised address very basic differences in theological understanding that have become a pervasive "hidden agenda" in conflicts with the church of our times.

IV.
Chronology with Documentation

Background:

The Tenth General Chapter approved a statement concerning the relationship of the Sisters of Mercy within the church which called for efforts to bring about the full potential of the Church by taking responsibility for leadership for change. Statements of Tenth, Eleventh, and Twelfth General Chapters called the Sisters of Mercy of the Union to serious consideration of efforts toward systemic change and to active participation in the development of the Church's understanding of issues critical to contemporary people.

1978

The first instance of Sisters of Mercy of the Union in political office in modern times began quietly in *November 1978* when Sister Elizabeth Morancy was elected to the State Legislature of Rhode Island as representative of District #18.

1980

Sister Elizabeth Morancy was re-elected to the State Legislature of Rhode Island as representative of District #18.

1982

On *May 7, 1982*, Sister Arlene Violet met with Bishop Louis Gelineau to inform him of her intention to announce her candidacy for the office of Attorney General of the State of Rhode Island.

On *May 13, 1982,* Sister Arlene Violet met with Sister Noel Blute, Provincial Administrator of the Sisters of Mercy of the Union — Province of Providence, to inform her of her intention to announce her candidacy for Attorney General.

On *May 14, 1982,* Sister Arlene Violet announced her candidacy for Attorney General.

On *May 18, 1982,* William Brodhead, Congressional Representative from District #17 of the State of Michigan announced he would not seek re-election.

Within twenty-four hours of the announcement Sister Agnes Mary Mansour called Sister Helen Marie Burns, Provincial Administrator of the Sisters of Mercy of the Union — Province of Detroit, to seek consultation of herself and the Administrative Team relative to seeking this public office.

In *June, 1982,* the Provincial Administrative Team reviewed Canon 139.2, the document on *Religious Life and Human Promotion,* the current instances of women religious serving in public office, the charism of the Sisters of Mercy, current ministerial directions of the Community, and shared with Sister Agnes Mary their support for her candidacy and their opinion that she was free to seek public office. Both she and they agreed that she would inform Archbishop Edmund Szoka of this decision prior to any press release. Unfortunately, the news leaked to the press before a *scheduled* meeting between Archbishop Szoka and Sister Agnes Mary occurred. The Archbishop, while not offering his approval, did not oppose her candidacy.

On *July 3, 1982,* Sister M. Theresa Kane, president of the Sisters of Mercy of the Union, received a letter from the Sacred Congregation for Religious and Secular Institutes (SCRIS) signed by Archbishop Augustine Mayer, O.S.B., indicating SCRIS "has been appraised concerning the candidature of Sister Arlene Violet" and seeking to ascertain "your position concerning Sister Arlene's candidature."

See Document #1

On *July 14, 1982,* Sister M. Theresa acknowledged the letter from SCRIS and indicated she was in a process of reflection and consultation and would communicate with them at a later date (see December 1983).

On *August 2, 1982,* Sister M. Theresa addressed a letter to several consultants (canonists, theologians, and others) regarding the inquiry from SCRIS. She and the Administrative Team sought advice "toward the development of a well-reasoned statement, an apologia, if you will, for the inclusion of political ministry among the works appropriate to contemporary women religious." On the same day, Sister M. Theresa addressed a letter to the Provincial Administrators and members of the Mercy Church-Institute Committee seeking their advice relative to the letter from SCRIS.

On *August 10, 1982,* Sister Agnes Mary was defeated in the primary election in her bid for the congressional seat in District #17.

In *November, 1982,* Sister Arlene Violet was narrowly defeated in her bid for Attorney General.

Sister Elizabeth Morancy won her *third* term in the state House of Representatives.

In *December, 1982,* Mercy Church-Institute Committee moved toward finalization of a position paper relative to elective office for religious.

Early in December, Sister Agnes Mary informed Sister Helen Marie that Governor-elect Blanchard was considering her for a state-level cabinet appointment.

Archbishop Szoka in a telephone conversation with Sister Helen Marie expressed his approval for the appointment and reflected his concern — should it be the Department of Social Services — for a clear stand relative to the abortion issue. Both agreed that Sister Agnes Mary should discuss this matter personally with Archbishop Szoka.

Approximately *December 20, 1982,* Sister Agnes Mary called Sister Helen Marie to say that the appointment to the Department of Social Services was confirmed and that she had not yet been able to set up an appointment with the Archbishop.

On *December 27 and 28, 1982,* Sister Agnes Mary left messages at Archbishop Szoka's office that she was trying to set up an appointment with him. By now she and the Provincial Administrative Team were aware that a public announcement of the appointment would be made on December 29, 1982.

On *December 28, 1982,* Sister Agnes Mary informed Sister Helen Marie that she had not been successful in reaching Archbishop Szoka. Sister Helen Mary agreed to continue trying while Sister Mary traveled to Lansing for the press conference scheduled the morning of December 29.

On *December 29, 1982,* Sister Helen Marie reached the Archbishop by telephone to inform him of the appointment to be announced later that day. Later that day Sister Agnes Mary reached the Archbishop by telephone to discuss with him the appointment and his concerns relative to the abortion issue. Both differ on their understandings of that conversation (see chronologies of Sisters of Mercy, Bishop Bevilacqua, and Sister Agnes Mary's Critique of Bishop Bevilacqua's Chronology. . . published in *Origins,* Vol. 13: No. 12).

On *December 31, 1982,* an article in the *Detroit Free Press* quotes Archbishop Szoka's approval of the appointment "as long as she makes clear her opposition to abortion. Sister Mansour is a Catholic. She follows the teachings of the church, but she cannot control the laws of the state. . . and Medicaid funding is a matter of law."

1983

On *January 10, 1983,* both the Provincial Administrator (Detroit) and the president received a steady, though not overwhelming, stream of letters regarding the announcement of Sister Agnes Mary's appointment. Media coverage in Michigan and elsewhere throughout January and February raised controversy relative to Sister Agnes Mary's appointment and Medicaid funding for abortion. Coverage and correspondence is favorable and unfavorable.

Sister Agnes Mary revised her statement on abortion, developed for her unsuccessful congressional bid. Consultants for the revision included politicians, theologians, and bishops.

On *February 8, 1983,* Sister Agnes Mary called Sister Helen Marie to share her decision to begin to respond to requests from the media. She had, until this time, deliberately avoided all efforts by media persons to draw her into conversation.

On *February 11, 1983,* the Sisters of Mercy, Province of Detroit, became aware of an ad in the *Wall Street Journal* and other major newspapers depicting Sister Agnes Mary and Archbishop Szoka as "baby killers."

Early February, Sister Helen Marie, aware that Sister Agnes Mary's confirmation hearing could generate additional media coverage, called Archbishop Szoka's office to inform him of the circumstances surrounding the hearing and to offer her willingness to meet with him before the hearing if he desired. Both concerns were given to his secretary to be forwarded to the Archbishop. No response was received.

On *February 14, 1983,* the Archbishop met with Sister Agnes Mary at his residence. This session lasted about one hour. Archbishop Szoka reported that he said he intended to publicly state his opposition to her continuing as Director of the Department of Social Services and to call for her resignation unless she clearly stated her opposition to Medicaid funding. Sister Agnes Mary understood him to say that he would have to go to her religious superiors so that they could ask her to change her position.

On *February 23, 1983,* at 8:45 a.m., Sister Helen Marie Burns received a letter from Archbishop Szoka informing her that he had withdrawn his support for Sister Agnes Mary's appointment and would ask for her resignation at a news conference at 10:15 a.m. that same morning. The news conference was held as planned.

See Document #2

On *February 28, 1983,* Archbishop Szoka met privately with two members of the Provincial Administrative Team — Sisters Maurita Sengelaub and Mary Rebecca Lorenz — in order to understand the action(s) of the Archbishop and to ascertain his willingness to meet with the entire Administrative Team later that week.

On *March 4, 1983,* Archbishop Szoka, Father Kevin Britt, and Bishop Dale Melczek met with the entire Provincial Administrative Team. The meeting offered no resolution to the matter.

On *March 5, 1983,* the Provincial Administrative Team issued a press release that indicated that there was not sufficient clarity at this time for them to judge that Sister Agnes Mary's resignation would be for the greater good.

On *March 8, 1983,* Sister Agnes Mary testified before the Michigan State Senate Committee. She was confirmed as Director of the Department of Social Services. In a prepared statement she testified that while she was opposed to abortion she could tolerate Medicaid funding and did not see the elimination of such funding as the way to change the abortion question.

On *March 10, 1983,* Archbishop Szoka presented a report of the situation to the Holy See through the Apostolic Delegate.

Extensive media coverage happened locally and nationally — *New York Times* ad, *Time* magazine, Catholic newspapers, local newspapers, *Origins,* etc., as well as radio and television shows.

On *March 23, 1983,* Archbishop Pio Laghi, Apostolic Delegate, held a meeting with Sister M. Theresa Kane, President of the Sisters of Mercy of the Union, and Sister Emily George, a member of the General Administrative Team. The Apostolic Delegate presented a letter to Sister M. Theresa from himself indicating that the Sacred Congregation instructed her as President to require Sister Agnes Mary to submit her resignation as the Director of the Department of Social Services.

See Document #3

On *March 27, 1983,* Sister M. Theresa informed Provincial Administrators of the letter delivered by the Apostolic Delegate and sought consultation from them. Consultation with some of the Michigan Bishops continued as well as efforts to keep the latest action of SCRIS from the news media.

On *April 4, 1983,* Sister M. Theresa met with Sisters Helen Marie and Agnes Mary to review the circumstances occasioned by the recent letter

from the Apostolic Delegate and to explore their individual recommendations relative to the circumstances.

On *April 6, 1983,* the General Administrative Team met to review consultations and to determine their response. They determined to request
a formal reconsideration of the case.

On *April 10, 1983,* Sister Agnes Mary requested a leave of absence from
the Sisters of Mercy of the Union.

See Document #4

On *April 11, 1983,* Sister M. Theresa addressed a letter to Archbishop
Laghi requesting a formal reconsideration of the decision reached by
SCRIS. She asked that the request and documentation prepared by the
Detroit Provincial Administrative Team be submitted to the Holy See.
She also informed him that the request for leave had been granted.

See Document #5
See Document #6

On *April 12, 1983,* the Apostolic Delegate sent by special courier to
SCRIS the request for reconsideration of the decision. On the same day,
the Detroit Administrative Team submitted documentation to the
Bishops of Michigan seeking their advice on the "next best step." Both
the Provincial Administrative Team and the General Administrative
Team granted Sister Agnes Mary leave of absence effective April 20, 1983.

According to the time-line of Bishop Bevilacqua, on *April 13, 1983,*
Archbishop Mayer, Secretary of SCRIS, asked Bishop Anthony Belivac-
qua to serve as ad hoc delegate in the matter of Sister Agnes Mary
Mansour. Archbishop Laghi addressed a letter to Sister M. Theresa indicating the documentation had been sent to Rome by special courier.
Archbishop Laghi thanked her "for the sensitivity you showed in responding to my request for an early reply to the inquiry about action to be
taken regarding Sister Agnes Mary Mansour."

On *April 15, 1983,* Bishop Bevilacqua met with Archbishop Mayer to
discuss the nature, scope, and contents of a Pontifical mandate under
consideration in the matter of Sister Agnes Mary Mansour.

On *April 16, 1983,* Cardinal Pironio addressed a letter to Bishop Bevilacqua which appointed him ad hoc delegate with the mandate to approach
Sister Agnes Mansour directly and to require, in the name of the Holy
See and by virtue of her vow of obedience, that she immediately resign
as Director of the Department of Social Services.

See Document #7

On *April 26, 1983,* Sister M. Theresa received a letter from the Apostolic Delegate informing her that "in response to her request for an appointment to discuss the case of Sister Agnes Mary Mansour, the Cardinal Prefect of SCRIS refers her to Bishop Bevilacqua who has been appointed the ad hoc delegate of SCRIS for this entire matter."

See Document #8

On *April 27, 1983,* a letter from Bishop Bevilacqua dated April 25, 1983, was hand-delivered to Sister Agnes Mary. This letter stated that Bishop Bevilacqua had been appointed ad hoc delegate at the direction of the Holy Father and that it was his responsibility to inform her of the decision of the Holy See in her regard.

See Document #9

On *May 1, 1983,* Sister M. Theresa and two members of the General Administrative Team were present in Rome to attend the UISG Assembly and subsequent annual meeting. On her arrival, Sister M. Theresa requested in conversation with an official of SCRIS a meeting with Cardinal Pironio relative to the Mansour case. No response was made to that request.

On *May 9, 1983,* Bishop Bevilacqua met with Sister Agnes Mary Mansour at the Provincial House of the Sisters of Mercy, between 4:00 — 7:00 p.m. He showed her the mandate received from the Holy See and read the mandate to all present. After discussion, argumentation, reflection, and prayer, Sister Agnes Mary requested dispensation from vows. Bishop Bevilacqua granted her request by virtue of the authority given him as ad hoc delegate. Sister Emily George called Sister M. Theresa in Rome to apprise her of the Vatican's decision and Sister Agnes Mary's response.

See Document #10

On the morning of *May 11, 1983,* Sister Agnes Mary held a press conference to accompany a press release stating her decision. In the afternoon the Provincial Administrative Team held a press conference to acompany their press release stating regret for the situation and support of Sister Agnes Mary. Bishop Bevilacqua released a statement to the press (see *Origins,* Vol. 13: No. 2).

On *May 12, 1983,* a succinct summary of events was sent to the Sisters of Mercy of the Province of Detroit by the Provincial Administrative Team.

On *May 14, 1983,* while still in Rome, Sister M. Theresa addressed a letter to Cardinal Pironio and Archbishop Mayer notifying them that a formal process of appeal of the decision and the process of SCRIS regard-

ing Sister Agnes Mary Mansour had been initiated at the Office of the
Apostolic Signatura. She also met that day with Archbishop Mayer and
other officials of SCRIS relative to the Constitutions of the Sisters of
Mercy of the Union. At the close of that meeting, Sister M. Theresa
introduced her concern relative to the Mansour case.

On *May 14, 1983,* Sister M. Theresa addressed a letter to the Apostolic
Signatura to formally appeal "both the decision and the process of SCRIS
which led to Sister Agnes Mary Mansour's decision."

On *May 18, 1983,* Sister M. Theresa (now returned to the States) informed
the Provincial Administrators of the formal appeal, indicated that to date
SCRIS had not responded to the formal request for reconsideration submitted on April 11, 1983, and recorded a difficult meeting with Archbishop
Mayer on Saturday, May 14, 1983.

On *May 18, 1983,* Sister M. Theresa addressed a letter to Archbishop
Laghi in which she registered concern for two sections of the precept:
Part I, Article 13, and Part I, Article 14.

See Document #11

On *May 18, 1983,* Sister M. Theresa addressed a letter to Cardinal Pironio
registering a formal appeal *with* SCRIS regarding the decision concerning
Sister Agnes Mary Mansour. Additional canonical counsel advised that
this appeal should precede the appeal to the Apostolic Signatura. She
listed four reasons for the appeal.

See Document #12

On *May 19, 1983,* a letter from the office of the Apostolic Delegate acknowledged receipt of the May 18 letter, but indicated any concerns relative
to "the matter of the former Sister Agnes Mary Mansour" should be
submitted to Bishop Bevilacqua.

On *May 20, 1983,* Mercy Center Washington released a press statement
concerning the appeal; Sister M. Theresa sent a letter to the Sisters of
Mercy of the Union summarizing the most recent events regarding "the
Mansour cse." Sister Emily George addressed a letter to Bishop Bevilacqua to object to certain misrepresentations in his press statement immediately following May 9, 1983.

On *May 23, 1983,* Sister M. Theresa addressed a letter of concern to
Archbishop Roach, President of the National Conference of Catholic
Bishops. Among other matters, she stated her distress that Bishop
Bevilacqua was appointed delegate and received his mandate before there
had been a response to the request for reconsideration. She also wrote
a letter to Bishop Bevilacqua forwarding the concerns addressed to
Archbishop Laghi on May 18. In an additional letter to Bishop Bevilacqua

she requested a copy of the mandate given to him by SCRIS and a copy of the minutes of the May 9 meeting forwarded to SCRIS; registered her disagreement with portions of his press release; and indicated that to date no response had been received from SCRIS to the points raised in her letter requesting reconsideration.

On *May 31, 1983,* Sister M. Theresa met with the Detroit Provincial Administrative Team to offer support, review the situation, and explain the appeal process.

On *June 6, 1983,* Bishop Bevilacqua informed Sister M. Theresa of the events of May 9, 1983.

See Documents #13

On *June 6, 1983,* SCRIS informed Sister M. Theresa that the Sacred Congregation could not accept her request for an appeal because Bishop Anthony Bevilacqua acted in the name of the Holy See.

See Document #14

On *June 7, 1983,* Bishop Bevilacqua acknowledged receipt of Sister M. Theresa's letter of May 23, 1983, and indicated that the minutes of the May 9 meeting would not be forwarded to her as "the minutes were substantially incorporated into the report requested by SCRIS and at the present time they must be considered property of the aforementioned Congregation."

On *June 17, 1983,* Sister M. Theresa formally initiated a process of appeal through the Apostolic Signatura regarding the decision and pro- cesses which led to Sister Agnes Mary Mansour's dispensation. Separate letters informed Archbishop Laghi and Cardinal Pironio of the appeal.

See Document #15

On *July 1, 1983,* in separate letters, Bishop Bevilacqua informed Sister M. Theresa that "the request of confidentiality which may have been attached up to this date by the Holy See. . . is hereby no longer considered binding" and forwarded a copy of the dispensation granted to Sister Agnes Mary Mansour as requested earlier. Once again, he refused a second request for the minutes of the May 9 meeting.

See Document #16

On *July 11, 1983,* Sister M. Theresa received a hand-delivered letter from the Office of the Apostolic Delegate. The letter was dated July 4, 1983, and was from the Apostolic Signatura. The letter informed her "that the Signatura Apostolica is unable to consider the recourse which you intend to present because. . . Bishop Bevilacqua was acting under express command of the Holy See."

See Document #17

On *July 5, 1983,* Bishop Bevilacqua replied at length to the concerns addressed to him by Sister M. Theresa in a May 23 letter.

On *July 13, 1983,* Sister Theresa addressed letters to Archbishop Laghi and Bishop Bevilacqua asking for a joint appointment with the General Administrative Team to reflect together on the events of the last few months.

On *July 19, 1983,* Sister M. Theresa addressed a letter to Cardinal Sabattani requesting "to know from the Apostolic Signatura what canonical recourse is possible in light of the July 4 communication."

Minutes from the meeting of *August 1, 1983,* revealed a lengthy discussion with attempts to understand apparently contradictory data. In a memo to Provincial Administrators regarding the meeting, Sister M. Theresa said, "I believe the meeting was a difficult but worthwhile endeavor on our part."

The Evening Bulletin in Rhode Island carried a story indicating that Bishop Gelineau "said that he had told Sister Arlene Violet she unquestionably will be violating church law if she runs again for Attorney General in 1984.

On *August 23, 1983,* Sister M. Theresa received a letter from the Apostolic Signatura reiterating its earlier position "that there is no possibility of recourse of any kind."

The second session of the Eleventh General Chapter of the Sisters of Mercy of the Union was held in Cincinnati, Ohio, from *September 1-6, 1983.* The Eleventh General Chapter approved a task force to undertake a study of political ministry as an appropriate expression of the charism of the Sisters of Mercy and a resolution expressing the delegates concern regarding the dispensation of Sister Agnes Mary Mansour (see narrative).

On *October 17, 1983,* Sister M. Theresa addressed a letter to Archbishop Laghi and Bishop Bevilacqua recording subsequent reflections of the General Administrative Team since the August 1 meeting.

On *October 26, 1983,* Sister M. Theresa received a letter from SCRIS requesting a reply "as soon as possible" to their *July 3, 1982,* request for her position relative to the candidature of one of your Sisters for the political office of Attorney General of the State of Rhode Island.

See Document #18

On *November 18, 1983,* a memo was sent to Provincial Administrators informing them of the October 26 letter from SCRIS and seeking consultation on this matter as well as any reflections concerning Sister M. Theresa's intent to request a papal audience regarding "the Mansour case."

Consultations concerning the October 26 letter were received from Provincials and canonists throughout the month of November.

On *November 26, 1983,* Sister M. Theresa received a letter from the Apostolic Delegate indicating he had received word "from the Holy See that the Holy Father . . . has made his mind clear on the application of certain provisions of the newly revised Code with regard to Miss Agnes Mary Mansour. In her case, the provision of Canon 690. . . does not apply." The new code of Canon Law allows the decision for readmission of former members to rest with the General Administration of the religious community. This power is rescinded relative to Agnes Mary. Mid-January consultation was sought from several canonists relative to the waiver of Canon 690 in Agnes Mary's regard.

See Document #19

In November, media coverage in Rhode Island and elsewhere began to escalate concerning the possible candidacy of Sister Arlene Violet for the office of Attorney General of the State of Rhode Island.

On *December 4, 1983,* Sister Arlene Violet submitted a letter to Sister M. Noel Blute and the Provincial Administrative Team: "with deep pain and with limited freedom of choice, I write this letter to request a dispensation from my vows."

On *December 21, 1983,* Sister M. Theresa addressed a letter to Archbishop Mayer in response to the July 3 inquiry. The letter indicated the action of the Eleventh General Chapter relative to the appropriateness of political ministry in light of the Mercy charism and informed him that Sister Arlene Violet had decided to withdraw from the religious congregation.

See Document #20

On *December 27, 1983,* Sister M. Noel Blute addressed a letter to Sister M. Theresa informing her of a December 23 meeting with Bishop Gelineau in which he stated that he had had consultation on the canon concerning reinstatement and that such reinstatement was not possible without recourse to Rome. The Bishop also asked to meet with the Provincial Administrative Team and Sister Arlene on January 3, 1984. The Mercy Administrative Team approved Sister Arlene Violet's request for dispensation. The request was forwarded to SCRIS on January 6, 1984.

1984

On *January 3, 1984,* Sister Mary Noel Blute, members of the Provincial

Administrative Team and Sister Arlene Violet met with Bishop Gelineau, Bishop Angell, Msgr. Varsanyi, Father Matano, and Father Evans regarding the political issue as it related to the Sisters of Mercy and the Church, especially in the diocese of Providence.

On *January 5, 1984,* Bishop Gelineau released a press statement regarding priests and religious in politics and the case of Sister Arlene Violet. (see *Origins,* Vol. 13: No. 34).

On *January 6, 1984,* Sister M. Theresa sent a letter to Pope John Paul II seeking the privilege of a private audience "in regard to the pastoral situation involving the administration of the Sisters of Mercy of the Union and Sister Agnes Mary Mansour." The letter was sent with a cover letter to Archbishop Laghi asking his assistance in seeing that the request was forwarded through the Secretary of State.

Sister M. Theresa also sent a copy of her letter to the Holy Father to Archbishop Quinn and Bishop Malone for their assistance in the matter.

A letter dated *January 9, 1984,* and mailed from the Apostolic Delegate's office on January 23 informed Sister M. Theresa that SCRIS had received her letter of December 21 but "wish to receive your own decision in your responsibility as supreme moderator of a religious institute bound by the common law of the Church." An inquiry was made also regarding the nature of Sister Arlene Violet's withdrawing — by exclaustration, leave of absence or dispensation. (This letter was mailed from the Apostolic Delegate's office on January 9, 1984, and received January 23, 1984.)

See Document #21

On *January 10, 1984,* in a memo to Provincial Administrators, Sister M. Theresa informed them of the action relative to the waiver of Canon 690 in Sister Agnes Mary's regard; of her December 21 reply to SCRIS; of her January 6 petition for a private audience with the Holy Father.

Replies from Archbishop Quinn and Bishop Malone offered suggestions concerning the letter of request for a papal audience. Consequently, Sister M. Theresa revised her original letter and submitted a second request.

On *January 20, 1984,* Sister Arlene Violet announced her candidacy for Attorney General and her decision to request dispensation from vows. The news articles in Rhode Island linked the candidacy of Sister Elizabeth Morancy with Bishop Gelineau's stand on political office. Both Sister Noel Blute and Mercy Center Washington released statements to the press.

On *January 27, 1984,* Sister M. Theresa repeated her request for a papal audience in a revised letter which spoke more generally to the purpose of the audience. Again, Archbishop Laghi was asked to facilitate the request.

See Document #22

On *February 14, 1984,* Sister M. Theresa wrote to Archbishop Mayer to ask for a response to the January 6 request for dispensation from vows by Sister Arlene Violet and to clarify that "the decision of the General Chapter to authorize a study regarding political ministry reflects and incorporates my personal position."

See Document #23

On *February 15, 1984,* Sister Elizabeth Morancy addressed a letter to SCRIS seeking clarification "as to what are my options in the present situation as a three term state legislator, member of a religious order who wishes to run again but has been asked not to seek re-election by the Bishop of the diocese."

See Document #24

On *March 6, 1984,* a letter from E. Martinez acknowledged that the Holy Father had received Sister M. Theresa's request for an audience. The Holy Father was not completely clear what expectations she had of such a meeting and so requests that she "outline in greater detail the scope of your proposal."

On *March 9, 1984,* SCRIS responded to inquiry of Sister Elizabeth Morancy encouraging her "to lovingly obey Church law and . . . fulfill what is prescribed."

See Document #25

Archbishop Mayer in a letter dated *March 12* asked Sister M. Theresa to urge Sister Elizabeth to persevere in her vocation as a Sister of Mercy and to communicate her decision to the Apostolic Pro-Nuncio as soon as possible.

A letter from Archbishop Mayer, dated *February 29, 1984,* enclosed dispensation papers for Sister Arlene Violet indicating that the original request had not included a vote of the General Council as required by Canon 691.1. "We ask that you notify us in writing about the vote of your council so that our file will be complete." The letter further stated that Canon 690.1 has been waived in regard to Sister Arlene Violet (again, the power given to the community in regard to re-admission is rescinded in her regard) and requests again, a reply concerning Sister M. Theresa's personal position on sisters holding political office. (The letter was received at Mercy Center Washington in a SCRIS envelope mailed from the Apostolic Nunciature on *March 13, 1984).*

See Document #26

On *March 23-27, 1984,* Twelfth General Chapter of the Sisters of Mercy

of the Union was held in Cincinnati, Ohio. This was a Chapter of Elections as well as a Chapter of Affairs. The Twelfth General Chapter approved the request from the appropriate Church authorities of an indult granting Sister Elizabeth Morancy dispensation from Canons 672 and 285, Section 3, in order to permit her to continue in public service; and extended to Sister Arlene Violet love and concern and pledged continuing efforts to clarify the role of women religious in political ministry.

On *April 3, 1984,* Sister M. Theresa addressed a letter to Archbishop Mayer recording the vote of the General Council relative to Sister Arlene Violet's request for dispensation from vows and the acceptance of this dispensation by Sister Arlene. She again referred to her February 14 letter as her response to the inquiry regarding political ministry.

See Document #27

On *April 19, 1984,* Sister M. Theresa wrote a letter to Pope John Paul II outlining her rationale and purpose in seeking a private audience.

See Document #28

On *April 24, 1984,* a packet of materials and brief was sent to Rome to petition an indult granting a dispensation for Sister Elizabeth Morancy to continue in public office.

See Document #29

On *May 7, 1984,* a letter from Archbishop Laghi to Sister M. Theresa indicated that he had been informed by the appropriate officials in Rome that the petition for indult had been denied.

On *May 9, 1984,* SCRIS replied in writing that the petition for an indult granting a dispensation for Sister Elizabeth Morancy to be a candidate for political office had been denied. In a separate letter, Archbishop Hamer suggested that he did not find Sister M. Theresa's personal position on Sisters holding political office in any correspondence. "If you had addressed this question with us, perhaps some of the difficulties involved in the Mansour, Violet, and Morancy cases could have been avoided."

See Document #30

On *June 21, 1984,* Sister M. Theresa notified Archbishop Laghi that Sister Elizabeth Morancy had requested a dispensation from her vows.

On *June 28, 1984,* Sister M. Theresa responded to the May 9 letter of Archbishop Hamer retracing once again the record of her expression of her personal position on Sisters of Mercy holding political office.

See Document #31

In *July, 1984,* Sister M. Theresa Kane completed her term of office as General Administrator for the Sisters of Mercy of the Union.

On *August 3, 1984,* the Apostolic Pro-Nuncio communicated to Sister M. Theresa the denial of her request for a private audience with John Paul II.

See Document #32

Document #1

SACRA CONGREGATIO   July 3, 1982
.PRO RELIGIOSIS
ET INSTITUTIS SAECULARIBUS
————
Prot. n. 51772/82

Sister Theresa Kane, R.S.M.
Administrator General
Sisters of Mercy of the Union of the United States
1320 Frenwick Lane, Suite 500
Silver Spring, Maryland 20901, USA

Dear Sister,

This Sacred Congregation for Religious and Secular Institutes
has been appraised concerning the candidature of Sister Arlene Violet,
R.S.M. for the political office of Attorney General of the State of Rhode
Island.

We come to you as Sister Arlene's general superior to ascertain
your position concerning Sister Arlene's candidature, especially in the
light of Canons 139 and 592, as well as this Sacred Congregation's
document of 1980 entitled Religious and Human Promotion. I.D. ("Involvement in politics").

We request that you forward your reply to us through the good
offices of the Apostolic Delegate.

Wishing God's blessings on you personally and on all the Sisters
of Mercy of the Union of the United States, I remain

Sincerely yours in Christ,

+ A. Mayer
        Lu.

Document #2

ARCHDIOCESE OF DETROIT
1234 WASHINGTON BLVD.
DETROIT MICHIGAN 48226

CONFIDENTIAL

OFFICE OF THE ARCHBISHOP

February 23, 1985

Dear Sister Helen Marie Burns,

I intend this letter for yourself and your Provincial Council. I am writing about the matter of Sister Agnes Mary Mansour. I want to begin by reviewing briefly the history of the present situation insofar as it involves me.

Early in December, 1982, you very thoughtfully called me to inform me that Sister Mansour was being considered for a State cabinet level appointment by the newly elected Governor. You indicated that nothing was certain but you wanted to know what I would think about such an appointment. I responded that I would not object if the appointment were to a field of endeavor in which the Sisters of Mercy had traditionally served and ministered. You assured me that such would be the case and mentioned that if she were appointed, it would probably be to the Education Department or the Department of Social Services. You empha- sized, however, that nothing was certain at that time. I responded that if the appointment were to the Department of Social Services, Sister Mansour would have to be very clear in her statements about abortion. You told me that you would express that caution to her and would suggest that she discuss this matter with me personally. I told you I would welcome such a discussion with Sister Mansour and would like to clarify this matter with her.

I heard nothing further from you or from Sister Mansour. My secretary told me that Sister Mansour called my office on December 27 and 28. On both days, I was occupied all day and into the evening with meetings and appointments. Sister Mansour did not indicate her reason for calling. I, of course, did not and could not know that she had the appointment and that the announcement was imminent. On the morning of December 29, I tried to call Sister Mansour. Almost simultaneously, I was informed by another source that her appointment was to be announced that day. I kept trying to reach her both in Detroit and Lansing but without success. I finally reached her by late afternoon. By that time, the announcement had been made and unfortunately she had already expressed some comments to the press which were confusing and objectionable.

I was surprised and disappointed that she didn't try to meet with me earlier, as you had suggested. In any event, when I spoke to her that day, I pointed out the absolute necessity for her to take a clear stand against medicaid payments for abortion. I pointed out the necessity of this position because of the teaching of our Church and also because of the moral obligation of opposing anything that encourages abortion. I'm sure you can also appreciate the moral problem of coopera- tion. There is the further moral consideration of the genuine scandal that anything but a strong position against medicaid abortions would produce. I told Sister Mansour that she must take a position of opposing medicaid payments for abortion. I also told her that if she could not take such a position, she should not have the job of director of Social Services. She told me she would try to follow my advice.

On that basis, I did not object to her acceptance of the appointment. I expected that she would clarify her position. You know the kind of adverse publicity I received for keeping my word to you and for thinking that Sister Mansour would follow my advice.

As the weeks passed, Sister Mansour said nothing--nothing to clarify her
position and nothing to indicate her opposition to medicaid payments for abortion. During this time, she did not make any attempt to contact me. Finally,
on February 7, I had my secretary, Father Kevin Britt, contact Sister Mansour
and tell her that I would like to have a private meeting with her that week.
She responded that she was so tightly scheduled that week that a meeting would
be impossible. She did say, however, that she could meet with me the following
Monday, February 14. I arranged to meet with her privately at my residence
on that date at 11:00 a.m. I spent about an hour with her trying to explain the
moral necessity for her to clearly oppose medicaid payments for abortion and to
state her intention to work for changing this situation. I also informed her
that the position she was expressing to me was morally objectionable and indefen-
sible. I finally had to tell her that if she did not change her stance, it
would be necessary for me to object publicly to her retaining the appointment
as director of Social Services and to call for her resignation.

Two days later, February 16, her picture and an interview appeared on the
first page of the Detroit News. It is clear to me that she has not changed her
position. In fact, she clearly states that she does not plan to ask the State
to stop providing abortions to poor women. She said she feels "more harm could
come from halting State funding" at this time. She makes no reference to the
irreparable harm to the unborn infants, a harm that is irreversible for them in
their loss of life.

For eight weeks, I waited, expected, hoped and prayed that Sister Mansour
would change her position. She has not. Consequently, I can no longer tolerate
her position nor can I keep silence. I am enclosing a copy of a statement I am
making to the media this morning at a news conference I have called for 10:15 a.m.

I truly regret that I must take this action. I assure you I do not take it
lightly. I have consulted many good, informed Catholic people. The scandal is
real; the confusion is genuine. But, most of all, her moral position, in my
judgment is clearly wrong.

I also assure you that I have not been influenced in my judgment by the
vicious attacks of fanatics or the scurrilous advertisements that have appeared
in various newspapers. I believe I sincerely gave Sister Mansour every opportunity to take an acceptable position. I am grateful to you for the courtesy
you extended me by informing me of the possibility of her appointment.

I believe I also owe you an explanation of the canonical situation. The
legislation involved is covered basically in the present Code of Canon Law
(still in effect), canons 139 and 592, as well as the more recent instruction
of the Sacred Congregation for Religious of March, 1980, on "Religious and
Human Promotion". I have personally studied these documents very carefully.
I have also consulted canonists in the United States as well as in two foreign
countries. They have unanimously agreed that Sister Mansour needs the permission of both her religious superiors and the local bishop not only to run for
elective office, but also to accept appointment to public office. The same
applies for her retention of the office. She does not have my approval.
Accordingly, she will be acting contrary to Church law and discipline if she
continues in office.

It is now the responsibility of you and your Provincial Council to inform
Sister Mansour that, because of my disapproval, she may no longer retain her
position as director of Social Services. I have no further direct jurisdiction
in the matter. It is up to you and your Council to provide for her compliance
with Church law.

I think that I must also, in all honesty, inform you that I know this whole matter has already been reported to the Holy See. I know because people have sent me copies of their letters. Because of these letters and the wide-spread publicity, I have no doubt that I will be asked to give a report on this whole matter. It is my personal opinion that the Congregation for Religious will intervene if you and your Council have not taken whatever action is necessary to bring about Sister Mansour's resignation. How and in what manner that intervention may occur, I don't know. I hope you understand that I am only expressing a personal opinion because of my desire to be fully honest in my dealings with you. I do not wish in any way to imply a threat.

I pray for Sister Mansour every day. I will also continue to pray for you and all the Sisters of Mercy who have always had a special place in my heart.

With all best wishes, I am

Sincerely yours in Christ,

+ Edmund C. Szoka

Archbishop of Detroit

Sister Helen Marie Burns, R.S.M.
Provincial Administrator, Detroit Province
Sisters of Mercy
29000 - 11 Mile Road
Farmington Hills, Michigan 48018

Enclosure

Document #3

APOSTOLIC DELEGATION

UNITED STATES OF AMERICA

No. 268/83/3

This No. Should Be Prefixed to the Answer

3339 MASSACHUSETTS AVENUE, N.W
WASHINGTON, D. C. 20008

March 23, 1983

Sr. Mary Theresa Kane, RSM
President of the General Administrative
Team of the Sisters of Mercy of the Union
1320 Fenwick Lane
Suite 500
Silver Spring, Md. 20910

Dear Sister Mary Theresa:

The Sacred Congregation for Religious and Secular
Institutes has written to me under the date of March

22, 1983 concerning the refusal of Sr. Agnes Mary
Mansour, RSM, to resign her post as the Director of
the Department of Social Services in the State of
Michigan, after Archbishop Edmund C. Szoka informed
her through the Provincial Council in Detroit that
she did not have his necessary approval as the local
Ordinary to hold a public office. As you know, such
approval is mandated by the discipline and law of the
Church.

A careful and deliberate study of all factors
has led the Sacred Congregation to support the decisions
of the Archbishop of Detroit, whose judgement has been
pastoral and sound. For this reason, the same Sacred
Congregation hereby instructs you, the President of
the General Administrative Team of the Sisters of
Mercy of the Union, to require Sr. Agnes Mary Mansour
to submit her resignation as the Director of the Department of Social Services in the State of Michigan. My
superiors have indicated to me that this decision is
final and is to be implemented without delay.

Both the good of Sr. Agnes Mary Mansour and the
Church call for the use of every means possible to
carry out this action with all discretion and sensitivity. You can rely on my assistance and support in this
regard.

Permit me to offer my encouragement and assure you
of my prayers for you and the Sisters of Mercy, who have
made unparallelled contributions to the unity and up-
building of the Church over these many years.

With every good wish, I remain

Sincerely yours in Christ,

Archbishop Pio Laghi
Apostolic Delegate

Document #4

April 10, 1983

Sister Helen Marie Burns, RSM
Provincial Administrator
29000 Eleven Mile Road
Farmington Hills, Michigan   48018

Dear Sister Helen Marie:

Having given much thought and reflective prayer and dialogue to the
circumstances that both the community and I now struggle with, I would
like to offer the following comments and requests.

From the beginning of my considering and finally accepting the appointment as Director of the Michigan Department of Social Services, I have
acted in good faith seeking the necessary approvals and communicating
in every instance honestly and openly. It was my understanding that
the needed approvals were granted knowing the abortion controversy
regarding medicaid funding existed and knowing my public stance on it.
Accordingly, I made in equally good faith a commitment to the Governor,
the Department of Social Services, and the poor and needy of Michigan to
service that is in keeping with the special mission of our community.
The human crisis of our state makes this commitment particularly acute
at this time.

Having said this, I am also painfully aware of the continuing strain
within the Catholic community and the need for some appropriate relief.
I would like, therefore, to respectfully request a simple leave of absence
from the Sisters of Mercy. This, hopefully, will establish the necessary
distance from public identification of the religious community with the
controversy and allow me to honor my current commitment to the people of
Michigan.

Secondly, as a matter of justice, I would further request that the leadership of our congregation continue to pursue opportunities to dialogue and
present our side of this case to Archbishop Szoka, the Apostolic Delegate
and the Sacred Congregation for Religious and Secular Institutes.

I regret the suffering that I have caused so many and will appreciate as
immediate a response as possible.

Thank you for your consideration and sensitive concern and support throughout these difficult days.

Sincerely,

Agnes M. Mansour, RSM

Document #5

Sisters of Mercy of the Union

April 11, 1983

Most Reverend Pio Laghi
Apostolic Delegate to the United States
3339 Massachusetts Avenue, NW
Washington, DC 20008

Dear Archbishop Laghi:

On April 10, 1983, Sr. Agnes Mary Mansour informed Sr. Helen Marie Burns and me of her decision to seek a leave of absence from the Sisters of Mercy of the Union. She did so after much prayer and reflection; believing that it is in the best interest of all concerned. It is with profound sadness that she has come to such a serious moment in a life led so faithfully within the religious congregation. Today, April 11, the councils of both the Detroit Province and the Mercy Administrative Team granted Sister's request for a simple leave of absence from the religious community.

It is with deep sadness that I communicate this to you. Sr. Helen Marie Burns and Sr. Agnes Mary Mansour will determine when in the immediate future the announcement of this decision will be made since it requires great sensitivity to the persons and public involved.

Even before I received word of Sister's decision, the Administrative Team had decided to request the SCRIS officials to reconsider the action they have taken. It remains our judgment that the issues raised by your March 23, 1983, communication are of even greater urgency in light of Sr. Agnes Mary's personal decision; we, therefore, reaffirm our decision to seek reconsideration.

I am enclosing a formal letter to this end and respectfully ask that you forward it to SCRIS.

These days have been a cause of suffering to so many concerned with this particular situation. I hope and pray that the suffering experienced now will be a source of enlightenment and purification for our future pastoral efforts.

Sincerely in Christ,

Sr. Mary Theresa Kane

Sr. Mary Theresa Kane, RSM
President

Pro.n. 268/83/8

Document #6

April 11, 1983

Most Reverend Pio Laghi
Apsotolic Delegate to the United States
3339 Massachusetts Avenue, NW
Washington, DC 20008

Dear Archbishop Laghi:

Your letter of March 23, 1983 has been very present to me during these past two weeks. After serious reflection, consultation and prayer, it is the request of the administrative team to ask for a formal reconsideration of the decision reached by the Sacred Congregation for Religious. I respectfully submit this request through you on behalf of the Sisters of Mercy of the Union. My reasons for seeking reconsideration are as follows:

1. Your letter of March 23 indicated that "a careful and deliberate study of all the factors" resulted in a judgment by SCRIS. SCRIS, however, has not reviewed the Sisters of Mercy documentation. Sr. Helen Marie Burns and the Detroit Provincial Team in consultation with Sr. Agnes Mary Mansour have carefully documented their story of these past months. We consider their data integral in understanding the factors involved. I explained to your secretary that the documentation will arrive on Tuesday, April 12; it will be hand delivered to your office for inclusion with the request to SCRIS.

2. Your letter further stated that Sr. Agnes Mary Mansour refused to resign her position. At no time prior to March 23 was Sister asked by the religious congregation to resign. The judgment about refusal is incorrect and is cause of injustice to Sr. Agnes Mary.

3. The law of the church states that the approval of the ordinary and of the religious superior are needed for acceptance of public office. I request a written interpretation of the church law in a case when only one of the required approvals is given.

4. Archbishop Szoka's withdrawal of approval has harmed both personal and corporate reputations since the Sisters of Mercy are perceived as being in defiance. This has been a source of grave concern to us.

5. Sr. Agnes Mary, Sr. Helen Marie and I consulted with several canonists and theologians relative to Sister's position regarding abortion, notably Medicaid funding. The consultations indicate that Sister is clearly within the tradition of the Church. Sister also supports the U.S.A. bishops in her public position on the Hatch Amendment. If SCRIS judges Sister's articulation unacceptable, I will appreciate receiving the reasons in writing.

---

6. A few Michigan bishops have personally expressed serious pastoral concern about Archbishop Szoka's actions. Moreover, they believe that more harm will be done by Sister's resignation. Accordingly, they desire that the matter be returned to the local level for resolution.

Archbishop Laghi, I have reflected on the Holy Father's recent World Day of Peace Message, "Dialogue for Peace: A Challenge for our Time." It is in a spirit of dialogue that I respectfully request an appointment with SCRIS to discuss the preceding concerns. I ask to be accompanied by one or two sisters. During the May UISG meeting, I expect to meet with SCRIS officials regarding the Constitutions and am willing to meet with them on this issue also. However, I will accommodate myself to a time convenient for them even before the May appointment.

I pray that we can resolve the present conflict in a compassionate, peaceful, non-violent and dialogic manner. I know, Archbishop, of your eagerness to do the same. Be assured of my continued cooperation, concern and prayers. May the Risen Christ be with each of us during this particular pastoral journey.

Sincerely in Christ,

Sr. Mary Theresa Kane, RSM
President
Religious Sisters of Mercy of the Union

cc:
Most Reverend Eduardo Cardinal Pironio
Cardinal Prefect
Sacred Congregation for Religious

Most Reverend Augustine Mayer, OSB
Secretary
Sacred Congregation for Religious

Pro. n. 268/83/8

Document #7

SACRA CONGREGATIO
PRO RELIGIOSIS
ET INSTITUTIS SAECULARIBUS

Prot. n. 5527/83

April 16, 1983

His Excellency
Most Reverend Anthony J. Bevilacqua
Auxiliary Bishop of Brooklyn
P.O. Box C
75 Green Avenue
Brooklyn, N.Y. 11202 U.S.A.

Your Excellency,

At the request of this Sacred Congregation for Religious and Secular Institutes, the Most Reverend Apostolic Delegate in Washington, D.C. on March 23, 1983 instructed the President of the Sisters of Mercy of the Union to require Sister Agnes Mary Mansour, R.S.M. to resign as the Director of the Department of Social Services in the State of Michigan. This request was made after His Excellency, Archbishop Edmund Szoka of Detroit had unsuccessfully required on February 23, 1983 that Sister Agnes Mary resign her public office. To date, Sister Agnes Mary has not resigned. In fact both the general and provincial superiors of the Sisters of Mercy of the Union, with their respective councils, on April 11 accepted a request of Sister Agnes Mary for a "leave of absence" and to continue in her public office.

Therefore, this Sacred Congregation, at the direction of the Holy Father, now appoints Your Excellency as its ad hoc delegate with the mandate to approach Sister Agnes Mary directly and to require, in the name of the Holy See and by virtue of her vow of obedience, that she immediately resign as the Director of the Department of Social Services in the State of Michigan.

Moreover, Your Excellency's formal request should be given to Sister Agnes Mary in writing with a clear indication of the consequences of a negative response.

Thanking Your Excellency for your generous acceptance of this sensitive and important assignment and assuring you that our full cooperation and prayers accompany you in it, I remain

Sincerely yours in Christ,

E. Card. Pironio, Pref.

+ A. Mayer
Secr.

Copies: Their Excellencies
Most Reverend Pio Laghi
Most Reverend Edmund Szoka
Most Reverend John Quinn

Document #8

UNITED STATES OF AMERICA

3339 MASSACHUSETTS AVENUE
WASHINGTON, D.C. 20008

April 26, 1983

268/83/8
No. ....

This No. Should Be Prefixed to the Answer

Strictly Confidential

Sister Mary Theresa Kane, R.S.M.
President
General Administrative Team
Sisters of Mercy of the Union
Mercy Center Washington
1320 Fenwick Lane Suite 500
Silver Spring, Maryland 20910

Dear Sister Mary Theresa:

        In response to your request for an appointment
to discuss with the Sacred Congregation for Religious
and Secular Institutes the case of Sister Agnes Mary
Mansour, R.S.M., the Cardinal Prefect, after a careful review of all available information, refers you
to the Most Reverend Anthony Bevilacqua, Auxiliary
Bishop of Brooklyn, who has been appointed at the
direction of the Holy Father the ad hoc delegate of
the same Congregation for this entire matter.

        With this special mandate Bishop Bevilacqua
has initiated steps to communicate the decision of the
Holy See to Sister Agnes Mary and will be available to
you after the initial interview with Sister Agnes Mary
to explain his task and the manner in which he is
proceeding.

        I will appreciate your treating this information
as deserving the strictest confidence.

        With prayerful good wishes, I remain

                        Sincerely yours in Christ,

                        Apostolic Delegate

Document #9

ROMAN CATHOLIC DIOCESE OF BROOKLYN

POST OFFICE BOX C

BROOKLYN, NEW YORK 11202

OFFICE OF THE CHANCELLOR
75 GREENE AVENUE

April 25, 1983

STRICTLY CONFIDENTIAL

Sister Agnes Mary Mansour, R.S.M.
Department of Social Services
State of Michigan
300 South Capital Street

Dear Sister Agnes Mary Mansour:

This morning I received a special mandate from the Holy
See. This mandate, given by the Sacred Congregation
for Religious and Secular Institutes at the direction
of the Holy Father, appoints me ad hoc delegate and con-
veys to me the responsibility of informing you of the
decision of the Holy See with respect to your holding
the office of Director of Social Services in the State
of Michigan.

In order that I may carry out my responsibility of showing
you my mandate and of communicating to you in person as
soon as possible the decision of the Holy See, I shall be
able to meet with you next week on any of the following
three days: Wednesday, May 4 - Thursday, May 5 -
Friday, May 6.

For the location of our meeting, I am willing to come to
any house of Religious Women in the Archdiocese of Detroit
that would be convenient for you.

At the meeting, you may feel free to have with you two
Religious Sisters from your Province. I myself will be
accompanied by two companions.

I would appreciate it if you would telephone me as soon as
possible to inform me which of the three listed dates
would be suitable as well as to arrange the time and location of the meeting. You can reach me in my Office between 9:00 A.M. and 4:30 P.M. at (212) 638-5500, Ext. 215.
If for some reason I am not in my Office, may I ask that
you leave a message with my secretary, Mrs. Florence
Mulvihill, and I will return the call as soon as I return.

In this matter I ask that strict confidentiality be maintained and that all publicity of any kind be avoided. I am
certain that you are sensitive to the dimension of this
question.

Let us join in prayer that the will of God and the good of
the Church will inspire our thoughts and motivate our actions.

With prayerful best wishes, I remain

Sincerely yours in Christ,

+ Anthony J. Bevilacqua

Anthony J. Bevilacqua
Ad Hoc Delegate of the Holy See
Auxiliary Bishop of Brooklyn

ROMAN CATHOLIC DIOCESE OF BROOKLYN
POST OFFICE BOX C,
BROOKLYN, NEW YORK 11202

OFFICE OF THE CHANCELLOR
75 GREENE AVENUE

PERSONAL AND CONFIDENTIAL

May 9, 1983

Sister Agnes Mary Mansour, R.S.M.
Provincialate House
29000 Eleven Mile Road
Farmington Hills, Michigan 48018

Dear Sister Agnes Mary:

May I, first of all, thank you for your cooperation in
agreeing to meet with me today at the Provincialate
House of the Sisters of Mercy-Detroit Province.

The purpose of our meeting is to give me the opportunity
of showing you my mandate from the Holy See appointing
me, at the direction of the Holy Father, as its ad hoc
delegate. As ad hoc delegate of the Holy See, I was
given the responsibility of communicating to you the decision of the Holy See in regard to your position as
Director of Social Services in the State of Michigan.
This decision is contained in the Formal Precept of the
Holy See, which I present to you.

As the factual section in the Precept demonstrates, there has been an extended period of dialogue of various dimensions and on various occasions among the parties involved in this matter. But dialogue must within a reasonable time end with the arrival at a conclusion. We are now at that point of arrival and moment of a conclusive decision.

I fully appreciate the anxiety that you must have undergone between my first communication to you and this exposition of the decision of the Holy See. Unfortunately, the nature of the process and commitments on the part of both of us made this interval unavoidable.

While the process requires that I submit to you formal directives verbally and in documentary fashion, please be assured that my role and the manner in which I carry it out is motivated by the sincerest pastoral and human concern for you. Since I was first apprised of my task in this matter, I have prayed for two intentions. I prayed that I would be able to fulfill my responsibility with as little pain as possible for you and in the way Christ would want me to. Because of the nature of this role and my awareness of the limitations of my abilities, I needed to pray much for this intention and I needed to ask many others to pray for my intentions.

The intention that I asked others to pray for and the intention of my own prayers were equally for you. As delegate of the Holy See, I have a responsibility to carry out in your regard. As a person and Bishop, I feel a very strong compassion for you for I feel you are suffering. And so, I pray that the peace that you desire will come to you by your realizing the need to be in union with Christ and the Church through obedience to Christ's Vicar and your Supreme Moderator.

At the same time, I ask for your understanding and patience and especially for your prayers that in all that I do during this process may be done in accordance with the will of God, for your peace, for the welfare of the Congregation of the Sisters of Mercy and for the good of the Church.

With prayerful best wishes, I remain

Sincerely yours in Christ,

+ Anthony J. Bevilacqua

Most Rev. Anthony J. Bevilacqua

Document #10

MOST REV. ANTHONY J. BEVILACQUA
AD HOC DELEGATE OF THE HOLY SEE
75 Greene Avenue
Brooklyn, N.Y. 11238

* *

FORMAL PRECEPT OF THE HOLY SEE TO SISTER AGNES MARY MANSOUR, R.S.M.

* * * * * * * * * * * * * * * * * * * *

IN NOMINE DOMINI. AMEN

* * * * * * * * * * * * * * *

I   Facts

1.   Early in December, 1982, Sister Helen Marie Burns,
Provincial Superior of the Detroit Province of the Sisters
of Mercy, received a call from Sister Agnes Mary Mansour,
indicating that Governor-Elect Blanchard was considering
her for a State Cabinet level appointment. Sister Helen
Marie Burns called Archbishop Edmund Szoka, Archbishop of
Detroit, to inform him of the possible appointment of
Sister Agnes Mary Mansour. Archbishop Szoka responded that
if the appointment were to the Department of Social Services,
Sister Agnes Mary Mansour would have to be very clear in her
statements about abortion. Both agreed that there should be
a personal discussion between Archbishop Szoka and Sister
Agnes Mary Mansour on the position of Sister Agnes Mary
Mansour on the abortion question .

2.   About December 20, Sister Agnes Mary Mansour called
Sister Helen Marie Burns that the appointment had been confirmed. Sister Helen Marie Burns states that Sister·Agnes
Mary Mansour also told her that she had not been able to
set up an appointment with Archbishop Szoka and that she continued efforts to call the Archbishop so that he would be
aware before any public announcement was made. The announcement was set for December 29.

3.   Archbishop Szoka states that he was told by his secretary that Sister Agnes Mary Mansour had called his office on
December 27 and 28. He was occupied all day on both days.
He further states that, unaware of the imminent announcement
of her appointment, he tried to reach Sister Agnes Mary
Mansour on the morning of December 29. Shortly after,
he received word that the announcement of the appointment
was to be made that day. He finally reached Sister Agnes
Mary Mansour in the afternoon after the announcement of
her appointment.

4.   Archbishop Szoka states that in the telephone conversation with Sister Agnes Mansour on December 29, he
pointed out the absolute necessity for her to take a clear
stand against medicaid payments for abortion and that if
she could not take such a position, she should not have the
job as Director of Social Services. Archbishop Szoka also
states that Sister Agnes Mary Mansour told him that she
would try to follow his advice and that on that basis, he
did not object to her acceptance of the appointment.

5.   After waiting for several weeks for Sister Agnes Mary
Mansour to clarify her position on medicaid funding for
abortion, Archbishop Szoka arranged to meet her on February 14, 1983. Archbishop Szoka describes this meeting as
one in which he spent an hour with her trying to explain the
necessity for her to oppose medicaid payments for abortion
and in which he also told her that if she did not change her
stance, he would have to object publicly to her retaining
the appointment and to call for her resignation.

6.   On February 23, 1983, Archbishop Szoka sent a letter to
Sister Helen Marie Burns informing her that after waiting
eight weeks for Sister Agnes Mary Mansour to change her position, he can no longer keep silence. He informed her that
Sister Agnes Mary Mansour no longer has his approval and that
if she continues in office she will be acting against Church
law and discipline which requires that she have permission of
the local Bishop and that of her Religious Superiors. In a
statement publicly issued that same day, Archbishop Szoka
called for the resignation of Sister Agnes Mary Mansour. He
also informed Sister Helen Marie Burns that it was her responsibility and that of her Council to notify Sister Agnes
Mary Mansour that she may no longer retain her directorship
and to provide for her compliance with Church law.

7.   In the same letter of February 23, 1983, Archbishop Szoka
told Sister Helen Marie Burns that because of the situation,
the scandal was real and the confusion was genuine.

8.   On February 28, 1983, Archbishop Szoka met privately
with two members of the Provincial Council of the Sisters of
Mercy and reviewed the whole situation with them.

9.   On March 4, 1983, Archbishop Szoka met with Sister
Helen Marie Burns and her Administrative Team to review the
whole situation again.

10.   On March 5, 1983, the Provincial Administrative Team of
The Sisters of Mercy, issued a statement regarding Sister
Agnes Mary Mansour. In the statement, the Administrative
Team concluded that there was not sufficient clarity at that
time for them to judge that her resignation would be for the
greater good. They also expressed their belief that Sister
Agnes Mary Mansour was acting according to a well-formed con-
science.

11.   On March 8, 1983, Sister Agnes Mary Mansour testified
before the Michigan State Senate Committee at the Confirmation
hearing that while she was opposed to abortion, she could
tolerate Medicaid funding for abortion through the Department
of Social Services.

12.   On March 10, 1983, Archbishop Szoka, in response to a
request from the Apostolic Delegate, presented a report of the
situation.   In that report, Archbishop Szoka emphasized that
the good, sensible Catholic people were confused, disturbed
and dismayed by the spectacle of a Catholic nun in the position of director of a department which pays for abortions
and refusing to state her opposition to such payments. In
his opinion, the situation was genuinely scandalous. This
report was forwarded to the Sacred Congregation for Religious
and Secular Institutes by the Apostolic Delegate.

13.   On March 23, 1983, the Apostolic Delegate, Archbishop
Laghi, personally communicated verbally and in writing to
Sister Theresa Kane, President of the Religious Sisters of
Mercy of the Union, the decision of the Holy See in regard
to Sister Agnes Mary Mansour.   In accordance with this decision, the Apostolic Delegate, in the name of the Holy See,
requested Sister Theresa Kane that she require that Sister
Agnes Mary Mansour resign as Director of the Michigan Department of Social Services. In response to an inquiry from
Sister Theresa Kane, the Apostolic Delegate explained the
canonical consequences of refusal to obey.

       The Apostolic Delegate gave Sister Theresa Kane ten days
to respond in writing. As a result of two further requests
by Sister Theresa Kane for postponements, twenty days elapsed
before Sister Theresa Kane sent her written reply of
April 11, 1983.

14.   In her letter of April 11, 1983, to the Apostolic
Delegate, Sister Theresa Kane requested a formal reconsideration of the decision reached by the Holy See She
asked that documentation of the situation prepared by
the Detroit Provincial Team be submitted to the Holy See.

15.   In her letter of April 11, 1983 to the Apostolic Delegate, Sister Helen Marie Burns expressed the hope that a
report of the Sisters of Mercy regarding Sister Agnes Mary
Mansour which she enclosed would be reviewed. She also
wished to correct a statement in the Apostolic Delegate's
letter of March 23 to the effect that Sister Agnes Mary
Mansour had refused to resign her position. At that point
in time, Sister Agnes Mary Mansour had not refused to resign her post since she had not been asked to do so by her
religious congregation.

16.   On April 11, 1983, both the Detroit Province and the
Mercy Administrative Team granted the request of Sister
Agnes Mary Mansour "for a simple leave of absence from the
religious community."

17.   On April 12, 1983, the Apostolic Delegate submitted to
the Sacred Congregation for Religious and Secular Institutes
the request of Sister Theresa Kane for a reconsideration of
the case.

18.   In his letter of April 13, 1983, the Apostolic Delegate
assured Sister Theresa Kane that the documentation report
prepared by the Sisters of Mercy had been sent to the Holy
See.

II Law

1.   Canon 139, §2 : "Without an Apostolic Indult, clerics
shall not... accept public offices that entail secular jurisdiction or administrative duties."

2.   Canon 139, §3 : "Without permission from their Ordin-
aries, clerics shall not... assume secular offices that impose the obligation of rendering an account."

   a.   The term, "secular offices", according to some
        canonists does not necessarily exclude public
        offices. (Brunini, The Clerical Obligations of
        Canons 139 and 142, p. 30. He also cites
        Ayrinhac and Maroto)

   b.   Cappello states that "secular offices"
        include all "municipal offices."
        (Summa Iuris Canonica, Vol. I, N.233, p.232)

3.   Canon 592: "All the religious are bound by the
obligations of the clergy set down in Canons 124-142,
unless the contrary is evident from the context or from
the nature of the law."

4.   Canon 499, § 1 :   "All religious are subject to the
Roman Pontiff as their highest Superior and they are
bound to obey him also in virtue of their vow of obedience."

   a.   The vow of obedience taken by a Religious by
        law subjects a Religious to the Holy Father in
        virtue of that vow. Therefore, any intention
        at the time of religious profession not to
        give obedience to the Roman Pontiff or a lack
        of intention of obedience to the Holy Father
        would render a religious profession invalid.

5.   Religious Life and Human Promotion (Document of
Sacred Congregation for Religious and Secular Institutes,
April 1978, N. 12) - "Active involvement in politics
remains an exception then, to be engaged in only by way of
substitution and to be evaluated according to special criteria. If exceptional circumstances require it, the individual cases must be examined so that, with the approval
of the authorities of the local Church and the religious
institutes, decisions can be made that are beneficial to
the ecclesial and secular community."

6.   Further observations on the involvement of Religious
in politics from "Religious Life and Human Promotion":

   a.   Footnote to the above quotation in N.12 quotes
        Pope John Paul II at Puebla: "You are re-
        ligious and priests, you are not social or
        political leaders or officials of a temporal
        power. Therefore, I tell you again - Let us
        not be under the illusion that we are serving
        the Gospel if we try to dilute our charism
        by an exaggerated interest in the wide field
        of temporal problems"

b.   No. 25: "In speaking of the variety of
     gifts and ministries, it should be noted
     that the laity and members of secular in-
     stitutes can take on apostolic, social and
     political responsibilities as individuals
     in accordance with the purpose assigned
     them by the Spirit.

     This is not the case with religious. They
     have freely and consciously chosen to parti-
     cipate completely in their mission of wit-
     ness, presence and apostolic activity in
     obedience to the common purpose and to the
     superiors of their institute."

7.   Leave of Absence

a.   Faculty N. 4 of list of faculties granted to
     Superiors General of Pontifical Law lay re-
     ligious institutes in the decree, Religionum
     Laicalium, of the Sacred Congregation for
     Religious and Secular Institutes, May 1, 1966:
     "With the consent of their council, to permit
     their subjects to be absent, for a just cause,
     from their religious house but not beyond a
     year. If this permission is given because of
     ill health, it can be granted for as long as
     the need perdures. If it is given for the sake
     of engaging inworks of the apostolate, it can
     be granted, for a just cause, even beyond a
     year, provided that the apostolic works engaged
     in are in conformity with the purposes of the
     religious institute and that the norms of both
     common and particular law are observed."

b.   Canonical Status of Religious Granted a Leave of
     Absence (James I. O'Connor, "Leave of Absence,"
     Review for Religious, Vol. 30, July 1971, p.637)

     i   Remains a full-fledged member of her
          religious congregation.

     ii   Status is distinct from that of an exclaus-
          trated religious.

     iii Retains active and passive voice.

     iv   Entitled to all notices from Superiors.

     v   Concerning vow of poverty, needs general
          permissions in money matters. Because
          she is bound by vow of poverty, she
          cannot legitimately be allowed to keep
          and use funds or their equivalent in
          excess of normal living needs and use.

     vi   As for the vow of obedience, the religious
          remains bound to her superiors and must
          report to them as stipulated.

III Precept of the Holy See

1. After a careful and thorough examination of all the documentation presented to the Sacred Congregation for Religious and Secular Institutes by both Archbishop Edmund Szoka and the Sisters of Mercy-Detroit Province relating to the case of Sister Agnes Mary Mansour, the Holy See has rendered its decision in this matter.

2. In virtue of a special mandate given to me, Most Reverend Anthony J. Bevilacqua, by the Sacred Congregation for Religious and Secular Institutes at the direction of His Holiness, Pope John Paul II, I have been appointed ad hoc delegate of the Holy See to communicate personally to you,Sister Agnes Mary Mansour, R.S.M., a Religious of the Sisters of Mercy-Detroit Province, the decision of the Holy See regarding your position as Director of Social Services in the State of Michigan.

3. In virtue of this mandate and as ad hoc delegate of the Holy See, I hereby require, in the name of the Holy See and by virtue of your vow of obedience to the Holy Father that you immediately resign your position as Director of the Department of Social Services in the State of Michigan.

4. Should you refuse to obey this precept to resign immediately, as Director of the Department of Social Services in the State of Michigan, I shall be compelled to initiate immediately the canonical process that subjects you to the penalty of imposed secularization entailing dismissal from the religious Congregation of the Sisters of Mercy and the loss of your canonical status as a Religious Sister.

+Anthony J. Bevilacqua

Most Rev. Anthony J. Bevilacqua
Ad Hoc Delegate of the Holy See

Given at the Provincialate House of the Sisters of Mercy-Detroit Province in Farmington Hills, Michigan this 9 day of May, 1983, in the presence of:

S. Sharon Holland IHM

Notary

Joseph A. Galante

Notary

MOST REV. ANTHONY J. BEVILACQUA
AD HOC DELEGATE OF THE HOLY SEE
75 Greene Avenue
Brooklyn, N.Y. 11238

Most Holy Father,

　　I, Sister Agnes Mary Mansour, professed of simple perpetual
vows in the Congregation of the Religious Sisters of Mercy of the
Province of Detroit in the Archdiocese of Detroit, request of Your
Holiness, through your delegate Most Rev. Anthony J. Bevilacqua,
an indult of secularization so that I may freely and legitimately
return to secular life.

　　I, Most Rev. Anthony J. Bevilacqua, in virtue of the authority
given to me as ad hoc delegate of the Holy See, at the direction of
our Holy Father, having received the request of Sister Agnes Mary
Mansour for an indult of secularization and having weighed her
reasons for making this request hereby grant the indult of secularization .

　　By this indult she is released from her vows and all other
obligations of her religious profession and she is thereby separated
from her religious congregation.

　　This Indult of Secularization takes effect immediately.

Most Rev. Anthony J. Bevilacqua
Ad Hoc Delegate of the Holy See

Petitioner

Given at the Provincialate House
of the Sisters of Mercy-Detroit
Province in Farmington Hills, Mich.,
this __9__ day of May, 1983, in the
presence of:

Notary

Notary

Document #11

May 18, 1983

Most Reverend Pio Laghi
Apostolic Delegate to the United States
3339 Massachusetts Avenue, N.W.
Washington, D.C. 20008

Dear Archbishop Laghi:

Upon my return from Rome, I reviewed the precept given to Sister Agnes Mary Mansour on May 9, 1983. Through this communication I wish to register my concern about parts of it that involved me personally.

        Part I: #13. The length of time required for my response was never stated by you. You never indicated a ten day response. I never requested a postponement; I requested an extension. In response to my inquiry about canonical consequences, you never indicated any consequences which would be directed to Sister Agnes Mary.

        Part I: #14. I never received a response to my request for reconsideration; the questions I raised and the interpretations requested have not been answered.

In a conference with Archbishop Mayer, I conferred briefly about the matter. Archbishop Mayer indicated that I had been uncooperative; that I had deliberately delayed my response to you and that my lack of cooperation had compelled SCRIS to act quickly--even taking action when I was out of the country. I quoted from your letter of April 13 acknowledging my prompt reply. At no time have I been uncooperative nor have I refused to require Sister's resignation.

I am deeply troubled by the events which have occurred, especially on May 9, 1983.

A formal canonical appeal has been initiated. I hope and pray that this Holy Year will be an opportunity for reconciliation between the Sisters of Mercy and the members of the hierarchy.

                          Sincerely in Christ,

                          Sister M. Theresa Kane, R.S.M.
                          President

Prot.n. 268/83/8

Document #12

Sisters of Mercy of the Union

May 18, 1983

Most Reverend Eduardo Cardinal Pironio, Prefect
Most Reverend Augustine Mayer, OSB, Secretary
Sacred Congregation for Religious
Piazza Pius XII, 3
Rome, Italy

Dear Cardinal Pironio and Archbishop Mayer:

On May 14, 1983, I registered in person an appeal with the Apostolic Signatura regarding the case of Sister Agnes Mary Mansour, R.S.M. Upon my return to the United States from Rome--my first opportunity to review the documents given Sister Agnes Mary, R.S.M., by Bishop Anthony Bevilacqua on May 9, 1983--I have been advised by canonical counsel that this appeal must first be directed to the Sacred Congregation for Religious and Secular Institutes since you authorized Bishop Bevilacqua as ad hoc delegate in this case. I am accordingly informing the Apostolic Signatura of the redirection of my appeal at this time.

On behalf of the Mercy Administrative Team of the Religious Sisters of Mercy of the Union in the United States of America, I formally and respectfully appeal your decision regarding Sister Agnes Mary Mansour. I submit this appeal for the following reasons:

1. Sister Agnes Mary Mansour requested and signed a dispensation from perpetual vows on May 9, 1983, under serious constraints and circumstances (vis). Sister was not informed by Bishop Bevilacqua that she had the right to appeal this decision nor was she told that she had the right to obtain canonical counsel before she signed her dispensation. Sister's letter of request for a dispensation clearly indicates that her decision was done under constraint (vis). Canon 645, par. 4 states:

   > the religious has the right of recourse against the dismissal to the apostolic see and pending the recourse, the dismissal has no juridic effect.

   Although Sister Agnes Mary Mansour was not canonically dismissed, she requested and accepted the dispensation only to avoid enforced dispensation (dismissal).

2. At no time in the process was Sister provided an opportunity to defend herself and her reputation. Canon #650, par. 3 states:

   > the religious has full freedom to present her defense and it must be faithfully entered in the record of the case.

3. On February 23, 1983, when Archbishop Szoka informed the Provincial Council that he had withdrawn his approval of Sister's appointment, Sister Agnes Mary Mansour was not residing or working in the Archdiocese of Detroit. There is question here of Archbishop Szoka's canonical jurisdiction.

On May 9, 1983, when the precept was delivered to Sister Agnes Mary Mansour I was out of the country attending the U.I.S.G. meeting in Rome. I was never informed officially by you or your ad hoc delegate either before or after that date that such severe action was contemplated or implemented. Further when I met with Archbishop Pio Laghi on March 23, 1983, he gave no indication of the canonical consequences to Sister Agnes Mary directly. Finally, I have not heard from you regarding my request of April 11, 1983, that SCRIS reconsider its actions regarding Sister Agnes Mary in light of the questions I then raised.

Vatican II directed us to respect administrative processes in view of the principle of subsidiarity and of the attention that need be given to the particular law of each religious institute. Most importantly, the highest law of the church--"lex suprema cura animarum"--requires that an appeal be made since the law has been violated as indicated in the instances listed above. I ask that you apprize me of the procedures that will carry this appeal forward.

Sincerely in Christ,

Sister M. Theresa Kane, R.S.M.
President

Prot.n. 268/83/8

Document #13

ROMAN CATHOLIC DIOCESE OF BROOKLYN
POST OFFICE BOX C
BROOKLYN, NEW YORK 11202

OFFICE OF THE CHANCELLOR
75 GREENE AVENUE

June 6, 1983

Sister M. Theresa Kane, R.S.M.
President
Sisters of Mercy of the Union
1320 Fenwick Lane - Suite 500
Silver Spring, Maryland 20910

Dear Sister Mary Theresa:

I wish to inform you of the events that occurred on Monday, May 9, 1983, when I carried out my mandate as Ad Hoc delegate of the Sacred Congregation for Religious and Secular Institutes at the direction of Pope John Paul II in the case of Sister Agnes Mary Mansour.

I agreed to meet with Sister Agnes Mary Mansour at the
Provincial House of the Sisters of Mercy-Detroit Province,
located in Farmington Hills, Michigan. The meeting took
place at 4:00 P.M. on Monday, May 9, 1983.

Present as my notaries were Monsignor Joseph A. Galante, and
Sister Sharon Holland, I.H.M. Present with Sister Agnes Mary
Mansour were Sister Emily George and Sister Helen Marie Burns.

After opening the meeting with a prayer, I expressed my gratitude to Sister Agnes Mary Mansour for.agreeing to meet with
me. While acknowledging that the meeting involved canonical
formalities, I attempted to place the meeting in a context of
pastoral concern. I tried to do this by summarizing verbally
the points contained in the letter which I addressed and gave
to Sister Agnes Mary Mansour.

I then showed to Sister Agnes Mary Mansour my mandate of
April 16, 1983 appointing me as <u>Ad Hoc</u> delegate of the Sacred
Congregation for Religious and <u>Secular</u> Institutes at the direction of Pope John Paul II. I also read the mandate to all
present.

Upon completion of the reading of the mandate, I then presented to Sister Agnes Mary Mansour a copy of the Formal Precept which I had prepared. I read the original of the Formal
Precept to all present,and asked Sister Agnes Mary Mansour to
follow the reading with the copy that I had given to her.
After I had completed the reading of the Formal Precept,
Sister Agnes Mary Mansour certified by her signature that the
copy that I had given to her corresponded with the original
that I had read. I then gave to her the original Formal Precept signed by myself and my two notaries. I received back
from her the certified copy which was then signed by myself
and my two notaries.

At the conclusion of the reading of the Formal Precept, Sister
Agnes Mary Mansour stated that she wished to ask for a dispensation from her vows. I asked her if she was making this
request freely. She responded that she was making it freely
knowing the usual intent of the question. She immediately
added, however, that she did not feel that it was really a free
decision in the sense that I offered her no other choice. While
it was true that the only choice offered to her was to resign
or be separated from her Religious Community, I told her that
such a choice was not a deprivation of her freedom. She also
responded that asking for a dispensation from her vows had
been an option that had been considered since the whole matter
began.

A discussion took place between myself and Sister Agnes Mary
Mansour, Sister Emily George, and Sister Helen Marie Burns.
The main issues that the Sisters raised and were discussed
were the following:

        1. The issue. that the process was unfair and
     that there was insufficient dialogue.

        2. The issue of the Magisterial teaching on
     funding for abortion.

3. The issue contained in their statement
that Archbishop Szoka had given Sister Agnes Mary
Mansour permission to accept the position as
Director of Social Services at a time that he
was aware of her position on Medicaid funding
for abortion.

4. The issue of why Sister Agnes Mary Mansour
was different from other lay Catholic persons in
public office who held the same position on Medicaid funding for abortion.

After a reasonable amount of time given to the discussion of
the above issues, we returned to the request of Sister Agnes
Mary Mansour for a dispensation from her vows. I attempted
to dissuade her from making this choice and tried to persuade
her to resign from her public office. Sister Agnes Mary
Mansour was firm that she wished to ask for the dispensation.
When Sister Agnes Mary Mansour did not ask for any time to
pray over her decision to seek a dispensation, I recommended
that she reflect on her decision in Chapel. Sister Agnes
Mary Mansour, Sister Emily George and Sister Helen Marie Burns
left the room.

During the absence from the room, Sister Helen Marie Burns
returned on two occasions to ask for clarification. Among the
points for which clarification was asked was the question as
to whether Sister Agnes Mary Mansour would still be considered
in disobedience to the Holy Father by seeking a dispensation
and what would happen to the Precept by requesting a dispensation. Since at all times Sister Agnes Mary Mansour retained
the right and freedom to request a dispensation from her vows,
I responded that by seeking and receiving a dispensation she
would not be considered as being in disobedience to the Holy
Father and the Precept to her to resign her office would no
longer be applicable.

After more than an hour, Sister Agnes Mary Mansour, Sister
Emily George and Sister Helen Marie Burns returned to the meeting room. Sister Agnes Mary Mansour presented me with her
signed petition for secularization. Without even reading the
petition, I once again tried at length to dissuade her from
making the choice of asking for a dispensation and I tried to
persuade her to resign her office as Director of Social Services.
I once again asked if she was free in making her decision to
ask for a dispensation. I again asked if she had given previous
sufficient reflection to this decision. The response that
I received was that they had been considering this option
of a dispensation since February 23rd when Archbishop Szoka
withdrew his permission for her to remain in public office.
They told me that they had considered this option because
from that date they had to consider all the options.

I asked Sister Agnes Mary Mansour once again if she wanted
more time to reflect on her decision. I told her that I was
willing to remain in Detroit and return the next day in order
to give her more time to reflect. In fact, I told her I
would give her as much time as she wanted so that she could
be certain that she was making the right decision. Sister
Agnes Mary Mansour responded that she wanted the dispensation
and she wanted it immediately.

Realizing that Sister Agnes Mary Mansour was firm in her request for immediate secularization, I granted it to her as I was empowered to do. This dispensation was signed by myself and by Sister Agnes Mary Mansour and witnessed by Sister Emily George and Sister Helen Marie Burns. The approximate time of the granting of the dispensation was 6:15 P.M.

It was agreed that any statement on what transpired on May 9th would be first made by the Sisters of Mercy. We agreed that confidentiality would be respected until 11:00 A.M. of Wednesday, May 11, 1983.

I and my two notaries left the Provincial House at approximately 6:30 P.M.

The above report represents what I consider to be the essential substance of the events that occurred in my meeting with Sister Agnes Mary Mansour on May 9, 1983.

As I promised Sister Agnes Mary Mansour at our meeting on May 9, 1983, I shall continue daily to remember her and all the Sisters of Mercy in my Mass and prayers.

With prayerful best wishes, I remain

Sincerely yours in Christ,

Anthony J. Bevilacqua
Auxiliary Bishop
<u>Ad</u> <u>Hoc</u> Delegate of the Holy See

Document #14

SACRA CONGREGATIO
PRO RELIGIOSIS
ET INSTITUTIS SAECULARIBUS

June 6, 1983

Prot. n. 55271/83

Sister M. Theresa Kane, S.S.E.
President
Sisters of Mercy of the Union
Mercy Center
1320 Fenwick Lane, Suite 500
Silver Spring, Maryland 20910   U.S.A.

Dear Sister,

This Sacred Congregation for Religious and Secular Institutes has received your letter of May 18 in which you submit an appeal to this Sacred Congregation against the process involved in the case of the dispensation of Sister Agnes Mary Mansour from her vows as a Sister of Mercy of the Union in the United States.

After a review of the case, we must inform you that this Sacred Congregation cannot accept your request not only because of the lack of foundation of your three affirmations but also because His Excellency, Bishop Anthony Bevelacqua acted in the name of the Holy See under the direction of the Holy Father.

Wishing the blessings of the Lord and the intercession of Our Lady of Mercy on you and on all the Sisters of Mercy of the Union. I remain

Sincerely yours in the Redeemer,

E. Card. Pironio, Pref.

+ A. Mayer
    Seu.

Document #15

June 17, 1983

Most Reverend Aurelio Sabattani
Cardinal Prefect
Office of the Apostolic Signatura
Piazza Della Cancellaria, I
Rome, Italy

Dear Cardinal Sabattani:

On May 18, 1983, I submitted a request for recourse to the Sacred
Congregation for Religious and Secular Institutes in the name of the
Religious Sisters of Mercy of the Union in the U.S.A. regarding the case
of Sr. Agnes Mary Mansour, R.S.M. On June 13, 1983, I received the decision
of SCRIS dated June 6, 1983, in which they indicated they were unable to
consider the request.

Today, June 17, 1983, as President and Administrator General of the
Religious Sisters of Mercy of the Union in the U.S.A., I formally seek canonical recourse through your office regarding the decision and processes uti-
lized which led to Sr. Agnes Mary Mansour's decision on May 9, 1983. In
a spirit of fidelity and charity I request such recourse.

I have been advised by canonical counsel that this letter serves as
the required documentation to be filed within ten days of June 13, 1983.
I am enclosing the following materials for your initial review of the case:

    1.   mandate to Bishop Bevilacqua from SCRIS, April 16, 1983;
    2.   precept given to Sr. Agnes Mary Mansour on May 9, 1983;
    3.   Sister's letter of request for dispensation and a copy of her
         dispensation, May 9, 1983;
    4.   letter of recourse to the Congregation for Religious on May 18,
    5.   copy of the June 6, 1983, response from the Congregation for
         Religious.

If there are any deficiencies about the manner in which this recourse
is being made, please advise me and I will make the necessary adjustments
to comply with the canonical processes. It is my understanding that an
advocate approved by the Apostolic Signatura is required if the case is
accepted. I am willing to have an English-speaking advocate appointed by
you and I welcome an opportunity to discuss the potential advocate before
a final decision is made.

Thank you for your consideration of this request. In any community
of believers acting in sincerity and truth, conflict can and does arise.
It is my hope and prayer that all of us engaged in the present difficulty
will resolve the matter with respect and dignity for all.

As a courtesy, I am apprising SCRIS and Archbishop Laghi, our Apostolic Delegate, that I have initiated the canonical recourse with your office.

Sincerely in Christ,

Sr. Mary Theresa Kane, R.S.m.

Sr. Mary Theresa Kane, R.S.M.
President

Enc.

Prot.n. 55271/83

Document #16

ROMAN CATHOLIC DIOCESE OF BROOKLYN
POST OFFICE BOX C
BROOKLYN, NEW YORK 11202

OFFICE OF THE CHANCELLOR
75 GREENE AVENUE

July 1, 1983

Sister Mary Theresa Kane, R.S.M.
President
Sisters of Mercy of the Union
1320 Fenwick Lane, Suite 500
Silver Spring, Maryland 20910

Dear Sister Mary Theresa:

In the various phases of the events that transpired in the matter of Sister Agnes Mary Mansour, confidentiality was occasionally requested for certain communications and events, usually for a temporary period of time. The process has now reached the stage where there may be some confusion or doubt concerning whether this confidentiality still remains in force.

In certain instances, it is evident from the very nature or circumstances of the communication or event that the confidentiality has terminated. In other cases, there does not seem to be sufficient reason to continue the confidentiality. Therefore, in order to remove any confusion or doubt, I wish to inform you that the request of confidentiality which may have been attached up to this date by the Holy See or its representatives to any communication or event in the case of Sister Agnes Mary Mansour is hereby no longer considered binding.

Assuring you of my daily prayers for you and for reconciliation rooted in justice, truth and mutual trust, I remain

Sincerely yours in Christ,

Most Rev. Anthony J. Bevilacqua
Auxiliary Bishop of Brooklyn
Ad Hoc Delegate of the Holy See

Document #17

SUPREMUM
SIGNATURAE APOSTOLICAE
TRIBUNAL
—
PALAZZO DELLA CANCELLERIA
00120 CITTÀ DEL VATICANO

4 July 1983

Prot. N. 15363/83 CA

Dear Sister,

With reference to your letter of 17 June 1983, it is my duty to inform you that the Signatura Apostolica is unable to consider the recourse which you intend to present, because this is not a question of recourse against a decision of a competent Dicastery of the Roman Curia, as is provided for in the Apostolic Constitution "Regimini Ecclesiae Universae" n. 106, but your intention is to impugn the decision taken by His Excellency, Monsignor Anthony Bevilacqua, who was acting under express command of the Holy Father.

Furthermore, the letter of the Sacred Congregation for Religious and Secular Institutes, dated 6 June 1983, under protocol n. 55271/83, against which you intend to make recourse, is not an administrative provision of the Dicastery, but a communication which confirms what is asserted above, namely, that the Bishop, Monsignor Bevilacqua, was authorised explicitly by the Holy Father to invite Sister Massour to resign her public office and, if she refused to do so, to adopt the appropriate canonical measures.

Yours truly,

+ Leron Grocholewski
Secretarius

Humberto Giacco

Sr. Mary Theresa Kane, R.S.M.,
Mercy Center Washington,
1320 Fenwick Lane, Suite 500,
Silver Spring,
Maryland 20910,
U.S.A.

Document #18

SACRA CONGREGATIO
PRO RELIGIOSIS
ET INSTITUTIS SAECULARIBUS

October 26, 1983

Prot. n. 51772/82

Sister Mary Theresa Kane, RSM
President, Sisters of Mercy of the Union
1320 Fenwick Lane, Suite 500
Silver Spring, Maryland 20910   U.S.A.

Dear Sister,

On July 3, 1982 this Sacred Congregation wrote you concerning the candidature of one of your Sisters for the political office of Attorney General of the State of Rhode Island, in order to ascertain your position in the light of Canons 139 and 592, as well as this Sacred Congregation's document of 1980 entitled Religious and Human Promotion, I.D. ("Involvement in Politics"). You replied on July 30, 1982 that you had received our letter and that you were in the process of reflecting and consulting on the matter and, moreover, that you would be in communication with us at a later date.

So far, this Sacred Congregation has received no reply from you. We therefore request that you kindly send us your reply as soon as possible, in the light not only of the above cited norms but also

Canon 672 of the Revised Code with the additional canons to which it refers, especially Canon 285, n. 3. We ask that your response be sent to us through the good offices of the Apostolic Delegate.

Wishing God's blessings on you and all the Sisters of Mercy of the Union, I remain

Sincerely yours in the Redeemer,

+ A. Kaye

Document #19

UNITED STATES OF AMERICA

3339 MASSACHUSETTS AVENUE
WASHINGTON, D.C. 20008

CONFIDENTIAL

No. 923/83/2

This No. Should Be Prefixed to the Answer

November 26, 1983

Sister M. Theresa Kane, R.S.M.,
Mercy Center,
1320 Fenwick Lane, Suite 500,
Silver Spring, Maryland   20910

Dear Sister M. Thersa,

As you know the new Code of Canon Law goes into effect on Sunday, November 27, 1983.

I have received word from the Holy See that the Holy Father, as Supreme Moderator of each religious (cf. canon 590, par. 2), has made his mind clear on the application of certain provisions of the newly revised Code with regard to Miss Agnes Mary Mansour. In her case, the provision of canon 690, which permits a supreme moderator to readmit to an institute a member who had lawfully departed, does not apply. This is so in reference to Miss Mansour's re-admission to the Sisters of Mercy of the Union as well as her admission to any other Religious Institute.

With cordial regards and best wishes, I am,

Sincerely yours in Christ,

Pio Laghi

Apostolic Delegate

Document #20

Sisters of Mercy of the Union

December 21, 1983

Most Reverend Augustine Mayer, OSB
Reverend Basil Heiser, OFMC
Sacred Congregation For Religious
and Secular Institutes
Piazza Pius XII, 3
00193, Rome, Italy

Dear Archbishop Mayer and Father Heiser:

Your letter of October 26, 1983 received through Archbishop Laghi's
office is hereby acknowledged. The process of serious reflection and
consultation warranted by the complexity of the issue you raised in
your letter of July 3, 1982 has continued to the present.

Having consulted with select knowledgeable persons in the U.S.A. Catholic
community, I also considered it advisable to bring your request before
our Chapter of Affairs scheduled for this year. At the September 1983
convocation the delegates authorized the administration to set up a task
force to study the appropriateness of political ministry in light of our
Mercy charism. This study is in process and will take into account the
perspectives of our Sisters as these relate to our charism and particular
law, the reflections of others in the church, and the current code of
canon law as it calls us to a new mind about law, inculturation and other
pertinent topics.

Since your letter referred specifically to Sr. Arlene Violet, I wish to
inform you that Sister has decided to withdraw from our religious congregation.

In accordance with your communication, I am sending this letter through
the Apostolic Delegate's office.

May the peace of God permeate our lives and spirit during this graced
season.

Sincerely in Christ,

Sr. Mary Theresa Kane, RSM
President

Protocol no. 51772/82

Document #21

Letter mailed from the Apostolic Delegate's address: Jan. 23, 1984 (SMTK)

SACRA CONGREGATIO
PRO RELIGIOSIS   January 9, 1984
ET INSTITUTIS SAECULARIBUS

Prot. n. 51772/82

Sister Mary Theresa Kane, RSM
President
Sisters of Mercy of the Union
1320 Fenwich Lane, Suite 500
Silver Spring, Maryland 20910   U.S.A.

Dear Sister,

        We have received your letter of December 21, 1983 in reply
to our letter of October 26, 1983 in which we asked your position concerning
the candidature of one of your Sisters for the political office of Attorney
General of the State of Rhode Island, in the light of Canons 139 and 592,
as well as this Sacred Congregation's document of 1980 entitled Religious
and Human Promotion, I.D. ("Involvement in Politics").

        We appreciate the procedure of consultation that you have
initiated.   However, we wish to receive your own decision in your responsibility as supreme moderator of a religious institute bound by the common
law of the Church.

        We feel that our request made already July 3, 1982 has allowed
you sufficient time to reflect and consult on the matter.   Therefore, we
ask for your response as soon as possible.

        We note with regret that as you indicate Sister Arlene has
decided "to withdraw" from the Sisters of Mercy. We would like to know
how she is withdrawing, e.g. by exclaustration, leave of absence or dispensation of vows. Above all, we counsel you to use all your influence to preserve
and strengthen her vocation by living a common life in your Congregation.

        Awaiting your response through the good offices of the Apostolic
Delegate and assuring you of our ·deep concern in this matter and of our
best wishes for the new year, I remain

                    Sincerely yours in Our Lady of Mercy,

                            + A. Mayer
                              Pen.

Document #22

Sisters of Mercy of the Union

January 27, 1984

His Holiness
Pope John Paul II
Vatican City
Rome, Italy

Your Holiness:

    As we begin another year of Our Lord, I extend greetings of peace and joy, pledging prayers and fidelity to build God's kingdom through the living of the Gospel message.

    On June 30, 1984, I will complete my service as President of the Religious Sisters of Mercy of the Union. In this capacity I have served the religious congregations for seven years; I humbly seek the privilege of a private audience before I conclude my service. The honor of a private audience would be a source of blessing for the Sisters of Mercy, for my successor and for me personally.

    Your Holiness, I make this request in a spirit of charity and unity. Asking your blessing and assuring you of my prayers and fidelity, I am

Respectfully in Christ,

Sr. Mary Theresa Kane

Sr. Mary Theresa Kane, R.S.M.
President

Document #23

Sisters of Mercy of the Union

February 14, 1984

Most Reverend Augustine Mayer, OSB
Sacred Congregation for Religious
and Secular Institutes
Piazza Pius XII, 3
00193, Rome, Italy

Dear Archbishop Mayer:

After several months of serious reflection, prayer and consultation, Sr. Arlene Violet of the Providence Province requested
a dispensation from her perpetual vows. During the months of
Sr. Arlene Violet's discernment process, Sr. Mary Noel Blute,
the Provincial Administrator of the Providence Province, Sister
Arlene Violet and I were in close communication with each other.
The dispensation request was approved on December 27, 1983 and
forwarded to your office on January 6, 1984. It is my earnest
hope and prayer that the Sacred Congregation for Religious and
Secular Institutes will grant the dispensation as soon as possible.

The decision of the General Chapter to authorize a study regarding political ministry as outlined in my December 21, 1983 communication reflects and incorporates my personal position.

As always, I remain available to confer personally with you on
this and any other matter.

As requested, this letter is being sent through the office of
the Apostolic Delegate.

May the peace of God be with you always.

Sincerely in Christ,

Sister Mary Theresa Kane, RSM
President

Protocol No. 51772/82

Document #24

State of Rhode Island and Providence Plantations

REPRESENTATIVE
ELIZABETH MORANCY
'99 Godann Street
Providence Rhode Island .....

Post 2 State House
Providence Rhode Island 02903

House of Representatives

February 15,1984

Sacred Congregation of Religious

Vatican City

Dear Members of the Sacred Congregation:

I am asking for a clarification as to what are my options in the present situation as a three term State legislator, member of a religious order who wishes to run again but has been asked not to seek re-election by the Bishop of the Diocese.

Specifically, would you answer the following questions: 1)Given the events surrounding the cases of Sisters Agnes Mansour and Arlene Violet do I correctly conclude that a nun must resign from an Order if she feels she should serve in elective office; 2)Does the policy prohibit appointive office as well?

I am seeking clarification because I feel it is essential to know all the options before prayerfully making any decisions. Thank you for your attention to this request.

Sincerely yours,

Sister Elizabeth Morancy,RSM

Document #25

SACRA CONGREGAZIONE
PER I RELIGIOSI
E GLI ISTITUTI SECOLARI

March 9, 1984

Prot. n. 60407/84

Dear Sister Elizabeth,

This Sacred Congregation for Religious and Secular Institutes has received this week your letter of February 15, 1984 in which you seek certain clarifications that you feel are essential before prayerful making any decisions about your future as a Sister of Mercy. We thank you for seeking this advice and we respond to your questions without delay so that you will be able to make informed decisions and will be thereby strengthened in the Lord.

We will first answer your second question in which you ask whether the law of the Church regarding holding political office applies to appointive office as well as elective office. Canons 672 and 285, 3 of the Revised Code of Canon Law clearly apply to all priests, brothers and sisters who "assume public office which entails participation in the exercise of civil power". Therefore, our answer to your second question is affirmative.

You also ask if you "correctly conclude that a nun must resign from an Order if she feels she should serve in an elective office". Given the clarity and importance of the prescription involved, a religious, who has freely vowed obedience in the Church, should lovingly obey Church Law and with generous loyalty fulfill what is prescribed. If, unfortunately, a religious prefers to serve in an office not allowed by Church Law, he or she thereby chooses to resign from religious life.

In your letter, Sister, you state that you desire to be a candidate for re-election as State Representative in Rhode Island but that the Bishop of Providence has asked that you not seek re-election. You are indeed faced with a difficult decision. We urge that you persevere in your Call as a Religious Sister and obey the Canon Law and the Bishop who is the competent ecclesiastical authority in this matter. After listening to you and all the concerned parties and after considering the law and its particular application in your case, the Bishop has decided that the norm should be observed.

Be assured, Sister Elizabeth, of our deep concern and prayers for you as you open yourself to the Holy Spirit, realizing that your decision will have profound effects upon yourself, your religious family and God's People in Rhode Island.

Sincerely yours in Our Lady of Mercy,

+ Augustine Mayer
fcc.

Basil Heiser, ofmc.
Undersecy,

cc : Bishop Louis Gelineau
Sister Theresa Kane, R.S.M.

Document #26

SACRA CONGREGATIO   February 29, 1984
PRO RELIGIOSIS
ET INSTITUTIS SAECULARIBUS

Prot. n. 51772/82

Sister Mary Theresa Kane, R.S.M.
President, Sisters of Mercy of the Union
1320 Fenwick Lane, Suite 500
Silver Spring, MD 20910   U.S.A.

Dear Sister,

       This Sacred Congregation has received your letter of February 14, 1984 in which you ask that we grant as soon as possible a dispensation from perpetual vows for Sister Arlene Violet, a member of your Institute and of its Providence Province. We had previously received your original request, dated January 6, accompanied by documentation for the dispensation.

       We noted in the aforementioned documentation that an indication of the vote of your general council was lacking as required by Canon 691, 1. Therefore we have issued the enclosed Indult of Dispensation which presumes the consent of your council before the Indult is communicated. We ask that you notify us in writing about the vote of your council so that our file on the case will be complete.

       We wish that you would call to the attention of Sister Arlene the stipulation in the Indult of Dispensation that any future readmission by her to a religious institute will require the special permission of the Holy See, Canon 690, 1 notwithstanding.

       Moreover, we respectfully ask that you would send your reply to us through the good offices of the Apostolic Pro-Nuncio, as well as the response to our requests of July 3, 1982, October 21, 1983 and January 9, 1984 concerning your personal position on Sisters of your Institute holding political office, in the light of the Code of Canon Law and this Sacred Congregation's document entitled Religious and Human Promotion. We note that your December 21, 1983 letter to us, to which you refer us for your personal position on the question, only indicates the facts that you consulted with knowledgeable persons and that a study on the matter, commissioned by your last Chapter of Affairs, is under way.

       With assurances of our desire to be of assistance to you and all the Sisters of Mercy of the Union, I remain

                  Sincerely yours in Our Lady of Mercy,

                      + A. Mayer

Document #27

Sisters of Mercy of the Union

April 3, 1984

Most Reverend Augustine Mayer, OSB
Rev. Basil Heiser, OFMC
Sacred Congregation for Religious
and Secular Institutes
Piazza Pius XII, 3
00193, Rome, Italy

Dear Archbishop Mayer and Father Heiser:

On March 28, 1984 Sr. Arlene Violet, R.S.M. of the Providence Province
of the Religious Sisters of Mercy of the Union in the U.S.A. accepted and
signed her dispensation from her perpetual vows. On March 13, 1984 prior
to forwarding Sr. Arlene Violet's dispensation, the Mercy Administrative Team
unanimously approved the request for Sister's dispensation.

My communication of February 14, 1984 includes my personal position as
President of the Sisters of Mercy of the Union regarding political ministry.

A unique charism of the Sisters of Mercy is its vow of service to the
poor, sick and ignorant. Cognizant of this vow, the General Chapter authorized
a study of political ministry as I described in my December 21 letter. Until
the fruits of that study are officially promulgated through the competent
authorities of the religious congregation, I have no other personal position
on the matter.

MERCY COVENANT, our interim Constitutions adopted by the General Chapter
articulates a vision of apostolic service; as President I have exercised fidelity
to the articulation.

As in the past, I am willing to confer with you on this or any other
matter. Thank you sincerely for your continued dedication and service to
women religious. May the coming holydays of Lent be another opportunity for
us to experience the loving mercy of God.

                              Sincerely in Christ,

                              Sr. Mary Theresa Kane, R.S.M.
                              President

Per your letter of 2/29/84, this communication is being sent through the office
of the Apostolic Pro-Nuncio.

Document #28

Sisters of Mercy of the Union

Holy Thursday
April 19, 1984

His Holiness
Pope John Paul II
Vatican City
Rome, Italy

Your Holiness:

With profound gratitude I acknowledge your consideration of my request for a private audience as expressed in the March 6, 1984, letter from the Most Reverend Eduardo Martinez.

In a spirit of respect and candor, I will attempt to outline the rationale for my request; my hope is that the spirit as well as the substance of the proposal will be evident:

1. The Religious Sisters of Mercy of the Union is a large religious congregation serving throughout most of the U.S.A., parts of South America, Central America and the Caribbean region in the apostolates of health, education, and the social services. During these past twenty years the congregation has striven faithfully to renew its understanding of religious life in the spirit of Vatican Council II. Since October 1979, when I had the privilege and responsibility as President of LCWR, to greet you at the Shrine of the Immaculate Conception in Washington, D.C., some perceptual distortions regarding the quality of spiritual renewal about this religious congregation have resulted. A private audience with an opportunity for dialogue will serve to clarify concerns you may have about the Sisters of Mercy of the Union.

2. In the past four years, the leadership of this congregation has been involved with matters that have received some public attention, e.g., the tubal ligation study; and, political ministry, including the Mansour and Violet cases. An audience will provide an opportunity for you to speak about any of these topics and allow me to respond to concerns you may have about them.

3. The Twelfth General Chapter of Affairs and Elections has just concluded. An audience will enable me to express personally the many expressions of prayer and support for you, as well as renewed fidelity to the mission of the church, which came forth in so many ways from the Chapter Delegates.

4. An audience will provide an opportunity for the leadership of one U.S.A. religious congregation to engage in conversation with you about the recent study initiated through Archbishop Quinn's Commission. We desire to offer a perspective on the study and indicate our cooperation with it.

5. Finally, it is my ardent desire that this request for an
    audience, if favorably considered, will include my successor,
    Sr. Helen Amos and our respective Assistants, Sr. Emily George
    and Sr. Helen Marie Burns; with me these sisters represent the
    present and the future leadership for the Religious Sisters of
    Mercy of the Union. I believe that all of us will benefit very
    much from dialogue with you. Each of us desires your blessing
    upon us and our beloved religious congregation.

   In a spirit of trust and joy during this sacred paschal season, I respond
to the communication kindly extended through the Office of the Nunciature
on March 19, 1984, and I remain

                              Faithfully and Respectfully in Christ,

                              Sr. Mary Theresa Kane, R.S.M.
                              President

Document #29

LAW OFFICES OF

KECK, MAHIN & CATE

1333 NEW HAMPSHIRE AVENUE, N.W

WASHINGTON, D.C. 20036

TELEPHONE (202) 822-8975

April 24, 1984

CHICAGO OFFICE:

8300 SEARS TOWER
233 SOUTH WACKER DRIVE
CHICAGO ILLINOIS 60606
TELEPHONE (312) 876-3400
CABLE ADDRESS MAMSCOTT TELEX 25 3411
TELECOPIER (312) 876-3582

44072/200/001
202 822-8975

Most Reverend Jerome Hamer, O.P.
Sacred Congregation for Religious
  and Secular Institutes
Piazza Pius XII, 3
00193, Rome,
ITALY

Dear Archbishop Hamer:

     Attached is the Petition of the Religious Sisters of Mercy
of the Union in the United States of America, on behalf of the
Twelfth General Chapter of the Sisters of Mercy, requesting an
indult from you granting to Sister Elizabeth Morancy, R.S.M., a
dispensation from Canon 285, § 3, in order to permit her to continue
in public office. The 72 delegates at the Twelfth General Chapter
represent 4,300 members of the Sisters of Mercy of the Union.
The vote of the delegates in favor of a resolution requesting an
indult for Sister Elizabeth Morancy was 62 in favor, 5 opposed,
and 5 abstentions.

As explained in the attached Petition, there is extreme urgency in receiving your decision by April 29. We sincerely apologize for the shortness of time involved.

Thanking you in advance on behalf of the Sisters of Mercy for your attention to this matter, I am

Sincerely yours,

Peter M. Shannon, Jr.

Peter M. Shannon, Jr.,
J.D., J.C.L., S.T.L.

PMS:cw
15.011
Attachment

PETITION

TO THE

SACRED CONGREGATION FOR RELIGIOUS AND SECULAR INSTITUTES

FOR AN INDULT

GRANTING TO SISTER ELIZABETH MONRANCY, R.S.M. ,

A DISPENSATION

FROM CANONS 672 AND 285, § 3, CODE OF CANON LAW

1.

INTRODUCTION

A.   Procedural Background

On March 27, 1984, the Twelfth General Chapter of the

Religious Sisters of Mercy of the Union in the United States of

America passed the following resolution:

> That the Twelfth General Chapter request
> from the appropriate Church authorities an
> indult granting Sister Elizabeth Morancy a
> dispensation from Canons 672 and 285, § 3,
> in order to continue in public office.

This resolution was adopted by the Chapter delegates by a vote of

sixty-two (62) in favor, five (5) opposed, and five (5) abstentions.

By letter dated March 30, 1984 (see Attachment 1),

Sister M. Theresa Kane, R.S.M., President of the Twelfth General

Chapter and President of the Sisters of Mercy, formally retained
the undersigned, Peter M. Shannon, Jr., J.D., J.C.L., S.T.L., to
process the Chapter resolution. The undersigned attorney for the
Sisters of Mercy wishes to advise the Sacred Congregation for
Religious and Secular Institutes (hereafter "SCRIS") that, although
a civil lawyer, he is acting solely in his capacity as a canon
lawyer in pursuing this Chapter resolution. In other words, the
Sisters of Mercy as Petitioner in this matter have not contemplated
and will not contemplate any type of civil procedure, litigious
or otherwise.

By letter dated April 21, 1984 (see Attachment 2),
Sister Elizabeth Morancy, R.S.M., denoted her awareness of the
Chapter Resolution and her desire to obtain a dispensation to
continue her ministry in elective public office. Also by letter
dated April 21, 1984 (see Attachment 3), Sister Elizabeth Morancy's
Provincial Administrator, Sister Mary Noel Blute, R.S.M., expressed
in writing her continued support of Sister Elizabeth Morancy's
political ministry.

B. Urgency of Petition

Sister Elizabeth Morancy is completing her third term
as a State Legislator in Rhode Island. If she is to pursue a
fourth term in the Legislature, she must file written notice with
the State of Rhode Island by June 1, 1984. However, Sister Theresa
Kane and Sister Noel Blute learned recently from Sister Elizabeth
Morancy that, in her opinion, she must announce to her
constituents by April 29 whether or not she intends to run for a
fourth term.

We realize that SCRIS must act most expeditiously,
if a definitive answer from SCRIS is to be forthcoming and
received by the Sisters of Mercy on or before April 29. On the
other hand, we are convinced that a definitive answer, prior to

any announcement by Sister Elizabeth Morancy on April 29 would be
beneficial to all concerned, including the Diocese of Providence,
the Sisters of Mercy, and the constituents whom Sister Elizabeth
Morancy represents.

One final note should be mentioned and emphasized in
this regard. If in fact no answer is received by April 29 and if
in fact on April 29 Sister Elizabeth Morancy announces her candidacy
for a fourth term in the State Legislature, then the Sisters of
Mercy wish, _ipsis_ _factis_, to withdaw this petition for an indult
granting the dispensation to Sister Elizabeth Morancy to continue
in public office.

C. Meeting with Bishop Gelineau

On April 21, 1984, the undersigned met on behalf of the
Sisters of Mercy with Louis E. Gelineau, D.D., Diocesan Bishop of
Providence, Rhode Island, U.S.A. In the presence of the Provincial
Administrator of the Sisters of Mercy, Sister Noel Blute, R.S.M.,
I apprised Bishop Gelineau of the Chapter resolution and
Sister Morancy's request.

After a lengthy and meaningful exchange of views,
Bishop Gelineau stated that, while he is unwilling to dispense
Sister Elizabeth Morancy from the proscription of Canon 285, § 3,
he does recognize the right of the sisters of Mercy to request
such a dispensation from the Holy See. Should the SCRIS believe
that some exceptions to Canon 285, § 3, are in order and that
compelling circumstances warrant a dispensation for Sister Elizabeth
Morancy, then the decision of SCRIS, Bishop Gelineau has authorized
me to state, will be readily accepted by him. Bishop Gelineau
has also authorized me to state that he supports our request for
a SCRIS decision by April 29, if at all possible, believing it
beneficial for all concerned if a definite decision is received

before Sister Elizabeth Morancy makes any public statement on
April 29.

On April 23, 1984, Bishop Gelineau telephoned the
undersigned. During our telephone conversation he requested a
notation in this Petition that he is aware of the March 9, 1984
expression of law made by the SCRIS in answer to the February 15,
1984 inquiry by Sister Elizabeth Morancy. Therefore,
Bishop Gelineau stated that he would be surprised if the SCRIS
grants the requested indult. However, he again acknowledged the
right of the Sisters of Mercy to ask for a response from the
SCRIS in this matter.

II.

FACTS

Born on May 12, 1941 in Fall River, Massachusetts,
Elizabeth Morancy entered the Sisters of Mercy in 1959, was
received into the Community in 1960, took temporary vows in 1962,
renewed temporary vows in 1965, and made perpetual vows in 1967.

In 1978 Sister Elizabeth Morancy was elected to the
State Legislature as representative of District #18. She was
re-elected in 1980 and again in 1982. District #18 is a city
neighborhood in Providence, Rhode Island, of some 9,400 people.
The District contains a mixture of Black, Hispanic, Indo-Chinese,
and White, with most of the people being poor or working class
blue collar, and a small percentage being what would be termed
"middle class."

Sister Elizabeth Morancy's work as a Representative in
the State Legislature is part-time work for which she is compen-
sated in toto at the rate of $300 per year. Much of her time is
spent in working with and for the Hmong refugees from Laos, many
of whom have settled within District #18 in Providence.

The Visitor, the official newspaper of the Diocese of
Providence, in an article on January 12, 1984, described
Sister Elizabeth Morancy's work as a State Representative in the
following terms:

> She has worked extensively with the poor
> and minority groups in South Providence
> area. Issues she has tackled include the
> equality of women, housing discrimination,
> confidentiality of rape-crisis records,
> and the resettlement of refugees in
> Providence, especially those in the Hmong
> community.

In November 1981, Sister Elizabeth Morancy received from
Bishop Gelineau a diocesan award for her work with the handicapped. The award was specifically tied to her work in the State
Legislature, primarily her successful sponsorship of two bills
providing subsidy programs for parents of handicapped children.
Presently, Sister Elizabeth Morancy continues her social service
efforts within the Legislature, recently sponsoring for the
fourth time a fair housing bill for the State of Rhode Island.

III.

THE LAW

Canon 285, § 3, Code of Canon Law, prohibits clerics
from assuming public offices entailing a participation in the
exercise of civil power. Canon 672 stipulates that Religious are
bound by the prescriptions of Canon 285.

By letter dated February 15, 1984, Sister Elizabeth
Morancy wrote to the SCRIS inquiring, inter alia, whether a
Religious must resign from her Institute if she believes she
should serve in elective office. By letter dated March 9, 1984,
Archbishop Augustine Mayer, Secretary of the SCRIS, replied that
if "a Religious prefers to serve in an office not allowed by
Church law, he or she thereby chooses to resign from religious
life."

In accord with Canon 87, a diocesan bishop can dispense
from universal laws such as the law contained in Canon 285, § 3.
In the opinion of the undersigned, there is nothing in canon law
which would prohibit Bishop Gelineau from doing what he has done
in this situation, i.e., considering the resolution of the
Sisters of Mercy requesting a dispensation for Sister Elizabeth
Morancy, expressing unwillingness to grant the dispensation, but
recognizing the right of the Sisters of Mercy to request such a
dispensation from the SCRIS.

IV.
ARGUMENT

Under the new Code of Canon Law, which became effective
in November 1983, Religious may not assume political office.
However, this prohibition is not absolute, in the sense that,
like other merely ecclesiastical laws, exceptions can be made and
dispensations can be granted by proper ecclesiastical authority.
Thus, the prohibition against Religious assuming political office
is not an instance where "Roma locuta est; causa finita est!"

In this instance, Sister Elizabeth Morancy was elected
to public office in 1978, re-elected in 1980, and again in 1982.
For six years and three terms of office, her political ministry
has been sanctioned by authority within her Religious Institute
and has been tolerated, if not implicitly approved, by competent
diocesan authority. Her constituents, in the main poor or lower
middle class, find it strange, almost incomprehensible, that at
this juncture, after so many years of service on their behalf and
on behalf of the Church in her political ministry, Sister Elizabeth
Morancy would be directed to discontinue her political ministry.
The people in District #18 cannot comprehend how and why the same
Church, which encouraged Sister Elizabeth Morancy to represent

them in the State Legislature, now of a sudden forbids her from
pursuing her responsibilities, particularly where her very efforts
within the State Legislature have redounded not only for the good
of the people in District #18, but also for the good of the
Church.

The people in District #18, through Sister Elizabeth
Morancy's efforts, have come to look upon the Catholic Church as
an institution which proclaims justice for all people. Within
the United States, one of the major ways to proclaim and obtain
justice for all people is through the legislative process. This
is what Sister Elizabeth Morancy has attempted to do both by her
words and by her actions. Her people are rightly confused and,
if a dispensation is not granted so that Elizabeth Morancy can
pursue her political ministry as a Religious Sister, then in the
opinion of many, the people in District #18 may begin to question
the credibility of the Church in its asserted quest for justice.

In no uncertain terms, it can and should be stated that
this petition, although denominated a Petition by the Sisters of
Mercy, might be termed a petition by the poor, the deprived, and
the disadvantaged people whom Sister Elizabeth Morancy represents
so well in the State Legislature.

There can be no question about Sister Elizabeth Morancy's
commitment to her people and her commitment to her Church. Her
three terms in the State Legislature have been exemplary, not only
from an ecclesiastical standpoint, but more importantly from a
human standpoint. She has sponsored bills to aid the handicapped,
the aliens, the homeless, and the suffering. There has been no
trace of scandal in her work or in her service. Indeed, the
diocesan award which she received from Bishop Gelineau in 1981
attests to the public acclaim, both within and without the

Church, of her dedication and determination to build up the Body of Christ by a life of ministry and service.

In sum, if an exception is ever to be made to Canon 285, § 3, we respectfully contend on behalf of the Sisters of Mercy and their Twelfth General Chapter that the exception should be made for Sister Elizabeth Morancy to pursue her part-time ministry in public office. This exception would be eminently justified because it upholds the values which Pope John Paul II and his predecessors have identified as sometimes harmed by clergy and religious in public office. That is, Sister Elizabeth Morancy's activities within the Rhode Island state legislature bespeak unity rather than disunity in Roman Catholic belief and her activities continue to witness the spiritual realities and the spiritual mission of the Church.

Denial of a dispensation to Sister Elizabeth Morancy for continuation in public office would, we submit, smack of retroactive application of the new Code to an existing and approved ministry, but more importantly the grant of the dispensation would fulfill the positive and urgent need for Sister Elizabeth Morancy to puruse her legislative effort to provide, for example, fair housing, shelters for the homeless, advocacy of the rights of the handicapped and protection for the victims of sexual abuse. In a word, the requested dispensation would promote basic Christian values and basic human needs.

V.

CONCLUSION

Notwithstanding Canon 285, § 3, and by virtue of the reasons described above, the Sisters of Mercy hereby request that Sister Elizabeth Morancy be authorized by the Sacred Congregation for Religious and Secular Institutes to continue in public office.

Respectfully submitted on behalf of the Religious Sisters of
Mercy of the Union in the United States of America...

Peter M. Shannon,   Jr.,   J.D., J.C.L., S.T.L.
KECK, MAHIN & CATE
Suite 1220
1333 New Hampshire Avenue, N.W.
Washington, D.C.   20036
(202) 822-8975

W011.14

cc: Most Rev. Louis E. Gelineau, D.D.
     Sister M. Theresa Kane, R.S.M.
     Sister Mary Noel Blute, R.S.M.

Document #30

SACRA CONGREGATIO   Rome, May 9, 1984
PRO RELIGIOSIS
ET INSTITUTIS SAECULARIBUS
———

     Prot. n. 60407/84

Dear Sister,

          This Sacred Congregation has received the petition for an
indult granting a dispensation for Sister Elizabeth Morancy, R.S.M. to be a
candidate for election to political office in the State of Rhode Island. The
petition was submitted at your direction and at that of the General Chapter
of your Institute.

          The petition, dated April 24, 1984, did not reach this office
until May 3, 1984 Although it states on page 3 that, if a response is not
received before April 29, you wish, "ipsis factis", to withdraw the petition,
we did give it careful consideration and on May 4 we telephoned our decision
to the Apostolic Pro-Nuncio in Washington so that you would know our determination as soon as possible.

We denied the request for the reasons stated in our letter of March 9, 1984 and addressed to Sister Elizabeth of which we sent you a copy.

We again ask that you and Sister's Provincial Superior urge Sister Elizabeth to persevere in her vocation as a Sister of Mercy and obey Canon Law and the Bishop of Providence who is the competent ecclesiastical authority in the matter and who has made the correct decision, based on the law and sound pastoral reasons.

Be assured, Sister Theresa, of our deep concern and prayers for Sister Elizabeth, realizing that her decision will have profound effects upon herself, your beloved Congregation and upon the Church of Rhode Island. Moreover, please thank Doctor Shannon for us.

Sincerely yours in Our Lady of Mercy,

+ T. Emer. op.
Pro Sub

Basil Heiser, ofm c.

Sister Mary Theresa KANE
President
Sisters of Mercy of the Union

Document #31

Sisters of Mercy of the Union

June 28, 1984

Most Reverend Jerome Hamer, OP
The Sacred Congregation for
Religious and Secular Institutes
Piazza Pius XII, 3
00193, Rome, Italy

Dear Archbishop Hamer:

I have given serious consideration to your letter of May 9, 1984. During this month I had hoped to discuss it with Archbishop Pio Laghi as the representative of the Holy See, but Archbishop Laghi is away from his office at this time. Since I conclude my term of office within a few days my only recourse is to communicate with you directly. I regret that circumstances do not permit a personal conference about a matter of such import to all of us.

Charity calls us as religious persons to disagree respectfully regarding
a position such as I conveyed to you in my letters responding to your
inquiries about political office for Sisters of Mercy of the Union.
Charity, however, does not include ignoring or dismissing the position
of another as you have done in stating that I did not honor your request.
It is my considered judgment that I respectfully and thoughtfully put
forward my position on political ministry as I understand it in light
of my responsibilities as the President of my congregation. Because
the two most recent General Chapters have dealt with the issue of political ministry, including the authorization of a study, I believe that
I am faithful in reflecting the serious effort of these Chapters to come
to terms with the question of whether or not political ministry is
appropriate to the charism of the Sisters of Mercy.

In seeking a response to your recent letter I have sought counsel with
select, reputable canonists. It has been emphasized that the first
request from the Sacred Congregation concerning my personal position
on Sisters of Mercy holding political office occurred on February 29,
1984. The earlier correspondence you cited related specifically to my
position on Sister Arlene Violet seeking the office of attorney general
in the State of Rhode Island. In fact, by letter dated February 14,
1984, I informed the Sacred Congregation that I had forwarded Sister
Arlene's request for dispensation on January 6, 1984. Since Sister had
made this request, it seemed to me then and it appears to me now that
your inquiry regarding my personal opinion was in a real sense moot.

Significantly, however, I offered in my letter of February 14 to consult
personally with Archbishop Mayer on this or any other matter. I also
had written directly to His Holiness, Pope John Paul II, on January 27,
1984, requesting a personal audience before I conclude my term as President
of the Sisters of Mercy of the Union. When later asked by Most Reverend
Eduard Martinez, Substitute Secretary of State, to clarify my intent
for such a meeting, I indicated that political ministry was among the
concerns I wished to discuss with the Holy Father. Again, on April 3,
when I wrote to Archbishop Mayer and Father Heiser in response to their
February 29 letter, I indicated the action of our General Chapter
authorizing a study on political ministry and expressed my willingness
to confer with them on this matter.

I must further be candid with you about your linking my alleged refusal
to be cooperative with the three Sisters who were constrained to seek
dispensations from their vows. If any behavior on my part resulted in
serious consequences to them, a grave injustice has been done to these
women and attempts should be made to rectify the situation.

It is my ardent hope and prayer that personal and mutual dialogue between
you and my successor, Sister Helen Amos, will result in more effective
communication for the benefit of our three Sisters, for our religious
congregation, and for the whole church that has been affected by these
unfortunate events.

My administrative council concur with the sentiments I have expressed
in this letter.

May the Presence of a Gentle, Loving God be with us as we strive for
deepened union and charity.

Sincerely in Christ,

Sr. Mary Theresa Kane, RSM
President

Document #32

3339 MASSACHUSETTS AVENUE. N.W.
WASHINGTON. D. C. 20008-3687

APOSTOLIC NUNCIATURE
UNITED STATES OF AMERICA

No. 2987/84/8

This No. Should Be Prefixed to the Answer

August 3, 1984

Sister Theresa M. Kane, R.S.M.
Mercy Center Washington
1320 Fenwick Lane, Suite 500
Silver Spring, MD 20910

Dear Sister Theresa:

Earlier, in an effort to pursue your request for a private audience with His Holiness, Pope John Paul II, you submitted a detailed outline of the issues which you wished to raise in your visit with the Holy Father. Careful consideration has been given to the matters which you have proposed.

It has been determined that the questions which you had intended to present to the Holy Father, could all the more be referred for examination to the Sacred Congregation for Religious and Secular Institutes.

Thus, it has been deemed inopportune to honor your request for a private audience with His Holiness.

I would encourage you to address yourself to the attention of the Sacred Congregation for Religious in discussing your proposals.

With cordial best wishes and kind regards, I am

Sincerely yours in Christ,

Pio Laghi

Apostolic Pro-Nuncio

ROMAN CATHOLIC DIOCESE OF BROOKLYN

POST OFFICE BOX C

BROOKLYN, NEW YORK 11202

OFFICE OF THE CHANCELLOR
75 GREENE AVENUE

July 5, 1983

Sister Mary Theresa Kane, R.S.M.
President
Sisters of Mercy of the Union
1320 Fenwick Lane, Suite 500
Silver Spring, Maryland 20910

Dear Sister Mary Theresa:

In my letter of June 8, I informed you that your letter of
May 23, 1983 was being evaluated. The pressure of many obligations,
in addition to the requirements of an adequate study of the issues,
delayed this reply. I am grateful for your patience and understanding.

Because of the nature and length of the response to your concerns,
I thought it best to incorporate my observations in separate document
which is herewith included.

While I am the author of this report, I can assure you that it
reflects, to the best of my knowledge and ability, the mind and criteria
of the Holy See in this matter.

It is my prayerful desire that the blessing of reconciliation
flowing from truth, justice and mutual trust will soon be ours.

With prayerful best wishes, I remain

Sincerely yours in Christ,

Most Rev. Anthony J. Bevilacqua
Auxiliary Bishop
Ad Hoc Delegate of the Holy See

MOST REV. ANTHONY J. BEVILACQUA
AD HOC DELEGATE OF THE HOLY SEE
75 Greene Avenue
Brooklyn, New York 11238

****

RESPONSE TO CONCERNS OF SISTER THERESA KANE
WITH CERTAIN ITEMS IN THE PRECEPT OF MAY 9, 1983

****

I.   Concern with Part I:13

        In your letter of May 8, 1983, you expressed concern with a portion of
Item No. 13 in Part I of the Precept of May 9, 1983 given to Sister Agnes Mary
Mansour. The pertinent section reads: "The Apostolic Delegate gave
Sister Theresa Kane ten days to respond in writing. As a result of two further
requests by Sister Theresa Kane for postponements, twenty days elapsed before
Sister Theresa Kane sent her written reply of April 11, 1983."

        Concern of your letter of May 18, 1983, addressed to the Apostolic Delegate,
Archbishop Laghi, reads: "The length of time required for my response was never
stated by you. You never indicated a ten day response. I never requested a
postponement; I requested an extension. In response to my inquiry about canonical
consequences, you never indicated any consequences which would be directed to
Sister Agnes Mary."

        A. Preliminary Observations

        1. Your concern refers to a meeting of the Apostolic Delegate with
yourself and Sister Emily George that took place on March 23, 1983.
In this meeting, the Apostolic Delegate communicated to you the decision
of the Sacred Congregation for Religious and Secular Institutes
instructing you to require Sister Agnes Mary Mansour to resign her
public office. At the meeting, the Apostolice Delegate presented you
with the letter incorporating the Congregation's decision that he had
verbally transmitted to you.

        2. Since your concern refers to a conversation at a meeting at
which I was not present, my observations will rely solely on the
documentation of this case available to me.

        B. Observations Concerning the Time Period within which to Implement
            the Decision

        1. The letter of March 23rd, from the Apostolic Delegate addressed
to you: "My superiors have indicated to me that this decision is final
and is to be implemented without delay."

        2. Memorandum from the Apostolic Delegate on meeting of March 23, 1983 -
in this memorandum, Archbishop Laghi states that at the meeting of
March 23, 1983, he gave you ten days within which to respond in writing
to the decision transmitted to you. In reply to your request, he
accorded you an extension since you told him that you wished to go on
retreat during Holy Week. Therefore, you would not be ready to give
a response before about April 4th or 5th. Subsequently in response
to your telephone request for another extension, the Apostolic
Delegate gave you an additional four days. In that same telephone
conversation, you asked the Apostolic Delegate if the Sacred
Congregation for Religious and Secular Institutes would be disposed to
a reconsideration of the case and if there could not be some kind of
compromise. The Delegate rejected such a possibility and insisted
that he receive from you a clear "yes" or "no" reply.

        3. If a specified period of time required for your response was
never stated to you by the Apostolic Delegate, what would be the
meaning of your admission in your letter of May 18, 1983 in which
you state that you did not request a postponement but "I requested an
extension."

        C. Observations Concerning your Inquiry about Canonical Consequences

1. In the meeting of March 23, 1983, you inquired of the Apostolic Delegate what would be the canonical consequences to Sister Agnes Mary Mansour if she refused to obey the decision of the Holy See. The Apostolic Delegate responded that if Sister Agnes Mary refused to obey the order to resign her public office communicated to her, she could be dismissed from the community and could lose her canonical status as a Religious.

2. Since you, as the Superior of Sister Agnes Mary Mansour, made this inquiry, I am sure that it was presumed that you, as her Superior, would have communicated this information to her.

3. As a result of the instruction given to you at the meeting of March 23, 1983, you were obliged to transmit the decision of the Holy See to Sister Agnes Mary Mansour. In fact, at that meeting, you asked the Apostolic Delegate what would be the consequences of your refusal to obey. The Apostolic Delegate responded that in the event of your refusal to transmit the decision of the Holy See to Sister Agnes Mary Mansour, you yourself would be subject to serious canonical consequences. Once you transmitted the decision of the Holy See to Sister Agnes Mary Mansour to resign from her public office, it must be presumed that she would have at least a general awareness that her disobedience to this requirement from the Holy See in this grave matter could have serious canonical consequences. This same presumption would hold if Sister Agnes Mary Mansour from any other source became aware of this decision of the Holy See for her to resign her public office.

II.   Second Concern

Your second concern refers to Item No. 14 in Part I of the Precept of May 9, 1983. This item reads: "In her letter of April 11, 1983, to the Apostolic Delegate, Sister Theresa Kane requested a formal reconsideration of the decision reached by the Holy See. She asked that documentation of the situation prepared by the Detroit Provincial Team be submitted to the Holy See."

In your letter of May 18, 1983, you articulate your concern with this item: "I never received a response to my request for reconsideration; the questions I raised and the interpretations requested have not been answered."

A.   Observations on your Concern that No Response was Given to your Request for Reconsideration

1. In his letter of March 23, 1983, communicating to you the decision of the Congregation for Religious and Secular Institutes that you require Sister Agnes Mary to resign her public office, the Apostolic Delegate informed you that the decision was final.

2. In a telephone conversation subsequent to your meeting with the Apostolic Delegate on March 23rd, you asked the Apostolic Delegate if the Congregation for Religious and Secular Institutes would be disposed to a reconsideration of the case and if there could not be some kind of compromise. The Delegate rejected such a possibility and insisted that he receive from you a clear "yes" or "no" reply.

3. On April 12, 1983, your request for reconsideration was sent to the Congregation for Religious and Secular Institutes by special courier. While I was asked on April 13, 1983, to be Ad Hoc Delegate in this case, on that date no final decision in the case was

communicated to me. On April 15, in the evening before my departure
from Rome, I met with Archbishop Mayer at the Congregation for
Religious. At that meeting we discussed the nature, scope and contents
of a Pontifical Mandate that was still under consideration in the
matter of Sister Agnes Mary Mansour. It was evident from the meeting
that your request for reconsideration was being given careful attention.

4. In the letter of April 26, 1983, the Apostolic Delegate informed
you that in response to your request for an appointment to discuss with
the Sacred Congregation for Religious and Secular Institutes the case
of Sister Agnes Mary Mansour, the Cardinal Prefect refers you to me as
Ad Hoc Delegate of the same Congregation for the entire matter. The
same letter informed you that I would be available for a discussion with
you after the initial interview with Sister Agnes Mary Mansour. It must
be understood that if Sister Agnes Mary had not requested the dispensation
from her vows, the canonical process would have lasted for a number of
days. On any of these days, I would have been available to explain to you
the decision of the Holy See which would have been the response to your
request for reconsideration.

5. At the end of my meeting with Sister Agnes Mary Mansour on
May 9, 1983, Sister Emily George told me that you wished to speak with me.
I told her that I would be most willing. I awaited word from you. If you
had communicated with me, I would have explained to you the decision of
the Holy See which, as I've stated above, would have been the response
of the Holy See to your request for reconsideration.

B. Observations on your Concern that the Questions you Raised and the
    Interpretations Requested in your Letter to the Apostolic Delegate
    of April 11, 1983 Have Not Been Answered

Before presenting my observations on your questions, I wish to note
that some of your inquiries about this matter made in the letter of April 11th
transcend the circumstances of my involvement in this matter nor is there
documentation on these same inquiries available to me which would enable
me to give a knowledgeable response. Consequently, I can give no reply
to Items No. 4 and No. 6 in your letter of April 11, 1983.

In the following observations, I shall follow the listing of your
letter of April 11, 1983. For each item, I shall give your statement in
the letter followed by my observations.

1. STATEMENT -- "Your letter of March 23rd indicated that 'a careful
and deliberate study of all the factors' resulted in a judgement by
SCRIS. SCRIS, however, has not reviewed the Sisters of Mercy documentation.
Sister Helen Marie Burns and the Detroit Provincial Team in consultation
with Sister Agnes Mary Mansour have carefully documented their story of
these past months. We consider their data integral in understanding the
factors involved. I explained to your secretary that the documentation
will arrive on Tuesday, April 12th; it will be hand delivered to your
office for inclusion with the request to SCRIS.

RESPONSE   -- The documentation referred to in your letter along
with your request for reconsideration were sent to the Sacred Congregation
for Religious and Secular Institutes by special courier on April 12, 1983
and was reviewed by it.
2. STATEMENT -- "Your letter further stated that Sister Agnes
Mary Mansour refused to resign her position. At no time prior to
March 23rd was Sister asked by the Religious Congregation to resign.
The judgement about refusal is incorrect and is cause of injustice to
Sister Agnes Mary."

RESPONSE

a. I will stipulate that it is true that "at no time prior to
March 23rd was Sister asked by the Religious Congregation to resign."
However, it still remains true that Sister Agnes Mary Mansour refused
to resign her position. She refused to resign even though she was
fully aware of the demand and obligation to resign her public office.

b. On February 14, 1983, Archbishop Szoka informed Sister Agnes
Mary in a meeting with her that if she did not change her stance on
Medicaid funding for abortions, he would have to call for her
resignation. In fact, she never did change her position on Medicaid
funding for abortions.

c. In his letter to Sister Helen Marie Burns of February 23, 1983,
Archbishop Szoka told her that Sister Agnes Mary Mansour no longer
had his approval to retain her public office; that, therefore, she
would be acting contrary to church law and discipline if she continued
in that office. He then informed Sister Helen Marie Burns that it was
her responsibility and that of her Provincial Council to inform
Sister Agnes Mary that, because of his disapproval, she could no
longer retain her position as Director of the Department of Social
Services and that she and her Council were to provide for the
compliance of Sister Agnes Mary with church law. It must be
presumed that Sister Helen Marie Burns communicated to Sister Agnes
Mary Mansour this decision of Archbishop Szoka and his call for her
resignation.

d. In his public statement of February 23, 1983, a copy of
which was sent to Sister Helen Marie Burns, Archbishop Szoka called
for the resignation of Sister Agnes Mary from her public office
without delay. It must be presumed again that Sister Helen Marie
Burns communicated to Sister Agnes Mary Mansour this public statement of Archbishop Szoka. This public statement also appeared in
its entirety in the public media. It must be presumed that the
call of Archbishop Szoka for Sister Agnes Mary Mansour to resign
came to her attention through the public media.

e. You stated in your letter of April 11th that at no time
prior to March 23rd was Sister Agnes Mary asked by the Religious
Congregation to resign. However, Sister Agnes Mary was aware of
her obligation to resign. The Superiors of the Sisters of Mercy,
including yourself, stipulated that Sister Agnes Mary Mansour
needed the permission of ecclesiastical authority. Sister Agnes
Mary Mansour was also aware of the need for permission from
ecclesiastical authority for her to continue in office. Therefore,
when she learned that she was in public office without permission
of ecclesiastical authority, she also had to become aware of her
responsibility to resign.

f. It must be noted that the obligation of Sister Agnes
Mary Mansour to resign her public office was not contingent upon
her being asked by her Superiors to resign but rather was required
because she was in violation of church law and discipline since
she was in public office without permission of ecclesiastical
authority. The major responsibility of the Religious Superiors of
Sister Agnes Mary Mansour, as Archbishop Szoka stated in his letter
of February 23rd to Sister Helen Marie Burns, was "to provide for
her compliance with church law." The obligation of Sister Agnes

Mary Mansour to resign her public office became automatic once she was aware that she no longer had the approval of required ecclesiastical authority. It was not the obligation of the Superiors of Sister Agnes Mary Mansour to ask her to resign. Rather they had a certain responsibility to inform her that she could no longer retain her public office and an obligation to enforce the requirement of her resignation.

g. It is not presumption but fact that Sister Agnes Mary Mansour was aware that Archbishop Szoka had called on her to resign as Director of the Department of Social Services. In her statement of March 8, 1983, at the confirmation hearing of the Michigan Senate, Sister Agnes Mary Mansour referred to Archbishop Szoka and then spoke of "his demand of me and of my Religious Superiors that I resign..."

h. It must be concluded from what has been said that the judgement that Sister Agnes Mary Mansour has refused to resign remains a valid one and is not the cause of any injustice against her.

3. STATEMENT -- "The law of the church states that the approval of the ordinary and of the religious superior are needed for acceptance of public office. I request a written interpretation of the church law in a case when only one of the required approvals is given."

RESPONSE -- When church law requires the approval of two superiors for acceptance of a public office, canonists agree that the person seeking the public office must have the authorization of both required superiors. Therefore, if a person accepts or continues in a public office and does not have the approval of either required superior or has the approval of only one of the two required superiors, that person is in violation of church law.

4. STATEMENT -- "Archbishop Szoka's withrawal of approval has harmed both personal and corporate reputations since the Sisters of Mercy are perceived as being in defiance. This has been a source of grave concern to us."

RESPONSE -- This item transcends the circumstances of my involvement in this case nor is there any documentation pertinent to your concern. Accordingly, it is not possible for me to give a response.

5. STATEMENT -- "Sr. Agnes Mary, Sr. Helen Marie and I consulted with several canonists and theologians relative Sister's position regarding abortion, notably Medicaid funding. The consultations indicate that Sister is clearly within the tradition of the Church. Sister also supports the U.S.A. bishops in her public position on the Hatch Amendment. If SCRIS judges Sister's articulation unacceptable, I will appreciate the reasons in writing."

RESPONSE -- Since your letter of April 11th did not include the articulation of Sister Agnes Mary Mansour on Medicaid funding for abortions, I must presume that her position is that contained in the two public statements that she made while running for Congress in 1982 and in her testimony at the confirmation hearing before the Michigan Senate on March 8, 1983. Sister Agnes Mary Mansour issued a position paper on abortion and legislation in June 1982 and another one in July 1982. In both of these position papers she states "I am morally opposed to abortion." In the June 1982 paper, she also states "I do not think it

wise to support legislation aimed at outlawing all abortions." In the
July 1982 position paper, she stated "I do not think it wise at this
point in American history to support a Human Life Amendment." In both
of these position papers, she stated that "I would support the use of
federal funds for abortion. This for me would be a vote for the poor
rather than a vote for abortions." In her testimony on March 8, 1983
at the confirmation hearing, she stated "although I am opposed to
abortion, I can tolerate Medicaid funding for abortion through the DSS."

I can state unequivocally that, in accordance with the
magisterium of the church, this position of Sister Agnes Mary Mansour
on abortion and particularly on Medicaid funding for abortion is
unacceptable.

Your letter of April 11, 1983, does not include the names of
the canonists and theologians who were consulted relative to the position
of Sister Agnes Mary Mansour nor do you include their statements on her
position. You merely state that the consultations "indicate that Sister
is clearly within the tradition of the Church." It would be rash,
unfair, and unrealistic for me to make any comments on the unknown statements of unknown canonists and theologians. Therefore, I shall
limit myself to an enunciation of the tradition of the Church, particularly
relevant to public funding of abortion, as articulated through the
magisterial teaching of the bishops.

The teaching of the church on abortion is clear, consistent and
absolute. Abortion is always, without any limitation or qualification,
an intrinsically moral evil. (Declaration on Abortion, issued by the
Sacred Congregation for the Doctrine of the Faith, November 18, 1974).
The Second Vatican Council described abortion as an "unspeakable crime."
(Church in the Modern World, No. 51). If conformity with the application
of the principle of formal cooperation, it follows that direct funding
for abortion is also morally evil. Consequently, it is objectively
immoral for anyone to support or condone direct funding for abortion.

The following statements represent some of the magisterial
teaching of bishops relating particularly to public funding of abortion.
These statements are corroborative of the non-acceptability of the stance
of Sister Agnes Mary Mansour on Medicaid funding for abortions.

a. February 13, 1973, pastoral message of the Administrative
Committee of the NCCB -- Referring to the 1973 decision of the
Supreme Court on abortion, the pastoral message states: "No
court, no legislative body, no leader of government. can legitimately
assign less value to some human life. Thus, the laws that conform
to the opinion of the court are immoral laws, in opposition to God's
plan of creation and to the divine law which prohibits the
destruction of human life at any point of its existence. Whenever
a conflict arises between the Law of God and any human law, we
are held to follow God's law...Catholics must oppose abortion as
an immoral act. No one is obliged to obey any civil law that may
require abortion."

b. January 24, 1973, statement of the Committee for Pro-Life
Affairs, NCCB -- "We urge all state legislators to protect the
unborn child to the fullest extent possible under this decision and
to restrict the practice of abortion as much as they can."

c. November 18, 1970, Declaration on Abortion of NCCB --

"The child in the womb is human. Abortion is an unjust destruction
of a human life and morally that is murder. Society has no right
to destroy this life. Even the expectant mother has no such right.
The law must establish every possible protection for the child
before and after birth."

   d. November 18, 1974 -- Declaration on Abortion, Sacred
Congregation for the Doctrine of the Faith -- "No. 22. It must
in any case be clearly understood that whatever may be laid down
by civil law in this matter, man can never obey a law which is
in itself immoral, and such is the case of a law which would admit
in principle the liceity of abortion. Nor can he take part in a
propaganda campaign in favor of such a law or vote for it. Moreover,
he may not collaborate in its application."

   e. March 24, 1976, testimony of USCC on constitutional
amendments protecting unborn human life before the Subcommittee
on Civil and Constitutional Rights of the House Committee on the
Judiciary -- "It is a sad commentary on our society that the poor
and minorities obtain a higher percentage of legal abortions than
is appropriate to their representation in the general population.
The poor and minorities are targeted as population groups that
should receive more abortions than others. An elitist attitude
that is patronizing and sometimes punitive decides that abortion
is good enough for the poor. The underlying concept is that abortions
are cheaper than other health services associated with child bearing
and child rearing. The factual result is that the poor and minorities,
who necessarily depend on the government for health services, will be
automatically subjected to a coercive pressure to accept abortion as
a practical choice.

   The poor and minorities possess human dignity equal to that
of other human beings. Government funding of abortion as an alternative to normal health care constitutes a betrayal of the trust
that should exist between a government and the people it was
established to serve and protect. Poor women and their unborn
children have done nothing to merit the destruction that government
policy offers to them."

   f. January 22, 1977, pastoral letter of Bishop Leo T. Maher,
Bishop of San Diego on "Defense of Life and Religious Liberty." --
"Concern and respect for the poor and disadvantaged are obligations
of all Americans. But if human dignity means anything, the rapidly
growing social policy of aborting the children of the poor and
minorities must be rejected. We must - and we can - find new ways
to help the poor overcome poverty. We must - and we certainly can -
provide better maternity and infant health care to all women and
their children, unborn and born. There is no justification for
directly and deliberately destroying more than one million unborn
human beings each year for the sake of hypothetical social and
economic gains."

   g. January 22, 1978, pastoral letter of Cardinal Terence Cooke
on Human Life -- "However, some political and social leaders, as
well as publicists, continue to press their viewpoint that abortions
for the poor, funded by the government, are a right and even a
necessary solution to poverty and other social problems. Some say
that they are opposed to abortion personally, but will not impose
their moral belief on those who disagree. Others insist that abortion

is a legal right for all and that people who oppose it on moral
grounds should not have the freedom to present their belief in
the public forum.

We believe that human life begins before birth. Scientific
evidence increasingly indicates that life begins at conception.
All rights of the unborn person, and especially the right to life,
should be safeguarded by individuals and by governments, whose
essential duty it is to protect these rights."

h.   January 22, 1978, letter from the New York State Catholic
Conference on Proposed Legislation relative to Medicaid Funding
for Abortion -- "Literally millions of New York taxpayers are
vehemently opposed to having their money used to fund the killing
of unborn children."

i.   September 13, 1978, memorandum from the Michigan Catholic
Conference concerning Prohibition Against the Use of State Tax
Dollars for Elective Medicaid (Welfare) Abortions -- "The Michigan
Catholic Conference disagrees with Governor Milliken and with all
who believe that it is unjust discrimination to prohibit the use
of public funds for Medicaid abortions. Those who favor abortions
for poor women believe that destroying unborn children is somehow
beneficial to society. The killing of any innocent human being
can never be considered beneficial."

j.   June 21, 1979, NCCB and USCC Suit on Abortion Benefits
(This involved a class action suit brought by the NCCB and the
USCC asking relief from the legal obligation of many employers
to pay abortion-related fringe benefits. While not involving
Medicaid funding for abortions, it is related to this issue since
it involves financial payments for abortion.) -- "The moral,
ethical and religious convictions of the NCCB and the USCC find
the deliberate and unnecessary destruction of human life to be a
grave and morally abhorrent act. The statute challenged herein
compels the named plaintiffs to facilitate this practice through
provision of economic incentive in the form of fringe benefits.
The compulsion to participate in the trivilization of this practice
and moreover the compulsion to become the economic means through
which this practice is carried forward greatly offends the moral,
ethical and religious convictions of the NCCB and the USCC and the
class represented."

k.   June 30, 1980, statement of Archbishop Quinn, President of
the NCCB, welcoming the Supreme Court decision upholding the Hyde
Amendment -- "I welcome the Supreme Court decision today because it
leaves intact the laws which restrict the use of tax funds to pay
for abortions. These laws were enacted by the representatives of
the people after serious deliberation, and they represent the views
of the overwhelming majority of Americans. The issue in the dispute
over government funding of abortion, after all, is whether citizens
who object to abortion in conscience shall or shall not be forced
to subsidize abortion with their taxes...this is a victory for
freedom of conscience as well as for unborn life."

l.   July 1, 1980, statement by Bishop Roger Mahony, Bishop
of Stockton, on the Supreme Court decision upholding the Hyde
Amendment -- "This decision represents a major victory for unborn
children, and is at least a beginning step towards changing the

'abortion mentality' which has prevailed so thoroughly among the
judges of our country. It is ironic that Justice Thurgood Marshall,
in his vigorous descent to the majority opinion, claims that poor
women have been dealt 'a cruel blow' because they are 'most powerless members of our society.' He fails to realize that, in fact,
the most powerless and voiceless members of our society are the
millions of unborn children whose right to life is violated through
death-dealing abortion."

   m. September 11, 1980, pastoral letter of Cardinal Medeiros of
Boston on Abortion -- "The Second Vatical Council declares that
abortion is 'unspeakable crime.' Those who make abortions possible
by law - such as legislators - and those who promote, defend and
elect these same lawmakers - cannot separate themselves totally
from that guilt which accompanies this horrendous crime and deadly
sin."

   n. October 1, 1980, intervention of Cardinal Cooke on behalf
of the United States Bishops in Vatican City -- "All rights of the
unborn person - especially the right to life - should be safeguarded by governments and public officials, whose essential duty
it is to protect these rights. To claim a personal conviction that
human life begins before birth and to do nothing to nothing to
protect that life is moral escapism. To plan solutions of social
problems through the destruction of unborn life is callous pragmatism.
To claim abortion as a right for all and as a solution for poverty
is an insult to rich and poor alike. Neither poverty nor any other
social evil will be resolved by the expedient of abortion. Any state
or nation which promotes and finances the permissive abortion of its
potential citizens is bankrupting its future and denigrating its
present moral climate." (1980 Synod of Bishops)

   o. January 18, 1981, pastoral letter of Cardinal Cooke on
Human Life -- "We urge you to insist that our government officials
take the necessary legislative and administrative action to assure
that public funds are not used to destroy human life, even for the
mistaken reason of solving the problem of poverty and other social
ills."

   p. March 16, 1981, letter of New York State Catholic Conference
on Proposed Legislation relative to Termination of Pregnancy --
"As you are aware, the bishops of New York State and the New York
State Catholic Conference have for the past several years taken a
strong position in opposition to the funding of abortion through the
Medicaid program. The Medicaid program was established many years
ago to provide for the health of the citizens of this state and not
to fund the destruction of the lives of the unborn by means of
abortion.

   The purpose of this letter, as Chairman of the Assembly
Health Committee, is to inform you that we maintain our strong
opposition to abortion and the funding of it through the use of
Medicaid funds..."

   q. March 24, 1981, reaction of Cardinal Manning of Los Angeles
on Decision of the California Supreme Court Approving Payment for
Abortions -- "Today the Supreme Court of California authenticates
the murder of babies in their mothers' wombs because the mother
might be poor. What a crime of violence and injustice in the face
of God."

r. April 23, 1981, Interfaith Statement on the State Budget
and Medicaid Abortion signed by Bishop Patrick Ahern, Chairman of
the New York State Respect Life Committee -- "Furthermore, using
public funds for the crime of abortion literally forces millions
of New Yorkers to pay for what they really consider an immoral
and unjust assault upon innocent human life."

s. May 1, 1981, letter of the New York State Catholic Conference
on Proposed Legislation Relative to Funding for Abortions --
"At a recent press conference a statement was released by
representatives of three major faith groups voicing opposition to
Medicaid funding of abortion. This statement rightfully contends
that abortion is in no way a solution to the problems of the poor,
rather it is an assault on their families. The statement points
out the immorality and unjust nature of forcing millions of
New Yorkers who oppose abortion to finance this destruction of
human life.

The New York State Catholic Conference, on behalf of the
Catholic Bishops of New York State, endorses this interfaith
statement and joins with Bishop Patrick Ahern, Chairman of the
Respect Life Committee of the Catholic Conference, and one of the
co-signers of the statement, in urging the legislature to discontinue the allocation of state funds for abortions.

We again urge you to defend the lives of the unborn children
by deleting abortion funding from the state budget."

t. May 24, 1982, letter of New York State Catholic Conference
on Proposed Legislation Relative to Medicaid Funding for Abortion --
"Furthermore, millions of New York taxpayers are strongly opposed
to the use of state funds to finance services which are contrary to
their social, moral and religious convictions.

We firmly believe that the government should provide
assistance to families and children to enhance their lives and
serve their needs. The state should not provide funds to destroy
the lives of unborn children."

u. February 23, 1983, public statement of Archbishop Szoka of
Detroit calling on Sister Agnes Mary Mansour to resign her post as
Director of the Department of Social Services in Michigan --
"The Catholic Church teaches that abortion is the direct and
deliberate termination of an innocent human life. Consequently
no one has a right to funds from the state or from any other
source to obtain an abortion. Furthermore we believe that the
state is morally wrong in providing Medicaid funding for abortions."

"It is the position of the Catholic Church and my position,
that we must oppose and disapprove of anything that fosters or
permits the continuation of the evil of abortion, including Medicaid
payments for abortion. Sister Mansour's statement that 'more harm
could come from halting state funding' for abortion totally disregards
the irreparable harm of abortion to unborn infants, a harm that is
irreversible for them in their loss of life."

v. March 5, 1982, remarks of Archbishop Szoka at Pastoral
Council Meeting -- "The church's teaching on abortion is a given.

It's not open for discussion. And it's very clear that if we are
opposed to abortion we must be opposed to anything that aids,
abets, encourages or helps it. And Medicaid funding for abortion
obviously does it."

"I am not trying to make decisions for everybody, but
the doctrine that I am sworn to uphold as a bishop is a doctrine
of the Catholic Church. That doctrine on abortion has been expressed
again and again. The National Conference of Catholic Bishops, all
the bishops of the United States who constitute an authentic teaching
authority in the church, have spoken very clearly about our opposition
to Medicaid payments for abortion.

For many, many years the Michigan Catholic Conference, which
has on its board lay people as well as bishops, has publicly again
and again taken the stand of opposition to Medicaid payments for
abortion. And there is no way that I as a bishop of the Catholic
Church can do anything or refrain from doing something that could
be interpreted as though I do not support that teaching."

w. April 1983, statement of the Connecticut Catholic Bishops
on "The Legislator Faces the Abortion Problem" -- Connecticut
Bishops first of all addressed themselves to three unacceptable
stances that legislators might adopt on the question of abortion.
They identified the third stance as the pro choice viewpoint and they
observed: "That is an attempt to separate your personal anti-
abortion views from your legislative stance. You might see all
this as an 'no-win' situation and avoid problems by saying: 'I
am personally opposed to abortion, but I will not let my personal
views influence how I vote.' This is the pro choice approach
which some Catholic legislators have adopted....We find the pro
choice viewpoint on abortion bankrupt in both logic and morality.
This may seem to a legislator as a way to avoid the 'problem' of
abortion. But the pro choice legislator cannot really answer self
or others on the questions of when human life begins and why all
human life is not protected by law in our nation. And the pro
choice legislator is, in this fundamental area, not working to
overcome evil and do good."

The Connecticut Bishops recommend a fourth stance, that
is, 'one which some legislators consistently and courageously do
adopt and express in their public and private lives: the stance
of being pro life. Following God's law and a conscience obedient
to God's Law is not the easy. To follow one's conscience in an
amoral and secular society means great sacrifice. Heroism is
sometimes called for in doing what is morally right....We look to
you, our legislators to be principled and strong in fighting for
the right to life and the dignity in living of all God's sons and
daughters. It is no exercise of civil liberty to destroy one's
unborn child. We urge you not to avoid the question and to uphold
the sanctity of life in a caring, humane society. Join us in
favoring any legislative initiative that is designed both morally
and legally to inhibit and eliminate abortions."

6. STATEMENT -- "A few Michigan bishops have personally expressed
serious pastoral concern about Archbishop Szoka's actions. Moreover,
they believe that more harm will be done by Sister's resignation.
Accordingly, they desire that the matter be turned to the local level
for resolution."

    RESPONSE -- This statement transcends the circumstances and
scope of my involvement in the matter of Sister Agnes Mary Mansour,
nor is there any documentation available to me on this item. ·Therefore
I can make no observations on this statement.

July 5, 1983

Contributors

HELEN MARIE BURNS, R.S.M. is a member of the administrative team of the Sisters of Mercy of the Union, an order numbering 4200 Sisters in North and South America. She was Provincial of the Detroit Province at the time of the Mansour case and official witness to many of the events documented in this book. She was formerly a director of religious education and a teacher in secondary education in the Midwest.

FRANCINE CARDMAN is an Associate Professor of Historical Theology at the Weston School of Theology in Cambridge, Mass. She has lectured widely and published on questions of women's ordination and traditions on feminist theology and spirituality. She co-edited the collection, *The Wind is Rising* and is a founding member and faculty member of the Women's Theological Center in Boston, Mass. She is a member of the board of directors of NETWORK and past president of the North American Academy of Ecumenists.

THOMAS E. CLARKE, S.J. is a writer and lecturer now living in New York City. He taught systematic theology at Woodstock College for twenty years, and was a research fellow at the Woodstock Theological Center from 1977 to 1981. Among his publications are: editor of *Above Every Name: The Lordship of Christ and Social Systems,* Paulist Press, 1980, and co-author of *From Image to Likeness: A Jungian Path in the Gospel Journey,* Paulist Press, 1983. He has collaborated with the Sisters of Mercy of the Union over a period of many years, most recently as a theological resource person in their workshop, "The Communal Search for Truth."

JAMES A. CORIDEN is the Academic Dean at the Washington Theological Union where he also teaches canon law. He is a presbyter of the Diocese of Gary, ordained in 1957. He holds degrees in Theology, Canon Law and Civil Law, and has written several articles on matters of church discipline and ministry. He has been engaged in theological education for seventeen years.

BARBARA A. CULLOM is Co-Coordinator of Theology for Christians on the Journey at the Quixote Center in Mt. Rainier, Md. She holds a Ph.D. in Biblical Studies from the University of Notre Dame, and is an Associate Member of the Sisters of St. Joseph of Peace. In addition to scripture, her interests include feminism and the creation of community-oriented liturgy. She is married and has two daughters.

CHARLES E. CURRAN is a Professor of Moral Theology at the Catholic University of America. He is past president of both the Catholic Theological Society of America and the Society of Christian Ethics. His most recent books are *American Catholic Social Ethics: 20th Century Approaches; Directions in Catholic Social Ethics;* and *Directions in Fundamental Moral Theology.*

MONIKA K. HELLWIG, systematic theologian, is Professor of Theology at Georgetown University. Her published books include: *Jesus, the Compassion of God* (Glazier), *Understanding Catholicism* (Paulist), *Whose Experience Counts in Theological Reflection?* (Marquette University Press), *Christian Women in a Troubled World* (Paulist). She has frequently conducted workshops and summer programs for religious communities as well as other groups. She is the mother of three children.

MARY E. HUNT, Ph.D. is a theologian who directs the Women's Alliance for Theology, Ethics and Ritual (WATER) in Silver Spring, Md. She received her doctorate in philosophical and systematic theology from the Graduate Theological Union, Berkeley. Currently she is completing a book entitled *Fierce Tenderness Toward a Feminist Theology of Friendship.*

MADONNA KOLBENSCHLAG, H.M. is a senior fellow at the Woodstock Theological Center in Wash., D.C., and a Sister of the Humility of Mary. She has published and lectured widely on women's development and spirituality, and on religion and politics. She is best known for her book, *Kiss Sleeping Beauty Good-Bye,* and for her recent study of religious professionals in politics: *Between God and Caesar.* She holds a doctorate from the University of Notre Dame and was formerly a professor of American studies and a Congressional aide.

PHIL LAND, S.J. has been a staff researcher and lecturer of the Center of Concern, Wash., D.C. for the last ten years. He came to this work from twenty years in Rome, teaching Catholic social thought and economics of development at the Pontifical Gregorian University. Much of the years 1967-1975 were devoted to the Pontifical Commission on Justice and Peace.

RICHARD A. McCORMICK, S.J. is the Rose F. Kennedy Professor of Christian Ethics at the Kennedy Institute of Ethics, Georgetown University. He lectures frequently throughout the country on moral questions. His latest book is *Health and Medicine in the Catholic Tradition*. McCormick has served on many advisory boards, e.g., Ethics Advisory Board (DHEW), Ethics Committee of National Hospice Organization, of American Hospital Association, of American Fertility Society, and has been a regular contributor to *Theological Studies*.

DAVID J. O'BRIEN teaches at Holy Cross College and is a member of the editorial board of *Cross Currents* and the board of directors of the *National Catholic Reporter*. His most recent book is *Renewing the Earth: Catholic Documents on Peace, Justice and Liberation* (Image Books, 1977) which he co-edited with Thomas A. Shannon.

DAVID O'CONNOR, S.T., was ordained a priest as a member of the Missionary Servants of the Most Holy Trinity in 1955. He earned a doctorate in canon law from The Catholic University of America in 1958 and was a peritus at Vatican Council II, 1962-1965. From 1967-1973 he was councilor and secretary general of his religious institute. Presently O'Connor is associate professor and chair of the department of church law at the Washington Theological Union, Silver Spring, Md.

ROSEMARY RADFORD RUETHER is the Georgia Harkness Professor of Applied Theology at Garrett-Evangelical Theological Seminary and member of the Graduate faculty of Northwestern University in Evanston, Ill. Before that time she taught for ten years at the Howard University School of Religion and was visiting professor at Harvard Divinity School and Yale Divinity School. She received her B.A. at Scripps College and her M.A. and Ph.D. at Claremont Graduate School in Claremont, Calif. in Classics and Patristics. She is the author or editor of twenty books and numerous articles on feminist and liberation theology and ethics, and lectures frequently at universities and church conferences.

Her most recent book is *Women Church: Theology and Practice of Feminist Luturgical Communities* (Harper and Row, 1983).

ARLENE ANDERSON SWIDLER teaches religious studies at Villanova University. A co-founder of the *Journal of Ecumenical Studies,* she is the author of numerous articles in such publications as *National Catholic Reporter, Commonweal* and *Bible Today.* Most recently she co-edited (with Walter E. Conn) *Mainstreaming: Feminist Research for Teaching Religious Studies* (Univeristy Press of America 1985).